IN IT TO WIN IT

PETER ROEBUCK

IN IT TO WIN IT
The Australian cricket supremacy

ALLEN&UNWIN

To all my colleagues on The LBW Trust
Learning for a Better World
and all its sponsors, donors and students.

First published in Australia and New Zealand in 2006

Allen & Unwin
83 Alexander Street
Crows Nest NSW 2065
Australia
Phone: (61 2) 8425 0100
Fax: (61 2) 9906 2218
Email: info@allenandunwin.com
Web: www.allenandunwin.com

National Library of Australia
Cataloguing-in-Publication entry:

Roebuck, Peter, 1956- .
  In it to win it : the Australian cricket supremacy.

  Includes index.
  ISBN 978 1 74114 543 4.

  ISBN 1 74114 543 0.

  1. Cricket - Australia. 2. Cricket players - Australia. I.
  Title.

796.358650994

Typeset in 11.5/14 pt Galliard by Midland Typesetters, Australia
Printed and bound in Australia by Griffin Press

10 9 8 7 6 5 4 3 2 1

CONTENTS

'I think we have turned the corner in one-day cricket. I think that from now on we are going to be very, very hard to beat.'

Allan Border, at the 1987 World Cup

Letter to *The Times*

Sir,
Thirty years ago I returned from Australia where I had a job with an international oil company. Everyone from the directors to the shop floor lunched together and rank was temporarily suspended.

Back in England I took a job with a Midlands engineering group. There were five different levels of canteen and dining room.

Yours faithfully,
G.A. Dawson

PREFACE

Australians have always played cricket by their own lights. Unimpressed by an inheritance from a distant land, they embarked upon their own independent course. From the outset, Australian cricket's approach was founded in realism. By and large, it has lacked sentiment and charm, in which respect it reflects the nation. Snakes wriggle in the interior, sharks swim in the seas, grim-jawed competitors stand at gully, sardonic remarks poised on their lips. Robin Hood was the English champion, Ned Kelly his antipodean equivalent.

Australian cricket is the sound of sprigs on concrete, the sight of umpires with fingers raised high above their heads, the reading of the score the wrong way around, leg spinners ripping the ball with all their might, a slip cordon unemotionally chewing gum as a fast bowler reaches his mark, and sunscreen splashed across faces. It is a game of harsh light, fiery bowlers, forceful batsmen and lean fieldsmen, a game played across the nation.

Romance is scorned, the fancy talk heard elsewhere is loved in secret but noisily rejected. No need has ever arisen to revisit the heroes of Australian cricket because there are no illusions to crush. Recent books about English champions which have revealed flaws will upset those convinced the game is played by special people whereas, in fact, it is merely a special game. Australian cricket cut out the cant on the day Fred Spofforth first marked out his run, on the day his comrades heard English amateurs address their professional colleagues in disparaging tones.

Australian cricket is gritty and democratic. It belongs not so much to the bluebloods as the redbloods. It reflects the rigours of the climate and rejects the prim and proper. Australia expects its cricketers to be characters. They might be as dark as Lillee, as defiant as Border, as swashbuckling as Michael Clarke. Provided they are distinctive it hardly matters. Australia likes sport and sportsmen. Apart from Cathy Freeman, Makybe Diva and Ian Thorpe it does not, though, live and die with them. Australia enjoys the sporting moment and the triumph but is also capable of moving on. Greyness, skiting, whingeing and whining are frowned upon. The real desire is always to get on with the game. The old call, 'Ave a go yer mug!' reverberates. Indeed it expresses the national outlook. Australia may be unsettled by oddballs but it likes triers. The rise and fall of Steve Waugh was a matter of debate and his century reached at the last ball of the second day of the 2002/03 New Year's Test provoked widespread celebrations for it epitomised the toughness of life and the survival of the individual. And never mind that Waugh himself could be as cranky as a rudely awoken koala.

Aggression has been the other constant factor of Australian cricket. Defeat is the almost inevitable result for any Australian team reluctant to force the pace. Something in the national psyche rebels against the English custom of turning every game into a version of a cross-country run. An attacking approach is instilled from an early age—the need to score runs, to take wickets and to avoid wasting time. Woe betide the batsman who potters around like an ancient in a village sweet shop. From 'Terror' Turner to Lillee, from Trumper to Ponting, Australian cricket has been played from the front.

It has been a great and sustained tradition and the green cap coloured after the wattle has become its enduring symbol. Few sporting symbols adopted by teams have had as much effect upon opponents as this oddly shaped piece of headgear. The All Blacks have their war dance and their shirts, the Welsh sing, the Scots play their pipes, northern Europeans paint their faces and Englishmen clap their hands but none surpasses the power of the cap worn by the Australian cricketer.

Respectful of history, determined to channel its power, Waugh used the 'baggy green' to remind his players that they were part of a great tradition. To disgrace the cap was to betray a history and a nation. The cap perpetuates the myth that Australian cricket has but a single mind. Over the years there have been rebellions, all of them about money and power, and two of them (1884 and 1902) occurred before the baggy cap started appearing on distinguished heads. Once the cap was established, nothing was allowed to compromise the team or its motif. The baggy green cap has been a constant in changing times, timeless and defiant, not so much a relic as a reminder that some things are not for sale.

Over the years the cap has reflected an unchanging tradition that has taken us from Charlie Macartney to Brett Lee. It has been an eventful journey. Only when a generation arrives that believes it is above such reference points will the game start to fade in the wide brown land.

Australian cricketers have a reputation to maintain. Overseas, they are regarded as a hard bunch prepared to pay any price to prevail. Of course that is to oversimplify the matter. Yet there has indeed been a sense of the indomitable that has taken the nation from Warwick Armstrong reading a newspaper on the boundary to Ricky Ponting saving a Test match by batting almost an entire day. The Australians might lose but they never lie down. It is not allowed.

Australian cricket's recent domination has been a mixed blessing. Under three very different captains Australians have played the same forcing game, searching for wickets or boundaries. Others have copied them and, as a result, fewer matches have been left drawn. On the other hand the Australians' uncompromising approach has provoked conflict and eventually the game's rulers felt obliged to appoint referees to oversee matches and impose discipline. Australia has been respected but not loved, sometimes not even in its own backyard.

This book is the last in a series that has included my memoirs and a collection of character studies. It is a search for Australia through its cricket. It is also an account of the almost uninterrupted success enjoyed by Australia over the last two decades. That the run ended with defeat in the most memorable Ashes series ever played was a stroke of luck. In the event the 2005 Ashes campaign provided an insight into the nature of both countries and both teams.

Thomas Keneally has observed that the curiously Australian blend of democracy and authoritarianism started with the first governor, Arthur Phillip, who distributed provisions evenly between every inhabitant of the settlement—convict or free settler—and then sent out shooting parties to exact revenge upon hostile elements. Phillip could have been an Australian cricket captain.

My thanks go to Patrick Gallagher and Angela Handley from Allen & Unwin for their support, assistance and interest. Matthew Klugman and Alex McDermott made vital contributions by collecting material, offering suggestions and demanding rigour. Finally my thanks go to my fellow Australians for putting out the welcome mat all those years ago.

LIST OF SCORECARDS

1

PLAYING THE GAME

In so many ways it is odd that of all English games cricket most stirred the interest of a supposedly rebellious people. It was the game of the upper classes, the game of Lord's, 'Plum' Warner and Lord Harris. At least that was its reputation. Of course it was never as simple as that with cricket or with English sport in general. Fortunately those settling on a vast and inaccessible continent, whether by force or by inclination, had the sense not to confuse a game and its governors. After all men come and go. Naturally they took a dim view of aristocratic captains who treated paid players 'worse than dogs', as one player put it. Not having attended the average English private school or fagged for one of its more feared sixth formers, democratically minded antipodeans were inclined to object to such apparent assumptions of superiority. But they were sufficiently familiar with England and English cricket to realise that autocrats of this sort were few and far between. It was left to later film directors to make them seem typical of the upper echelons of that damp island.

Nor was English cricket quite the game of stiff upper lips, 'Bad luck, chaps!' and honey for tea portrayed by romantic writers, poets and other dimwits. The antipodean inheritance was by no means so lame. Indeed the English and Australian approaches to cricket have

1

never been as far apart as might be imagined from a reading of contemporary commentators and subsequent chroniclers. Inevitably, attention was drawn to differences that did indeed reflect the contrasting characteristics of the islands and their inhabitants, one huge and arid, the other tightly packed and wet. That, though, did not mean they had nothing in common.

English cricket never was quite the prudish haven of respectability imagined by numerous schoolmasters and moralisers. Indeed the moralising mostly came from behind lecterns and was intended to instil the correct values in boys destined to lead the Empire, and professionals presumed in need of direction. At the end of the 19th century, England's most eminent sporting hero was a bearded sometime doctor from Gloucestershire widely and justifiably regarded as one of the most unscrupulous sportsmen ever to put on a pair of boots. Nor is current English cricket as much a place for the faint-hearted as outsiders may imagine. Anyone supposing that English cricketers are not familiar with the livelier entries in the more broad-minded dictionaries or that they treat opponents with punctilious civility ought to spend an afternoon playing for Budleigh Salterton, a seaside town not exactly known as a hotbed of radical thought or confronting conduct. Any illusions that remained would not survive a night in the Budleigh bar, especially if the locals had decided the time was ripe for one of their notorious 'lock-ins'!

Despite its supposed association with the class system, Australians had more sense than to condemn the game of bat and ball as representing everything they detested. Instead they set out to dominate it and presently brought to the game an egalitarian streak that ultimately proved a boon. Taken as a whole, Australia's contribution to the game has been constructive.

Sooner or later cricket was bound to move away from its base in London, both in spirit and body. Fortunately the influence of ambitious factions determined to use their numbers and economic power to establish themselves as the game's true and inevitable rulers has been balanced by a strong dose of antipodean common sense. When England talks, some elements from its former colonies prickle with resentment. Australians speak from a different past and with a rougher tongue. Accordingly Australians such as David Richards, Malcolm Gray and Malcolm Speed have been better placed to represent the game's governing body than their English contemporaries. Nor did it take them long to move base camp to Dubai.

Sooner or later, too, the English and Australian hegemony was bound to be broken. Even in 2005, though, these two nations had much fuller fixture lists than India, long since the game's main source of cricketing revenue. Foreigners are expected to tour these primary nations in the middle of their seasons, and never mind the inconvenience. Old habits die hard.

By and large, and recent events notwithstanding, Australian players have likewise outstared their reputation as the most rugged members of the cricketing family. Certainly they have not travelled as badly as might have been predicted in the drawing rooms of Bloomsbury. At the time of writing the Chief Executive of the ICC is an Australian, as was the last Chairman, as are the coaches of Sri Lanka, the West Indies, Bangladesh, India and several English counties. Most counties are eager to fill their ranks with emerging Australians. The caricature of the vulgar antipodean dismissive of old England, suspicious of foreign lands and dark skins and hankering to put a raw prawn on the barbie is an amusing creation that does not survive acquaintance with the facts.

Nor is Australia any longer an Anglo-Saxon country. Melbourne and other Australian cities are host to many communities including large groups from various African countries. Although he sometimes seems reluctant to admit it, Prime Minister John Howard has presided over an influx of immigrants from a wide range of countries. He has also been responsible for a surge in government spending and administrative costs.

In any case the first settlers did not take much persuading to resume playing cricket at the earliest opportunity. They were never likely to abandon the better parts of their previous lives, among which games occupied an eminent position. After all they were not political refugees escaping a nefarious system but men, women and children from mostly humble backgrounds whose hungry hands had been caught in the till or whose worst instincts had got the better of them. They had not rejected and did not necessarily disagree with the disposition of their places of origin. Why should they refuse to play their games?

As Jack Pollard points out in his glorious work, *The Complete Illustrated History of Australian Cricket*, it was quite normal for cricket to be played in settled lands. 'Cricket was 69 years old in America,' Pollard writes, 'and had firm footholds in Canada, Scotland and India when Captain James Cook discovered the East Coast of Australia in 1770. Irish cricket was recovering well from Cromwell's edict that all bats, stumps and balls should be burnt.'

Before long most prisoners realised that the lot of the released convict in Australia was altogether more promising than that endured by labourers in Old Blighty. Moreover, there is a sense of equality on a playing arena that must have appealed to even the most disenchanted democrat. Boards may or may not be dominated by high-born fools, but once the boots or pads or Speedos have been donned there is only the cruelty of competition. As far as sport is concerned democracy is an irresistible force. Eventually even the wealthiest of athletic activities throws open its doors. Black women from poor parts of America have won the greatest tennis tournaments. A black man has become the best golfer the game has known. A man born in Madras has captained England's cricket team, a Christian has led Pakistan onto the field, a Muslim has taken charge of the Indian outfit, while Sri Lanka's side counts among the most cosmopolitan collection of characters ever to set foot on a cricket field. Working-class Australians wanted to play cricket, wanted to make it their game, and they succeeded gloriously. Australian cricket can be understood only as a blue-collar activity.

The settlers and freed convicts had no reason to turn their backs on cricket, or any other sport. Nor did they. On the contrary they seemed to relish them as one of the few remnants of happier times that could survive the voyage.

Cricket and rugby were brought to the distant continent upon the settlers' ships and slowly took forms that reflected the new terrain and the temperament of its peoples. Of course they were not played immediately, or not in any formal sense, because there were more pressing matters to consider, such as food, shelter, security and the creation of a functioning society. But the games did not pass away, and every ship brought a few more enthusiasts. Criminals and policemen, judges and guards, differ only upon the issue of law and order. Many of them like cricket. Pollard relates that the first cricket match in Australia was played in 1803 on a patch of ground later to be formalised and to prosper under the title of the Sydney Cricket Ground.

Even settlers instinctively hostile to English ways were not obliged to disdain the pastimes that were followed throughout their country of origin by youth and aged alike, aristocrat and artisan. Apart from anything else it was hardly sensible to deny oneself such pleasures as could be taken on this inhospitable terrain, and cricket was too enjoyable an activity to be abandoned to the wealthy and well born.

Australians had started playing cricket and before long were beating their supposed masters. In some respects the 'new' country's success was because it regarded cricket as a recreation to be played with every last ounce of strength at the players' disposal, but a recreation all the same.

England's cricketing history is altogether more complex and contains elements that partly explain the intensity of the conflict between the cricketing countries. As far as the English were concerned, sport was much more than a recreation. As the Empire spread, so the newly created games left the rough and ready fields of their origins and became instruments of power, tools to be used to spread Englishness and much else in the settled lands.

The games of the old country were taken up at the private schools where colonials were beaten and cold-showered into shape the better to remember their duties and to endure the awaiting hardships. Once the blue bloods had taken up these sports it was inevitable they'd take them over. Sport became a way of spreading an outlook some thought elevating and others dismissed as sententious. Regardless of the reasons for their spread, the games themselves reflected the peculiar genius of the English people.

By the same token the manner in which the English played their games expressed the tortured and inhibited character that emerged in Victorian times (against which fellows such as Denis Compton and latter-day Georgians such as David Gower and Ian Botham made their timely protests). England has seldom played any sport with abandon. Matches between the old and new countries have often resembled poetry readings given by Alfred Lord Tennyson and Banjo Paterson. Still, the games developed by a nation to whom the discovery of the ball was a breakthrough to put beside those of the wheel and orange marmalade count among the favours bestowed by the colonialists.

Of course the religious fanatics in America, familiar with perfidious Albion, regarded the colonial games with suspicion and set about creating their own entertainments. Baseball, basketball and gridiron are the dubious results of their defiance, games that have proved harder to spread than thick honey.

Australia was relaxed about its colonial inheritance because its background was so different. The settlers knew well enough that there was more to cricket than politics and country houses. Those were not its true origins. Gambling, controversy, chucking, fighting and drinking have a longer cricketing tradition than cucumber sandwiches. They also seem to be lasting the pace better. Neither early Victorian England nor its ball games were remotely as respectable as the advocates of the 'Golden Age' sometimes insist. No one reading Dickens or the social history of Taunton (or any other town), or an accurate history of sport could imagine otherwise.

English cricket was not as corrosively divided between rich and poor, upper and lower, as at first sight it seemed. Indeed it managed to retain its integrity despite the pressures of the times. During those Victorian years when members of different classes could not share a common dressing-room, hotel or carriage, cricket was alone among the national games in maintaining a single governing body and competition. These divisions were no more created by the game than were Indian castes, yet it could not ignore—let alone escape—them. Cricket did its best to alleviate the divisions, not through progressive thought but simple practicality and a common desire to play with and against the best regardless.

Inevitably a struggle for cricketing power did take place in England between paid players and amateurs convinced of their birthright and eager to maintain the status quo. Battle was joined in the middle of the 19th century, as increased access to the steam train enabled skilled artisans to take their services and abilities around the country in search of a pay packet. That the emergence of professional teams representing no one except themselves and eager to entertain crowds in the manner of a travelling fair occurred at the same time as the growth of the Trappist movement was no coincidence. Both had their roots in the same city, Nottingham, known for its miners, lace-workers and cricketers. Both had the same idea—that the craftsman ought not to be treated as factory fodder, that his skills were hard-won and valuable.

Neither the professional teams nor the Trappists lasted long. Neither survived the economic power and strength summoned by the patricians. Professional players did not have much chance, not in England, not in a mere game. No one was prepared to spill blood in pursuit of sporting freedoms. Nor were many prepared to pay money to watch even the most gifted players participate in meaningless matches, or not once the novelty had worn off. Moreover the working teams were inclined towards drink and disputation.

By the 1860s, English cricket acknowledged that it could not survive as an exhibition. It needed to organise itself properly and that required a central body to arrange fixtures, formulate rules, select teams and so forth. Trains brought national newspapers and contemporary heroes into people's homes and no sport determined to widen its appeal could ignore these developments. A governing body was needed to impose standards and to seize upon the opportunity presented by the popularity of the game.

The professional sides were doomed. Eventually English cricket was bound to be run from an office in London, and by the very types governing the rest of the country. These early travelling teams were replaced by a county structure and a ruling body that has survived almost intact to this day. Long before the first English touring teams arrived in Australia the game had put the workers back in their place.

Yet it was not as simple as that or Australians might have had reason to rebel. As games gathered ground in a suddenly shrinking country so England faced the task of accommodating a populace and an aristocracy both eager to play and yet bound by conviction or custom to respect the traditions that kept them apart. Soccer split between the Football League and the Football Association, professional and amateur. Likewise, professionals formed their own rugby code, playing 13-a-side, while the patricians and Celts developed their 15-a-side running game.

Cricket remained intact. Despite appearances it was not the least democratic game in the country. Quite the opposite. Only this apparently lofty game of bat and ball enabled all sections of society to play together. Australia did not inherit an arrogant activity, but an adaptable pastime that had put popularity before pride.

In its commitment to maintaining its unity cricket was obliged to accommodate the requirements of the age. Accordingly it insisted that players and gentlemen take to the field through different gates, change in different rooms, travel and stay in different hotels and appear differently on the scorecard. The amateur was Mr Bloggs while the paid player was J. Bloggs. Twice a year the supposedly opposing forces met in keenly but sportingly contested matches between the 'Gentlemen' and the 'Players'. Unsurprisingly, outsiders mistook this separation for snootiness, but these strategies were a way of allowing the rulers and ruled to play the same game and often for the same team.

Of course there was the possibility that experienced professionals might find themselves playing under a nincompoop born with a silver spoon in his mouth but not many amateur captains fitted that description, and those that did seldom lasted long. More common was the selfless leader who put the team first as the professionals gathered the runs and wickets needed to ensure a renewal of their contracts. By appointing a captain from the elite, cricket was merely reflecting its times. Despite the claims made on its behalf, sport has seldom been in the forefront of progressive thought. In those days it was regarded as essential that leadership be left in the hands of those born to lead.

What was disconcerting was not that divisions existed in the English version of the game a 'new' country took to its heart but how long they lasted. Until the 1950s, Somerset, my county, always searched for an amateur to lead the side and never mind that this sometimes meant appointing three captains in one year, as was the case in 1948 when two of the appointees were lawyers and one had served and once scored a century before breakfast in the Sudan. The previous year, R.J.O. Meyer, Headmaster of Millfield School, had been dragged from his duties and given the task of leading a collection of old pros and such promising lads as had escaped Hitler's guns. The thought of raising a professional above his station did not occur to a conservative and exclusively male committee of farmers, businessmen and what passed in the region for gentility.

Customs die hard and sportsmen are notoriously conservative. Not until 1960 was a black man considered worthy of captaining the West Indies. Not until a few years later was the last of the 'Gentlemen versus Players' matches held. By then thousands had died in wars fought to defend their country, among them many professional cricketers.

Although never comfortable with the class distinctions adhered to by their former colonial master and to a greater and lesser degree detected in its cricket teams, Australians looked past them. Not that Australian cricket was exactly a haven of advanced thought, a fact confirmed by the various disputes between players and Board and State Associations concerning low pay and the treatment meted out to those representing their country and responsible for scoring runs and taking wickets on its behalf.

Not until the 1970s and the start of the Chappell era would Australian cricket finally reject the former colonial power or, at any rate, the manner in which it played cricket. Ian Chappell, especially, would become the voice of cricket radicalism in his country, as would Sunil Gavaskar, Imran Khan and Arjuna Ranatunga in theirs. In their own way, these men were freedom fighters in whites. Chappell would dismiss county cricket as breeding 'safety-first' mediocrities, regard with suspicion those affecting rectitude and detest authorities prepared to pay players a pittance.

Although some aspects of the rebellion led by the Chappells are now disapproved of, especially the element of breast-beating, Australia's recent cricketing achievements cannot be understood without reference to that turbulent period. Nor can their meaning be grasped without an appreciation of the particularities of the Australian experience with the game of bat and ball.

2

SETTING THE SCENE

Australians have always competed hard in their chosen sports but a considerable period passed before Australian cricket teams assumed the air of invincibility that at various times in the last 20 years has accompanied them onto the field. Fortunately much less was expected of Australia's competitors in the nation's formative sporting decades. Of course an emerging country will take time to settle into the rigours of international competition. Apart from anything else facilities may be threadbare, organisation may be wanting, intent may be missing, identity may not have been forged. A new nation has a thousand decisions to make, many of them subconsciously, through actions as opposed to thought. Not everything can be settled around a table. Australia had to determine its interests and its destiny, on and off the field.

Maturity and desire were not the only factors in the spluttering rise of Australian sport. As trains had given English professionals the opportunity to take their talents around the country, so the development of affordable air travel released aspiring antipodean sportsmen. Nowadays it is nothing to cross the Nullarbor for a match, even a 20-over stoush, sometimes along the way catching a glimpse of famous television commentators as they sample the fare available in the front cabin.

Aeroplanes have made an enormous contribution to Australian sport, encouraging frequent interstate engagements (from which some of the players occasionally emerge unscathed) and swift inter-continental travel. Suddenly overseas was not a destination full of inhabitants with strange customs and forward defences but a place where skills could be pitted against the finest products of a different school of thought.

In Australia's emerging years sports followers were content to enjoy the achievements of their champions but regarded success as a bonus and not a birthright. Not until a more advanced, more united, more purposeful Australia repeatedly failed to make its mark at Olympic Games and Davis Cups did the nation become aghast. Before that a rash of defeats provoked a much milder reaction than the gnashing of teeth evident in countries persuaded that success is, or ought to be, a constant companion.

Until Australia grudgingly accepted that sport had to be approached with rigour, that fine competitors could not be simply collected from bush and beach, that excellence does not always arrive to order, that those playing on the ear might be beaten by better-organised opponents, the nation seemed satisfied with its occasional triumphs. There remained a lingering sense of a small nation sending its sons and daughters out to meet the might of the world. Triumphs were welcomed as confirmation that the new country had arrived, that the remote land could no longer be ignored. Disappointments were absorbed with a shrug. Australia wanted to compete, relished its victories and medals but understood that established buildings were not easily razed.

Not that Australians were often downcast. Doubtless it helped to boost morale that newspapers were willing to celebrate stirring performances by familiar faces and to give short shrift to everything else. Australia was able to feast upon crumbs.

Even now it can be illuminating to follow an Olympics from afar and then to read the antipodean version of events. Not long ago I watched an Olympics on African television and hardly heard an Australian name mentioned. Returning to Australia it came as a surprise to discover that Australia had, by its own estimation, dominated proceedings to such an extent that opponents were still reeling.

That most Australian newspapers rely upon provincial readerships adds to the effect. A small market forces owners and editors anxious to boost sales to appeal to local enthusiasms. An element of tub-thumping also creeps in as papers strive to survive the heat of competition. Any Australian rag unwilling to stoop to the dramatic or to reflect the interests of a wide range of readers is destined for the bankruptcy courts.

Nowadays Australia has a proud record in the athletic activities introduced by colonialists to entertain and, it was hoped, educate the inhabitants of distant lands. Results in a range of games confirm that this once-misbegotten continent has turned itself into a formidable sporting force. No opponent can expect an easy time from an Australian in any athletic activity, even soccer. But this was not always the case. Indeed it has been a hard road.

As late as 1987, Australia was still not the respected opponent it has become. The nation's sporting history depended not so much upon the achievements of its teams as upon the performances of a few champions, equine and human, who were either eliminated by the Americans or undermined by snooty Pommy captains. Or so locals persuaded themselves.

The anguish felt across the country about the fate suffered by Phar Lap, and the compromising of 'our Don' by an unprincipled toff revealed much about Australian pride and prejudice. It went beyond mere dismay, reached into the innards of the nation. A sense of injustice was created, a sense of persecution. A remote country desperate to make an impression on the rest of the world had been thwarted on the very cusp of achievement. Of course jealous opponents or, failing that, foreign bookmakers were to blame. Australian sportsmen convinced themselves that their most natural rivals, the yardstick by which success was measured, would stop at nothing to prevent the upstart nation making its mark. It is a sentiment that has never quite been subdued.

Few peoples have identified as strongly with their sporting sons as the Australians. Seldom has Australia's willingness to embrace its leading sportsmen been more clearly demonstrated than in the outpourings of emotion that surrounded the death of Sir Don Bradman and the sudden loss of David Hookes. If anything, The Don's passing provoked an even greater sense of loss than had been anticipated and never mind that he was once again approaching his century. The cortège was saluted by thousands of mourners and the service was followed by a vast audience on television and radio. Seasoned observers remarked that the occasion had been surpassed only by the death of Princess Diana, whose laying to rest was covered by every Australian television channel.

Hookes was an altogether different character—young, loud and abrasive where Bradman was old, discreet and cautious. Although entertaining, lengthy and often productive, his career could not be deemed an outright success. Yet his untimely death had an effect that reached beyond family, friends and the game of bat and ball and into the broader community. The South Australian Government gave him a State funeral attended by politicians, past players and ordinary citizens. Hookes had been loved. He was 'Hookesy', as Dean Jones was 'Deano' and the more elusive Bradman, 'The Don'. Nicknames play a larger part in Australian life than elsewhere. They reach beyond the secrets of sporting rooms and into the broader populace. They are a way of creating the legends and characters denied by history. Certainly it is hard to imagine as strong a reaction to the loss of two such contrasting sportsmen in any other predominantly Anglo-Saxon country. Many tears were shed by inhabitants who had not met either man but let them into their hearts. No one was bothered about these heroes' flaws. They had long since moved past all that.

Australia's isolation has been a limitation and a strength. It helps to explain the noise that emerges from the country's mouthpieces and sometimes its inhabitants whenever a favourable impression is made. Anonymity was regarded as a sort of death. The country craved attention. A new nation of little strategic importance burdened with a hostile terrain and an often cruel climate faced the daunting task of accommodating numerous settling peoples while also trying to remind a distant world of its existence. Governments have been presented with the challenge of turning into a united force peoples that had, for whatever reason, endured many hardships and travelled thousands of miles in search of a better life. Provinces that were far apart and fiercely independent had to be persuaded to cooperate, an attempt that might one day succeed. All this on a land that was largely uninhabitable.

Perhaps Australians have been strengthened by a sense of adversities faced and overcome. Perhaps they have accepted, too, that for better or worse the country is as they made it. There are no excuses; no one else is to blame, on the field or off it. An empty piece of paper is at once an intimidation and an opportunity.

Behind the tendency to rejoice in every success was a desire to confirm that the country was indeed a nation state whose citizens had much to appreciate and protect. How, otherwise, could federation succeed? How could a war be fought? How could taxes be imposed? What did it mean to be an Australian? Most of the States are substantially bigger than proud, independent and economically viable European nations. Australia needed its sport and its assertiveness to establish a sense of belonging.

England may suffer from the tiredness of age. Australia retains the nervousness of the new. Or it did until the recent development of a more deeply rooted sense of self-esteem reflected in the emergence of numerous comedies and comedians prepared to tease the customs and inhabitants of the land of their birth. *Kath and Kim*, *Skithouse* and *CNNNN* confirm that Australian humour is not limited to Dame Edna, Crocodile Dundee and other successful exports.

Of course it was this very uncertainty that led to the extremes evident in Australian life as men with reassuringly deep voices sang about beer even as tens of thousands of intrepid characters paraded through the main streets of Sydney in the annual Mardi Gras. Hardly had Australia put down its roots than it encountered the collapse of faith that has led to the current western replacement of lives with lifestyles and the conviction that the purpose of existence is neither service nor survival but the exploration of the self. In short, the new country had to rush through its formative period and plunge into a sceptical and self-absorbed world.

If the challenge has been met with a certain aplomb it is because many Australians did not believe much in the first place. Even at the national level, politics has been as much about personality as policy. Long ago Australia turned its back upon socialism and the rest of the secular faiths, except capitalism, and even that has been highly regulated. Apart from State rights, the predominant battle has been between conservatives and progressives, a battle that has raged with fury. Even the Catholics and Protestants did not fight as ferociously in Australia, not to the death, though the histories of Australian cricket and Australia itself cannot be understood without reference to the battle between the Micks and the Prots.

Gradually an approach to life has been found on this continent that suits the inhabitants, and it has been reflected in the local way of playing sport. It has helped that Australians are mostly uninterested in minor matters of gossip and innuendo. Indeed they are a curious mixture of warmth and wariness. Tolerant and generous of disposition, especially in financial matters, a point proven once again by their response to the 2004 tsunami, they are at the same time physically and emotionally defensive. A conversation between males generally consists of one fellow asking the other how he is going, whereupon his chum replies 'not too bad, mate', or, much worse, 'good', following which the discussion peters out. It is a cliche and a generalisation and it happens a lot.

As an old and proud country, England expects more from its citizens and feigns shock whenever a public figure is caught in a compromising position. Not all the English Puritans set sail for the Americas. For their part, Australians do not much care what happens in the bedrooms and parlours where men routinely make fools of themselves. Accordingly they were well placed to adapt to the age of disbelief that has led to the current dialectic lurch towards zealotry.

By and large Australians are more concerned about sports results than tittle-tattle or beliefs. The fortunes of local teams in familiar sports has long been of especial interest, not least because the faces of the players were so familiar that the greatest among them became folk heroes to a street, a suburb, a city and sometimes a state. Now and then they appealed to the entire country.

The tyranny of distance and the inability of most local players to leave an imprint anywhere except in the inflamed imaginations of devoted supporters also encouraged enthusiasts to concentrate upon the wellbeing of their local sides. Until improved communications revealed the possibilities and pleasure to be obtained from a broader approach, Australians relied on transistor radios, books, newspapers or word of mouth for their introduction to foreign sports and sportsmen. No second-hand report, though, could match the sight, sound and smell of a champion footy player taking a mark.

As much could be told from the subjects of the furious debates that arose in clubs where men and women could drink and play slot machines in the hope of hearing the superb sound of coins collecting in the till. As often as not the topics that aroused the most heated arguments concerned local engagements unlikely to provoke interest in the next city, let alone neighbouring states or nations. Australian newspapers focused upon the contrasting fortunes of teams and athletes celebrated in their own community and unknown beyond its boundaries. Often those communities were as small as they were committed. Passions were aroused on Saturday afternoons.

It was not even as if the same games were followed the length and breadth of the land. A rising 'star' could be famous in Melbourne and obscure in every other city of his homeland. Aussie Rules had not yet broken from its heartland, a breakout that had to wait till cable television operators began to search for an attraction, a breakout that remains only partially successful.

An Australian could become rich and famous through sport and yet remain anonymous in three-quarters of his own country, let alone the rest of the planet. That the same situation applied in the United States was no consolation. In any case the Americans were isolated by choice and the faith of the founding fathers. Australians wanted to succeed overseas, wanted to win admiration and gain experience and exposure. It was not pride that held Australians back so much as distance, cost and a lack of confidence that often remained hidden behind a loud veneer. School leavers able to afford the passage travelled in search of the reputed riches awaiting them in older and more sophisticated lands. Foreign standards and practices were accepted by all save the most spirited Australian rebel. Anyone able to label his product as having secured acclaim overseas could anticipate booming sales.

It was not easy for Australians to prosper both at home and overseas because they were so far apart. Most entertainers had to be content with fame in their own backyard. Not that they necessarily had the talent needed to find a following elsewhere. A few flourished far away but they seldom came back because it was too hard and too risky. Two of Australia's leading exports in the field of popular entertainment were a man who played the role of a Melbourne housewife and a gentle fellow who painted and played the wobble board. Neither could be called mainstream. Australia succeeded in the fringes.

As a result immense importance was attached to such international triumphs as did emerge, regardless of the field. Sporting victories over the old colonial power were celebrated with especial vigour by a nation as yet unwilling to raise its aspirations beyond the confines of its origins. The cacophony that greeted these conquests inclined opponents to think that, like their galahs, Australians made more noise than seemed fitting. They seemed to suppose that the world revolved around them. Certainly wins were celebrated without much sense of decorum. A prime minister once effectively gave the nation a day off after a local yacht had prevailed in a race sailed off Long Island. The English-born financier behind the team turned out to be a crook.

Mind you, in recent years the English have joined the revelry. Sooner or later the Georgian strain was bound to reassert itself. The Barmy Army was the first sign that sporting England no longer took itself quite so seriously. Events at Trafalgar Square on the Tuesday after England finally reclaimed the Ashes showed that, for all its - toffiness, England is as desperate to prevail on sporting fields as its opponents, and every bit as parochial. Moreover the English cricketers were given OBEs and MBEs for services rendered. Australians have to be satisfied with ticker-tape parades. By and large Australians realise they are self-absorbed. England seems entirely oblivious of its own narrowness.

Alone among Australian team sports, cricket was played in every corner of a vast continent. Inevitably this has bestowed upon the game of bat and ball an importance unmatched by rivals. Australia's cricket captain occupies a much more prestigious position than most of his foreign counterparts. During a Test match political leaders queue up to join the commentary team on ABC Radio, a team almost universally regarded as beyond compare. Some of these public figures even survive a few more years in office.

In contrast, when the Wallabies take to the field they represent their country yet are drawn primarily from two States and one Territory, and three cities, whence aspiring players must travel or else remain forever unknown. Although Melbourne will cheer anyone wearing the green and gold it has its own footballing code, its own heroes. Hardly anyone in Adelaide or Perth or Darwin knows the difference between a ruck and a maul (a disadvantage they share, in the opinion of some, with South African referees).

Tennis is the other national game and many triumphant days have been enjoyed. Indeed by the 1970s Australia had become the second most successful tennis country after America. But by the mid-1980s it had entered a fallow period. No one knew that there was a ratty child growing up in Adelaide intent on changing all that, a task he accomplished in style.

Cricket has long been Australia's predominant game. Over the decades its primary challenge has been to strike a balance between the English inheritance and local attitudes. Perhaps, finally, in a new century the right blend has been found. If so it has been a long process.

It took Australians a considerable time to put faith in their distinctive way of playing sport. Of course the same applied to clothes, theatre, comedy and so forth. Locals were slow to cast aside the tried and trusted ways brought on the ships or followed in prestigious magazines unleashed upon the British public from such respectable haunts as could be found in London's inner west. In some areas, Australia has been slow to cut the ties that bind, a hesitancy that sits ill with its self-image and reputation. Much to the astonishment of their former colonial ruler, Australia retains its foreign head of state and her dysfunctional family (this may be a tautology). Perhaps it is unsurprising that a new and remote nation seeking to construct a functioning society should start by copying a successful operation and only begin to put its customs aside when absolutely convinced that their time had passed.

Not that Australian cricket has ever lacked local flavour. Almost from the start Australia's approach reflected the heat and dust of the interior, the baked ground and vast open spaces that encouraged boldness even as England's drizzle, mud and enclosed fields preached caution. The Australian cricketer was the fellow defiantly chewing gum, his cap pulled over the back of his head, his eye glinting knowingly, his arms leathery and brown and his look fierce as he gave the ball a rip, sent down a bumper or cracked a straight delivery through mid-wicket. In short he was straightforward and uncompromising, a bloke disinclined to take things too seriously, fond of a beer, liable to put a dollar on a horse, reluctant to salute seniority but prepared to back his mates to the hilt.

When Justin Langer had a row with the captain of the South African team, Graeme Smith, it was over the visitors' grimness. As tough touring leaders are prone to do, Smith had been trying to play the Aussies at their own game. Unwilling to step back, unprepared to show any sign of fear, he bandied words with his hosts and did not disguise his hostility towards crowds and local papers. Before leaving South Africa he had described an Australian tour as a 'form of torture'. Australians enjoyed the banter and did not take it to heart, but they were puzzled by Smith's attitude. Here was this long-faced bloke acting tough and looking like an ambitious lieutenant in the British Army. Langer said, 'We're just trying to enjoy ourselves out here, mate.' Smith had not understood that Australians enjoy the badinage and the bumpers and so forth. To them, that is sport. He had mistaken it for naked hostility towards outsiders in general, and his team in particular.

The Australian male is happiest surrounded by his mates and that, too, has had its influence on the way sport has been played, for it is not true of the subcontinent or Europe or even England. A pack mentality has developed. Mike Brearley once said that to play against Ian Chappell's side was to take on a gang. To Australian ears it was a compliment. John Inverarity, one of the most civilised of men, instilled the same outlook during his tenure at Warwickshire. It is Australian cricket at its most potent: confrontational, uncompromising, an assertion of uncontained manhood.

Naturally the Anglo-Saxon male's apparently limitless enjoyment of the company of other men mystifies the female of the species. Playing sport and drinking in public houses count among the activities created by men specifically so that they could spend some time together. That sport, anyhow, also tests courage and allows participants to immerse themselves in a team adds to the effect. Not that life in a pub has always been a bed of roses. In the 19th century the most popular pastime in the pubs frequented by Somerset men consisted of two blokes standing on barrels and belting each other on the head with sticks till one gave way, whereupon another adventurer took his place and tried to take the crown.

The concept of 'mateship', of the Australian digger, has been somewhat idealised—yet the picture is not entirely mythical. Apart from anything else it provides a picture of the vision of Australia and Australianness, not that locals favour such a high-falutin' term. It is everywhere. Even the local currency is known as 'the little Aussie battler'. Australians wanted to be rid of the notion that a man's background mattered. The image of the ordinary bloke prepared to look the next man in the eye and shake his hand has a powerful effect upon the antipodean male.

Despite their rugged exteriors, though, Australia's sportsmen were more conservative than they were usually prepared to let on. They did not mind being regarded as wags but they did not want to be dismissed as roughnecks. Admittedly the Australians were never as polite as the Indians and Sri Lankans, where elders command so much respect, nor as philosophical as the West Indians, but they tempered their aggression—at any rate till the Chappells took charge—and showed a respect for custom and tradition that revealed a desire to be acceptable. No country appreciates Lord's more than the Australians. Over the years, Australian cricketers have cocked many snooks, most of them at pomposity, patronising attitudes, snobbery and hypocrisy. More than might be thought, though, they have given the ancients of the game their due.

In their own eyes, anyhow, and despite a reputation for verbal violence, Australians have played a sporting game. Often they had a point. Bodyline was not their creation, nor did they doctor pitches (or not much anyhow). In truth the Australians were seldom guilty of the sort of cynicism detected in those persuaded that victory was worth any price. When he chose to bombard the Australians in 1932/33, Douglas Jardine was not just expressing his spartan character, nor merely trying to stop Bradman. He was using a game to suppress a former colony whose people had offended him. He was an unyielding school prefect giving rowdy fourth formers a hiding. To his way of thinking it was his duty to ensure that England or, rather, Englishness prevailed.

That is not to say that Australians obeyed every sporting tradition foisted upon them. Specifically, their batsmen did not walk, or not until Adam Gilchrist's recent transformation. A defence can be made of the Australian point of view. Australian cricketers pride themselves on their lack of cant. 'Walking' was despised because it seemed to belong, as indeed it did, in a pulpit. Moreover it was open to abuse. Nothing irritates Australian players more than attempts to mislead the umpires, a trait detected in some of the supposed saints of the game.

Accordingly, Australian cricketers prefer to leave decisions to the umpires. As Steve Waugh once asked, 'Do you dob yourself in when you exceed the speed limit?' They do not trust the notion that a sports field is a different place where different rules apply.

Another Australian characteristic that surprises visitors is the acceptance of authority. Outsiders are puzzled that despite their reputation for rugged individuality, Australians meekly accept high levels of income tax—the issue was hardly raised at the last federal election yet tax rates are much higher than elsewhere and have been for decades—and instructions not to cross empty roads. Perhaps it is because Australia's inhabitants realise that the challenge of building a nation state upon a vast and empty land requires sacrifices. Moreover, most of the early arrivals were not pioneers but rejects. They were not there to create their utopia as much as to avoid the noose.

In addition, Australia began with a government in place. As Alex McDermott, a young Melbourne historian, points out: 'Normally that is not the case. A trade route opens up, people settle, a town forms, and then government reacts to it, and regulates it. In Australia there were no trade routes or emerging towns. Government started it all. Perhaps that is why we are so placid about bureaucratic intrusions into our lives.'

Naturally this willingness to respond to decisions made in high places is reflected on the field. Young sportsmen are taught to obey without demur the edicts of authority figures, whether blind, deaf or merely incompetent. Otherwise the entire thing falls down. Or so locals insist. Australians are mavericks as opposed to libertarians.

That being said, distance allowed cricket in Australia a more or less free rein to build a tradition of its own. Lord's and its dictates were a world apart from the patches of grass in Richmond and near the barracks in Sydney that were turned into playing arenas. Disapproving commanding officers might regret the raucous ways of the performers as they pitted their skills in bitter internal struggles or intense competition with an equally determined bunch from a distant city but their authority did not extend to the cricket field. In any case the officers themselves can hardly have been as prim and proper in the new continent as upon the parade ground at Sandhurst.

Gradually an Australian style of play developed. Partly it was a matter of temperament, partly a question of effectiveness. Propping and cocking might suit English batsmen trying to eke out runs on another damp pitch with the ball darting around and the committee watching, but it did not fit a brasher outlook. Nor were finger-spin or medium-pace dangerous on hard pitches of the sort that presently became familiar. In scorning both, Australian cricket reflected both an attitude to life that did not tolerate procrastination and a realisation that the prevailing conditions demanded different skills. Cricket became a young man's game partly because the nation was young and striving and partly because the grounds were too firm for ageing bones, the heat too cruel for the family man and the light too bright for fading eyes.

Aggression has been a distinguishing feature of Australian sport. As much could be guessed from the only game invented, or at least developed, in this neck of the woods. Aussie Rules is surely a singular expression of physical and tactical freedom. It is a game founded upon attack as league and soccer have defence at their core. It is a celebration of youth and courage that reflects a refusal to squeal and a rejection of the claustrophobic approach favoured in less spacious lands with duller climates. In effect Australia has tried to play every sport the way Aussie Rules is played.

In cricket, this has meant bowling thunderbolts or wrist-spin and either hooking and stepping down the pitch fearlessly or else serving as the trenchant counterpoint. Defensive batsmen were tolerated, provided they could be turned into characters in the manner of Bill Lawry or Ken 'Slasher' Mackay. Otherwise vim and vigour were expected, not the grim accumulation of runs associated with England, a nation capable of turning any activity into another form of suffering.

The Australian style of playing cricket did not reach its apogee until the Chappells took charge of the national team. For a long time, Australia was reluctant to look itself in the mirror. For better or worse, Ian Chappell put a stop to all that. The Chappell era (as the period from Ian Chappell's assumption of the captaincy in 1971 to the retirement of Dennis Lillee, Greg Chappell and Rod Marsh in 1983 has come to be called) and its aftermath forms the backdrop to the events of 1987 and Australia's subsequent triumphs. It both issued a challenge and showed the way forward.

3

THE CHAPPELL
CHALLENGE

When Ian Chappell became captain of the national side, Australian cricket started to reflect a country proud of its egalitarian background. Only by reference to the teams of the Chappell era can a proper appreciation be gained of the task facing their successors and, most particularly, the 1987 side as it tried to recover the single-mindedness of Australian cricket.

A fearless warrior of notably independent disposition and a temperament less constrained than most by niceties, Chappell defied the game's bureaucrats. He accused them of exploiting players and showing not the slightest interest in their wellbeing. In a different age he might have been a Spartacus or a Breaker Morant; instead he joined battle with cricketing authority. Abrasive, egocentric and adamant, he had the cut-throat's ability to breach the veneer of respectability and to penetrate to the core of human pretension. Never one to back down from a fight or retreat in the face of adversity, he inspired loyalty, turning his team into a gang.

Nowadays he is most often remembered as an undaunted leader and as an outspoken commentator. He was also a fine batsman. At the crease he was an honourable yet ruthless brigand, one minute dancing down the pitch to drive Bedi and Prasanna at Eden Gardens in Calcutta, the next stepping back to hook John Snow, and never mind that his grandmother had urged him to cut out the stroke as it was costing him his wicket too often. He batted at first wicket down and never shirked a challenge or gave second-best to a bowler. He had a withering tongue, a fixed idea of how the game ought to be played and how men ought to behave, and was quite capable, to his latter chagrin, of behaving like a lout on and off the field. By his own lights, though, he played the game. He saw the field as another place with its own rules. Certainly there was no humbug in him. No wonder Kerry Packer wanted him to be his captain when the revolution came. The stakes were high.

Chappell arrived in Australian cricket as a gum-chewing radical at a time when the game was run much as it had been for 50 years, by people more at home in the Melbourne Club than placing bets at their local TAB. He wore his collar turned up and, like Hemingway, asserted his manhood as if it were a shoe in need of constant polishing. He took over the national captaincy at a time when Australian fortunes were at a low ebb. Under his predecessors, Bob Simpson and Bill Lawry, the Ashes had been lost and dull cricket played. Scoring had slowed almost to a halt, the bowling lacked penetration, many matches were left drawn and sometimes entire series ended in stalemate. It was a far cry from the bright cricket played a decade earlier under the more dashing leadership of Richie Benaud.

Chappell took upon himself the task of restoring vigour to Australian cricket. He provoked as he progressed, challenging the common divide between official and player, a divide evident in more egalitarian countries such as Australia as they had long been in the mother country.

Until Chappell and like-minded thinkers such as Tony Greig in England and Clive Lloyd in the West Indies, without whom the revolution could scarcely have occurred, cricket had not seen the need to change, did not sense any threat or realise that the world was passing it by. Even then the game only cast aside its diehard tendencies under pressure from a rich and tough businessman whose rough manners hid an acute brain and a fondness for cricket, gambling and winning.

Times had changed. Bill Ponsford, Bill O'Reilly, Bill Woodfull, Bert Ironmonger and the rest kept playing till their hair turned grey, but those were slower days and cricket was less of a commitment.

Among the more misleading impressions given in recent times is that previous generations of Australian cricketers routinely retired at 30. In fact this applied mainly to those playing the game in the 1960s and 1970s. They had to find jobs, build careers. Previous generations were more generously accommodated.

As a cricketer, Chappell had nothing much to lose when the chance came to put the cat among the pigeons. His defiance of cricketing authority did not spring from any dishonourable motivation. Those involved in the uprising understood that they were bringing a deluge of abuse upon their heads. Thanks lay many painful years distant. In the meantime, many of the players had to be reassured constantly by Chappell and threatened by the businessman paying their wages.

Chappell was neither the instigator nor the leader of the revolt. Indeed if the Board had been willing to assign television rights to the highest bidder there could have been no revolt. In Kerry Packer, a television mogul every bit as suspicious of the establishment as himself, Chappell found a formidable ally and cricket officialdom faced an implacable foe.

Packer was a pugnacious and practical advocate of the free market. He was also an astute observer of mankind. Not for him the closed doors and cosy assumptions of the past. Like Chappell, he had attended an elite private school and understood the ways of the well-to-do. More than Chappell, he had suffered at the hands of the elect, had been dismissed as a brainless bully by glib schoolboys confident of their place in the order of things. Throughout he had felt patronised, and with reason: he had been. In fact he merely suffered from a reading disorder, but in those days few had heard of dyslexia. Nowadays the mistake could not so easily be made. Packer was never bookish, nor was he either a fool or an oaf. No one meeting him could think otherwise. He was a sensitive and secretly funny man with a tough brain and an awareness that money is power, and that power must be used unblinkingly or it is nothing.

By dint of his inheritance and by way of proving himself to the tormentors of his youth, Packer became an entrepreneur whose expression of interest and high-ball offer to cover cricket on his commercial station was abruptly rejected by the sort of people who had long raised his hackles. Hate can be a powerful force. After all it took Keating to the prime minister's office. Those incapable of hatred must find a force to match it or perish in the anonymity of lower achievement. Packer did not have the luxury of failure. Too much was at stake.

Neither Packer nor his captain belonged or had ever lived in the more ordered civilisation of Melbourne and therefore were not bound by its codes. Packer was a Sydneysider and therefore blessed, or burdened, with a freer and more combative spirit than those raised in Melbourne. Chappell moved to Sydney after being raised in Adelaide. The citizens of that fair city must accept their lot gracefully (the choice made by a large number of well-adjusted dwellers content to live in such an approachable place) or else try their luck in one of the larger settlements. Those trapped in between are inclined to make a loud noise through a fear that otherwise their deeds will pass unnoticed, their voice will go unheard.

Chappell and Packer found a veritable phalanx of prominent cricketers willing to entertain their proposal. The players' position had been weak ever since previous rebels had been crushed at the turn of the century, and never mind that their numbers had included some of the most impressive and best-loved cricketers their country has known. Victor Trumper may have been beloved of his people and may have been generous to a fault, his cortège may have been followed in mournful silence by half a city, but that did not save him from the wrath of the game's rulers when he dared to challenge their power.

Nor did it help Monty Noble, one of the most feared sportsmen of his generation, a cricketer who commanded respect wherever the game was played. Noble was an impressive man but, as far as challenging cricket officialdom was concerned, he was a pygmy. It was not always a case of greed or short-sightedness in high places, whether in Trumper's time, or in Chappell's. It is seldom quite as simple as that. Often it was more a matter of different approaches to the game, and to life itself. Repeatedly, experienced businessmen join cricket Boards whereupon they abandon everything they have learned by committing themselves to the maintenance of the amateur ideal (though a glance at the careers of W.G. Grace, C.B. Fry, Ranji and so many others could confirm that this was an illusion). Somehow they did not notice the financial problems this caused their players, or the number whose days ended in hardship.

Besides the curious idealism that comes over otherwise seasoned campaigners when their thoughts turn to sport, the fact remains that the administrator has wider responsibilities than the player and therefore is less likely to put his lot at the top of the agenda. Whereas the cricketer lives and dies with every ball, withdraws into a cocoon the better to perform his duties with the efficiency demanded by his wife or required by his own nerves (whichever is the stronger), the official must concentrate upon the overall health of the game.

Chappell and his men brought the power of industry to cricket in their country and irrevocably changed the lives of Australian cricketers. Of course it was inevitable that cricket developed along the same lines as industry. Workers' rights did not count for much until the unions, empowered by the ballot box, felt strong enough to look the bosses in the eye.

Professional cricketers started to receive their due when they formed associations designed to represent their views and argue their case. Until the World Series came along, the players' position was still weak. Anxious not to imperil their positions by appearing uncooperative, players tended to grumble but accept their lot. It was not so much feebleness as desperation. No one wanted to endanger his dream. Everyone knew there was only one show in town. Packer offered the players an alternative, a bargaining counter, a realisation that the time of 'like it or lump it' had passed and that they, as players, had lives to lead and something valuable to sell.

Packer also helped cricket to fill its own coffers by brightening up its image. Times were changing. No athletic endeavour could take for granted its audience or its place in the lives of the next generation. Maybe the surf was up. An intelligent follower of the game blessed with an original mind, and familiar with the way sport was presented in America, Packer reached beyond the initial dispute over broadcasting rights. Not that the rights were unimportant. In all the eulogies at his death, too little was made of the reason Packer wanted them in the first place. Obliged to show a certain amount of Australian content on his television stations, he knew that cricket would fill the gap. Whatever cost was involved was a small price to pay. Packer was a ruthless businessman who hired expensive lawyers and accountants to find loopholes whereby he'd pay as little tax as the edges of the law permitted. He did not pretend otherwise.

Moreover Packer knew that cricket was being undersold. It was a game but also a product to be packaged and marketed. Here, at last, was someone who properly appreciated and exploited cricket's potential. Night matches, chants, songs and coloured clothing made their debuts and before long the game was making a lot more money. Packer secured the broadcast rights, declared peace and shared the burgeoning profits with the game's awoken governing body. Inevitably the players began to demand, and eventually to get, their share.

Not that the game's renaissance in the 1970s was entirely due to a bunch of players and a wealthy businessman by temperament more inclined to ride with the Kelly Gang than to sup with Sir Henry. Cricket had already taken its first tentative steps towards renewal before Chappell's appearance as a swaggering batsman and occasional leg-spinner.

The first one-day international was staged at the MCG in 1970/71, years before the World Series rebellion. Admittedly it was an unscheduled attempt to entertain a crowd dismayed that their Test match had been ruined by rain. Still, a large crowd arrived and presently even the most reactionary supporter realised that the abbreviated form of the game was beyond suppression. One-day cricket had proved so popular in England that a second competition had been introduced, then a third. By the mid-1970s, county cricket had sprung back to life. Most of the game's greats, especially the West Indians, were playing in England. They needed the money, and the work. Cricket was moving in the right direction but, not for the first time, it was just a little slow. Packer galvanised it.

Chappell contributed far more to Australian cricket than confronting intransigent authority and improving the position of the leading players. He also built a team that counts among the strongest and best-loved in Australian cricketing history. About the only thing the team did not accomplish was the winning of the World Cup. They had only one opportunity and it took a great innings and a strong team to stop them, and that in the failing light. A memorable match at Lord's in 1975 ended narrowly in favour of an emerging West Indian side. Twelve years later a more modest and apparently weaker Australian outfit arrived in India determined to outdo their famous predecessors. In truth it was the only way they could draw attention to themselves, let alone secure a place in the minds and hearts of a cricketing nation loathe to forget the heroes of the previous decade.

But Packer and company could not have succeeded with any old Australian side. His timing was superb. He knew that Chappell had not merely formed a powerful side. One of the most significant attributes of the team that emerged from the darkness of the previous years was its ability to capture the popular imagination. Around the world the youth revolution had taken place, first as a break for freedom then, inevitably, as an industrial force. By their sheer weight of numbers, newly liberated youth offered a market neither industrialists, politicians, advertisers, radio stations, musicians nor publishers could ignore. Cricket needed to find a way to maintain its relevance in western countries. Most especially it needed to be 'cool'. Happily, Australian cricket has been lucky in this regard, has remained a game that can be played by the most image-conscious teenager. In recent times the dashing looks and fearless ways of Brett Lee and Michael Clarke have been a boon. Likewise the extraordinary feats of Adam Gilchrist and Shane Warne have helped the cause. Australian cricket has managed to remain sexy.

Much of the popularity and consequent success of Australian cricket over the last two decades can be traced back to the Chappell gang's ability to appeal to a younger generation eager for heroes and prepared to fly by its own lights. To coach and teach in Australia during the 1970s was to hear little else from the youthful sporting crowd than what fun it had been sitting among the larrikins on the Hill barracking for Lillee and 'Thommo' or rejoicing in the latest inspired intervention of their most particular hero, 'Dungog' Doug Walters.

Chappell's team contained characters capable of attracting the affection of young and old alike. The Chappells themselves were too lofty to seek the adulation of the masses, but several team-mates were both approachable and perfectly cast for the role of popular hero. Explosive pace bowling had long been part of the folklore and expectations of Australian cricket, yet Australia had not found a proper fast bowler for years, let alone a pair of them. Graham McKenzie had fought a lone battle, and he had been disconcertingly genial. Suddenly there was Dennis Lillee, all bristling moustache, menacing approach and fierce bumper. His deliveries hissed and spat like an enraged snake. At the other end was Jeff Thomson, with a slingshot action that made the ball rear like a stung cat. Together they terrorised the West Indians and the Englishmen, including Tony Greig, exactly the sort of batsman crowds loved to hate. And youngsters lapped it up. Not even Jimmy Barnes could create quite as much mayhem in a stadium.

They weren't the only attractions. Max Walker's tangled action, bull's heart and broad grin appealed to the larrikins while Ian Redpath's willowy frame and antique shop manner delighted the older brigade. Rod Marsh's earthy loyalty appealed even more than his undoubted ability behind the stumps.

But it was Doug Walters, that most Australian of sporting heroes, whose appeal was truly national. Like many before him, Walters came from the bush and brought with him its resolute lack of affectation. With his cards and cigarettes and grog, with his sense that he was one of the boys and might just as well have become a shearer or a roustabout as a champion batsman, he epitomised many of the ideals cherished by Australians while also fulfilling a sporting dream.

Walters was strong, silent, brilliant, instinctive, loyal to his mates and the common cause and seemed to belt the bowling around almost in his spare time, as an adjunct to his social activities. They talk about him still, though he has not played for his country for almost 30 years. That he did not in some respects fit the caricature hardly mattered. Of course he was never quite as off-the-cuff as his reputation indicated. On the contrary, he was a masterful player off the back foot and an astute thinker about the game. Before Test matches he'd practise long and hard in the nets. Once the match was underway, though, he did not want to waste energy in preparation. Gavaskar had the same approach, and no one ever called him cavalier.

Walters knew his game, knew himself and was prepared to be blinded or illuminated by these lights. Occasionally one could detect bewilderment in him, especially over repeated failures against the moving ball in England, yet never any sense of strain. Freedom from over-analysis was one of his strengths. He knew when—and how much—to think, and when to act. As far as Australians were concerned it was a most reassuring sight.

Walters was the ultimate exponent of an Australian approach to cricket that remained intact until the defeats of the early 1980s. Cricket and other sports had their strongholds, but there was no production line or any sense that players could be churned out on demand. By and large Australians dislike regimentation in sport and, naturally, this is reflected in the coaching. Foreign coaches might concentrate upon grip, wristwork, backlift and much else. Convinced that not much can go wrong for a batsman whose feet are moving quickly and correctly into position, Australians focus on footwork. It is part of a native talent for cutting every activity to its bare bones.

Obviously this approach did not start in the Chappell era, nor did it end with the retirements of the last few adherents. Australian batsmen have, mostly, avoided complexity. When they are playing well they may admit only that they are 'hitting 'em well'. When they are out of sorts they shrug and say they are 'hitting 'em well in the nets', and leave it at that. It is both an antipodean version of the power of positive thought and a reflection of the local reluctance to make a fuss.

Nor was it enough merely to start playing as Australians were supposed to play. As in theatre, opera, newspapers and much else, the need arose to dismantle the English way of thinking and to find another more contemporary and homegrown yardstick. Australian cricket had to start swigging beer and stop sipping cocktails.

Not until the Australians started to break free from their self-imposed cricketing limitations were they properly placed to take their legitimate position in the cricketing diaspora. Sooner or later Australia had to regard England as merely one of its regular opponents. Australia could not have won in India as it did in 2004 had not the players long since stopped thinking mostly about England and, for a spell, the West Indians.

Patently the appearance of Kerry Packer at Lord's cricket ground and in the London law courts—and especially his apocalyptic and hilarious question to the complacent occupants of cricketing office, 'we all have a bit of the whore in us, don't you think gentlemen?'—marked the end of the anglophile period. Clearly it was a statement of independence, even an amused battlecry, from a significant figure. Packer called the bluff of the entire cricketing establishment and directed against them the formidable powers at his disposal: the loyalty of well-loved players, a television channel, money, the scorn of the outsider and a nation belatedly trying to chart its own course. And the time was ripe for a brazen challenge.

Ian Chappell's swaggering bunch of bravadoes had much the same impact on the field as did Packer in the corridors of cricketing power. Plain as day, knowingly or unknowingly, they were a voice of sporting liberation challenging current mores. Supporters in the popular sections of the stands cheered their impudence even as their ruder actions provoked discomfort among those embarrassed by the rougher side of Australian life, and anxious not to give offence. If Bodyline and the war were not enough to convince traditionalists that the time had come to part company with their former colonial ruler, then England's entry into the European Community ought at the very least to have reminded them of geographic, economic and strategic realities. But the ties remain unbroken. As might be expected, Ian Chappell has advocated the cause of the republic as, more discreetly, has Steve Waugh, but the Queen of Australia remains on her throne; the nation's Head of State is still a foreigner.

Clearly Australian cricket had to rid itself of its post-colonial hang-up. Doubtless it helped the cause that the teams led by the Chappells kept winning. In any event the abrasive and nationalistic approach favoured by Australian cricketers since the Chappell era has caused only mild unease.

Ian Chappell turned his side into an uncompromising expression of Australianness, a veritable reflection of his chosen self. Far from apologising for the saltiness of the diggers or the coarseness of the larrikins on the hill, Chappell and his mixture of men embraced them. The concept of Australianness had been examined afresh and rein-terpreted without fear or favour.

Of course it is no coincidence that the disrespect shown by Packer and Chappell to the *idea* of England, as opposed to its representatives (neither has ever been rude to the Queen on the grounds that she is a likeable woman and it is hardly her fault—it was not even England's fault because it was the Australians who needed to wake up), was presently followed by the longest period of Australian domination the game has known.

Nor was it merely domination of the old foe. Ambition and imag-ination had been let loose and the Australians had accepted that putting such a premium on beating England indicated not defiance but deference. It meant that this vast, remote and supposedly inde-pendent island nation had still not thanked its progenitor and taken its leave. Plain as day, it was time to move on. Actually the time had long since passed. Had not the chilling words supposedly spoken by Winston Churchill during the course of the Second World War been burnt deep in the antipodean soul: 'You are expendable'?

Chappell, Walters, Lillee and the rest saved Australian cricket from conservative management, anglophilia and social irrelevance. As players and heroes, they set a standard by which their successors were bound to be judged. Nor did they go quietly into the dark night. On the contrary, they came back to the stage as commentators, journalists and coaches. The Chappell influence did not end. If anything, and for better or worse, it grew stronger. Not the least of the tasks facing subsequent Australian teams has been to escape from its shadow. And the only way to do that was to build a side with as impressive a record, as high a reputation and as dedicated a following as that won by Chappell's champions.

Border and his men took their first steps on that path in India in 1987. Ever since, the challenge of eclipsing the Chappell era has been a powerful if unspoken motivating force in Australian cricket. After all, most players have grown up hearing about little else.

4

DOWN IN THE
DUMPS

After the glories, controversies, rebellions and folk heroism of
the Chappell era, the game entered a troubled time in which
past and present, materialism and spirit fought over the
spoils. Chappell and his team had caught the imagination, brought
to life a game that might otherwise have slipped from the minds of a
new generation with a wider range of interests, and a higher level of
independence. Brighter, sexier cricket touched a nerve both with the
times and the disposition of the emerging players. Nor was it limited
to Australia. None of the impressive English cricketers to appear hereabouts was defensively minded.

Livelier cricket was sorely needed. Almost alone in the 1960s,
cricket became duller. In the age of Carnaby Street, Mini-Minors,
mini-dresses, taking flowers to San Francisco and the ever-widening
intake of herbs, the game seemed passé and might have foundered.
Bill Lawry, Bob Simpson, Geoff Boycott, John Edrich and dour
county professionals hanging on to their contracts were not well
placed to meet the challenge. What could they say to Mick Jagger and
Twiggy? Originally a game, cricket was fast becoming a craft. No
parent steered his son towards a career in cricket. Other sports were
struggling to escape the trap of controlled wages. Cricketers

remained impoverished participants in a game that took a long time to complete, demanded lots of valuable space and was used to living on tuppence. It might have become irrelevant. Instead it sprang back to life like a desert after rain.

If the 1960s was cricket's most forgettable decade, saved only by the élan of the West Indians, the 1970s were a riot. An outstanding World Cup lit up 1975 and another, almost as good, followed in 1979. Numerous brilliant players emerged, including many more from the Caribbean. India and Pakistan came to life, finding their own wristy, stylish batsmen, some notably engaging spinners and, in Pakistan's case, strong pace bowlers.

Yet it was not all sweetness and light. A change was coming over the game, a change that found its starkest expression in its most powerful team. The new West Indians were angrier and more ambitious than their predecessors. Popularity was not enough for them. Partly it was historic, an expression of the desire often detected in subdued nations and oppressed tribes to make their presence felt and, as elsewhere, sport provided the simplest and most obvious means to that end.

Boxing had long been the way out of the ghetto. Soccer was fast taking its place. Athletics was another alternative, as African long-distance runners left the sophisticates in their wake and powerful sprinters from the American mainland flexed their muscles. Cricket remained a sport with rules and a spirit that was emphasised wherever the game was played. Colonial countries tended to retain the idea of the gentleman's game longer than their mother country.

Such attitudes were hard to sustain as the game expanded. Once cricket started to confront struggle and poverty its manners were bound to be questioned. Money was the other factor, money brought by television. Cricket could not escape its times or its past. Once the colonial days ended, the surge towards combativeness, democracy, and the scramble for money was bound to follow.

Partly the harder edge detected in the game in the 1970s had geographic causes. Take the West Indians, once the most sporting of teams and now the most feared.

As the influence of the more restless islands, Jamaica and Antigua, increased, so attitudes changed until a team was formed that was not interested in laughter and losing. They wanted to win, an outlook shared by their Australian counterparts and Kerry Packer, the Kurtz-like privateer who employed them for a few years. In the latter part of the decade the two mighty forces met upon the field and, after suffering early and instructive defeats, the darker-skinned outfit prevailed.

Of course the sharper approach discovered in the West Indian game also emerged in music, that other great outlet of energy. A more demanding and politicised generation rejected the sympathetic sounds of the past in favour of the harder, prouder, more insistent tones of reggae, rap, and beyond. West Indian cricket reflected the state of mind not so much of supporters as fellow travellers. Alas the force faded as the players became ever more self-indulgent. They had forgotten about the hard work that supports the creation of black excellence, any excellence.

Not that the West Indians were alone in displaying extraordinary talents at this crucial juncture in the game's development, as it moved away from amateurism and authority and towards money and inter-nationalism. South African cricket was also flourishing, with great players such as the Pollock brothers still showing their form along-side the likes of Mike Procter, Eddie Barlow, Vincent van der Bijl and Barry Richards. Alas these men were destined to explore their abilities within the long shadow cast by apartheid. Not that any of them did much to upset the status quo.

England, Pakistan and India also produced marvellous cricketers and competitive sides. The old country might not have had the best team in the world in the game it invented since the time of 'Typhoon' Tyson, Len Hutton, Peter May and Jim Laker, but it had not yet fallen foul of the bad habits that would spread in the 1980s. Tony Greig, Alan Knott and Geoff Boycott counted among its leading lights, but were soon to be overtaken by Ian Botham and the 'three Gs', Gooch, Gower and Gatting.

The subcontinent was gathering the confidence and resolution needed to assert itself on and off the field. Gavaskar and Imran were cricketers of the highest calibre and the utmost intent and both turned into a shout a voice that had only fitfully been heard. They, too, were products of their times. Gavaskar constantly shored up the batting while tugging the beards of the older powers, and Imran prowled his domain like a lion as he licked his pride into shape.

In short the Australians were not the only nation playing compelling cricket in the 1970s. By the end of the decade they were not even the strongest side in the world, a position Clive Lloyd's West Indians would hold for another ten years. Australia was their main challenger, however, and it took the West Indies years to establish a conclusive superiority. Indeed it was not until Greg Chappell, Lillee and Marsh hung up their boots that the gap widened. Australia held their opponents in a short series played at home in 1981/82, a series memorable for Kim Hughes' epic century on a rotten pitch at the MCG, an innings that counts among the greatest ever played.

Kim Hughes and Greg Chappell were contrasting characters. Hughes was an erratic genius. Fond of a drink, forceful in his opinions, sometimes reckless on the field, the Western Australian had been blessed with exceptional talent but not the state of mind needed to exploit it. Chappell was a more rigorous type whose career was sustained by a pursuit of excellence. Where Hughes was brash, Chappell was calculating; where the younger man gambled, he sought absolute command.

Both could send spectators into raptures, Hughes with his opportunism, Chappell with his clinical polish. Hughes was the golden boy, the shallow son of the establishment; Chappell was the defiant past, at once a rebel and a conservative, a thinker and a man of action. Hughes' inability to control himself condemned him in the eyes of tougher, senior players, and prevented him fulfilling his talent. He needed to be led and to listen. Instead he was elevated to the captaincy.

The arguments that followed the slow disintegration of the Australian team of the 1970s were as painful as they were protracted. At first the decline was hidden by the excellence of the remaining players, among them Greg Chappell and Dennis Lillee. For as long as these players were wearing the baggy green, Australia was able to hold its position. Moreover some new talents had been discovered, notably Hughes and Allan Border. The future appeared to be in safe hands.

Under the surface, though, the cracks were widening and Australian cricket could not forever pretend they did not exist. Talent was as thinly spread as jam in wartime. Eventually the champions of the previous generation took their leave and then came the reckoning.

Their departure exposed frailties and fractures in the game across the country. Humpty Dumpty could not easily be put back together.

Australia was not prepared for its fall from grace. As a country it was not persuaded of the merits of systems and structures. England could keep its hedges, fences, little fields and endless need to categorise. Australia had started more or less from scratch, an immense opportunity but also a fearful challenge, and was obliged to choose its own path, construct its own buildings and, eventually, assert its independence. Something in the Australian outlook protested against specialist training. The idea of an 'elite' created discomfort in a land where passengers in taxis sat beside the driver and men batted at practice in order of their arrival.

Perhaps, too, a tendency had arisen for Australian cricketing success to be taken for granted. It is always a mistake. George Johnston in *My Brother Jack* called complacency 'the most insidious of vices'. Far from moving forwards, Australian cricket had missed the opportunity presented by the emergence of a gifted and popular side playing cricket that impressed old-stagers even as it inspired a fresh generation.

Upon the departures of the last of Chappell's gang, Australia was left with a limited and often bitter group of players. Leaderless, disillusioned, burdened with an administration still coming to terms with the upheaval of the Packer years and determined to reassert its authority, the players drifted towards trouble. A team lacking conviction, a nation lacking purpose, players lacking direction, all are inevitably bound for the rocks.

Not that the reconstructing of Australian cricket was ever likely to be a straightforward task. It may be a few years of defeat were needed to concentrate the minds of the cricketing community. Nor is it fair to heap all the blame upon the shoulders of the game's administrators. As if Australian cricket needed another headache, an unsanctioned tour to South Africa was being organised and would be joined by supposedly responsible and faithful servants of the national game. Ali Bacher and his unscrupulous associate and friend Joe Pamensky had sufficient resources at their disposal to be able to offer generous contracts to players willing to imperil their careers by playing cricket in Africa, against South Africa, during the southern summer. Superb organisers, and the most plausible of presenters, they were adept at feeding off the sort of petty gripes that betimes arise in every walk of life, especially among insecure and underpaid sportsmen. For their part, Bacher and Pamensky argued that they only wanted to keep cricket alive in their country.

Twenty years have passed since a group of Australian cricketers accepted an offer of US$100 000 to play a series of matches in South Africa. Threats of suspensions were not enough to stop them. Teams from the Caribbean, England and Sri Lanka had visited South Africa already to play unofficial Test and one-day matches. Most of the West Indians and the Sri Lankans understood that they were signing their cricketing death warrants. Many of them were marginal players raised in poverty and unlikely to enjoy any other significant pay days. Most of the English players were merely disgruntled. Graham Gooch, Mike Gatting and Geoff Boycott joined rebel tours, and Ian Botham signed a letter of intent. At the time, English cricket was riddled by racism. Senior figures at both the BBC and MCC had made money under apartheid. At one stage the entire selection committee had joined rebel tours.

The idea of raising an Australian rebel side had been hatched in 1982 after a meeting between Bacher and Bruce Francis, a former Australian opener. Candidates were not hard to find. Although the Packer revolution had changed the face of the game and the lives of established players, Shield cricketers were still trapped between amateur and professional and were therefore at loggerheads with old-fashioned administrators. Bitterness between Packer and establishment forces had also left its mark. Many respected Australian cricketers were ripe for the plucking. Nor were many of them concerned about racial equality or the ruthlessness with which the South African regime held its position.

Negotiations dragged on until October 1984, when contracts were signed in Singapore. From the outset it seemed like a rotten proposition yet the strength and seniority of the rebel squad was startling. Only England had been able to raise a more formidable outfit.

Former Australian captains Kim Hughes and Graham Yallop were the prize trophies. Senior cricketers such as Terry Alderman, Rodney Hogg and John Dyson seemed not to feel any loyalty towards Australian cricket or, at any rate, its Board. Steve Rixon, Mike Haysman, Greg Shipperd, Carl Rackemann and a dainty leg-spinner called Trevor Hohns added their names to the list.

To the fury of the rebels, three players withdrew at the last minute: Dirk Wellham, Graeme Wood and Wayne Phillips. Murray Bennett had already withdrawn owing to an uneasy conscience. Wellham, Wood and Phillips were paid off by forces anxious to maintain the credibility of Australian cricket and, first and foremost, to send a reasonable side to England to try to regain the Ashes in 1985.

Dismayed by his colleagues' betrayal, and infuriated by the under-handedness of men with whom he had shared dressing-rooms and, or so he had thought, doubts and dreams, Allan Border took a weak side to England in 1985. His team was trounced. Meanwhile the rebels were narrowly beaten by a white South African side (most black Africans, coloureds and Indians supported the visiting team from their confines in the worst parts of the stadiums) that included Graeme Pollock and Clive Rice. Hughes and company were happy that their wives were allowed to join the tour for Christmas.

Although there was enough money on the table to make a family man swoon, it said something about the parlous state of Australian cricket that so many significant players were willing effectively to withdraw their services from the game in the country of their birth. Nor was it merely a matter of a few renegades and creaky-boned ancients enjoying one last visit to the teller.

In some quarters it was argued that the tour was an inevitable extension of the 'every man for himself' principle supposedly espoused by a previous generation that had walked upright into the most bitter dispute in the history of Australian cricket. Ian Chappell and his supporters resented the implication. They did not see themselves as turning their backs on Australian cricket but as provoking it, challenging it, the better to serve players, public and nation alike. They contended that the South African rebels were not interested in anyone except themselves. It was an argument hard to refute.

Condemnation of the rebel tour was widespread, especially among those convinced that such visits encouraged an abhorrent system. Regardless of the moral issues raised, the tourists deserved censure because they were not trying to achieve anything except bigger bank balances. By walking out on Australian cricket they revealed not so much their independence as their superficiality.

After serving their bans, the rebel players returned to the main-stream game. Three of them coached international teams, several emerged as State coaches, two settled in South Africa and others became commentators. Hohns was appointed Chairman of the Australian selection committee. Eventually, democratic South Africa returned to the international fold. In the end a Players' Association was formed to rid the game of the grouses and grievances upon which the organisers had fed.

If nothing else, the rush to join a team of outcasts in South Africa confirmed the extent of the disturbances beneath the surface of Australian cricket. The rebel tours cannot easily be dismissed as merely reflecting badly on those involved. Although financial security was the main temptation, it did not work alone. Manifestly, a significant proportion of senior Australian cricketers felt sufficiently detached from cricket in their country to be able to walk out on it. This is not to deny that the money issue needed to be confronted. Sport has never accepted much responsibility for the wellbeing of its players, so it was hardly surprising that some might see fit to take care of themselves.

Patently the Packer rebellion had merely been the first stage of a much longer process whose aim was to change the shape of Australian cricket so that it better reflected the requirements of the people it served and was better placed to survive in the world in which it competed. Packer and company had helped to make the game more attractive and the lives of the leading players more lucrative, but the fundamentals of the game across the land had not been addressed. Sooner or later the gap had to be filled.

The tour to South Africa was not the only problem encountered in the traumatic period from 1981 to 1987. Between them the retirements of the last outstanding players of the previous period, the debilitations of the rebel tours and the failure to create a program capable of dealing with these challenges condemned Australian cricket to a long period of trial and tribulation. Calamity followed upon calamity. The Ashes had been lost by a distracted team led by Greg Chappell in 1977 and recovering them proved beyond subsequent outfits, most of them burdened with unconvincing leadership. England repeatedly displayed the bravado and charismatic dynamism that for a decade had been an Australian prerogative.

The defeats that came along in successive Ashes series and the failure to make an impression in the 1983 World Cup helped to focus the minds of sporting—and especially cricketing—Australians. Simply put, it was not good enough. Cricketing failure was taken to heart because cricket differed in one respect from other national and local activities. It was Australia's game, the national game, the common bond.

From government ministers to brickies sweating over cement, the game meant something. They all looked the same in a pair of whites. Dave Gibson opened the bowling for Eastern Suburbs in Sydney on Saturday afternoons and spent the rest of the week emptying rubbish bins until his numbers came up in the lottery, whereupon he bought a coastal property and put up his long-suffering feet. Australians can be accused of many things but snobbery is not among them.

Australian cricket has never been an elite sport to be pursued with particular enthusiasm in private schools and universities. On the contrary, those eager to advance their talent in the game were advised to serve their apprenticeship at clubs, to mix with adults from an early age, to learn to hit the ball harder and to take care of themselves, to endure the bumpers and curses, and to regard them as badges of honour. Youth cricket was not the critical test and did not long hold the attention of the more gifted youngsters.

Cricket was a national concern. From the Second World War onwards, every mainland State was represented and eventually Tasmania was considered strong enough to add its weight to the collective effort. Local stables might train champion horses, individuals might win Wimbledon or gold medals, but Australia could not hope for sustained domination in these activities. Winning at cricket was another matter.

Whether or not cricket struck a particular chord with Australians for reasons beyond the accidents of history must be left to the sociologists. Suggestions that the sight of Allan Border and Steve Waugh walking out to bat at the SCG, solitary figures undertaking one of the loneliest of sporting journeys, evokes the explorers as they packed their bags and went in search of inland seas or paths across the continent, seem fanciful.

Still, there has always been a hint of solitude in the Australian character, and an ability to endure that reflects the power of nature with its fires and droughts, and the harshness of a land better suited to eucalypts than more delicate flora. Alongside this sense of isolation (compounded by the distance between farms, settlements, civilisation and companions) is a desire for camaraderie that found its expression in the mateship ethic that has played such a part in the Australian conversation.

Perhaps cricket may satisfy a certain craving in the national character. More than most games, it isolates, examines and exposes the individual, pits him against the rest of the world and sometimes nature itself, against 11 opponents prepared to use fair means or foul to bring him down. Sylvester Stallone has seldom faced more overwhelming odds than the batsman as he marches to the crease.

An hour later the same player may surround himself with a bunch of mates with whom he can attempt to destroy an opponent. India's most famous indigenous game, Kabbadi, works on the same principle and it is no surprise that these two games have caught the imagination of locals.

On the other hand, Australians may, as most prefer to think, simply enjoy the delights to be obtained on the field of play, most especially the opportunity presented to belt the living daylights out of a ball, hurl it at the heads of opponents (and sometimes their stumps), spin it as hard as possible and meanwhile chirp away like a veritable aviary. Things can be done on a sporting field that, performed in any other arena, might attract the attention of the forces of law and order. Perhaps sport is popular precisely because it provides an arena in which men may test themselves and each other without having to bother unduly about the consequences. And afterwards men can continue to enjoy the company of men, without embarrassment and without any need to rush home to the nest.

Whatever the reason, Australia's commitment to cricket was longstanding and strong. Accordingly the failures of the 1980s were taken to heart. Communications and cooperation had improved to such an extent that it was possible to call a meeting of minds as a prelude to making a plan. The reconstruction of Australian cricket began with meetings and phone calls and winter nets and concerned citizens. It was no more an overnight sensation than was Rod Stewart.

The game's problems were obvious and not merely cyclical. Although the Packer rebellion had brought money into the game there was still no production line for players and not much of an internal structure. Australian cricket had depended upon its clubs and

States and most especially upon the emergence from the bush—and, sometimes, the beach—of a stream of gifted players.

Australians had relied upon happenstance, but Australia was no longer merely playing England twice every four years and numerous 'easy beats' in the intervals. Australia was playing the cricketing world, and the world meant business. Worse, Australia was sliding down the rankings. The cry went out. Something had to be done.

5

PANNING FOR GOLD

Australia's reliance on the unsolicited emergence of talent from every unsuspected corner of a vast and arid continent could not sustain the nation's yearning for success. As so often happens, an enterprise that began as an adventure was before long wearing the frown of expectation. Sooner or later Australian sport was bound to seek the regularity that structure alone can bring. Systems capable of providing opportunity and stimulating excellence were needed to release the nation's sporting ability or, as some might have it, show the country in a better light.

Cricket needed to put its mind to the task of sifting and sorting players so that latent ability was discovered, developed and brought into the mainstream, or else it could not compete with rivals that increasingly treated sport as an industry. The foreigners were on the right track. Over the past 20 years, few companies have grown their revenues and enriched their workers and stakeholders as impressively as has sport. Once sport cast off its inhibitions it spawned magazines, boosted the sales of satellite and cable television and became such a fashion statement that swimmers were persuaded to wriggle their way into the long suits recommended by clothes manufacturers.

Of course, the increase in revenue across a wide range of sporting activities has had a profound impact upon the manner in which those activities were pursued. As Bob Dylan once growled, 'Money doesn't talk, it swears'. Hitherto no one had quite known what to do with sport. At once it was a rainbow chased by westerners and a weapon seized upon by East European governments. Money changed all of that by changing the way the world was run. Capitalism prevailed in Europe, advertisers and industrialists started running the show and sport followed in their wake. The collapse of communism had the residual effect of reducing international tension, temporarily as it turned out. For the time being it was beyond the power of any government or sport to resist the tide of western affluence.

Once the political conflict was resolved it was just a matter of time before European nations started singing from the same book. Sport and capitalism became inextricably linked. Democracy replaced dictatorship. The western world became a gigantic marketplace. Moreover, sport was set apart from other activities such as music and fashion by its relative immunity to the influence of the world's dominant force. The Americans had been unable to convert Europeans or antipodeans to their favoured athletic pursuits. Soccer and athletics remained the world games, rugby was gaining toeholds in Europe and cricket was trying to shore up its base while also spreading into neighbouring nations.

Inevitably the rising tide of liberation brought numerous repressive regimes to their knees, thereby leaving the field open for sport to widen its interests. The previously intransigent apartheid government decided to sue for peace, a change of circumstances that especially affected the opportunities available to cricket and rugby. Ultimately the tide was stopped by the emergence of a highly motivated group of medievalist Islamists scornful of materialism and its effect upon their entrenched way of life.

For a few years the world was a calmer place. Vicious battles raged in the Balkans and Africa, yet these were local conflicts and did not indicate a deeper unease. It did not last. Eventually the evangelists went to war. Not until Fazeer Mohammad, the noted West Indian commentator, broached the subject on ABC Radio did most Australians realise that the Bible and Qur'an had so much in common, including numerous saints and prophets and events and precepts. Conflicts arise because the medievalists are fighting to preserve their relevance or, as they see it, the truths of their faith. Unsurprisingly they detest the internet and other avenues of free thought and expression.

Western Europe rushed into the arms of consumerism. As far as politics was concerned, it abandoned the old left as the new right and searched for a third way and found it in an agnostic version of politics that reflected a conviction that convictions were old hat.

Like other popular activities, sport was affected by these forces, though they were far beyond its control. Money brought increased competition, television brought exposure. The knocking down of the walls allowed the world to come out to play.

Of course it changed everything. It was not just the Packer rebellion that altered cricket in the last quarter of the 20th century. A game is a product of its times.

Before long the rise of India as an assertive, cosmopolitan and thankfully secular country once again altered the balance of the game. It could hardly have been otherwise. India has over a billion people and a fast-growing economy. It has mobile phones and a highly educated, ambitious and commercially minded middle class. It has the internet. It has nuclear bombs. Many of its millions follow the national game and national team, many have televisions, and quite a few have bulging pockets. Cricket could not pretend otherwise. Ever since, it has been a question of making the changes work. Cricket no longer belonged in southwest London. Nor could the older powers take for granted their supremacy, on the field or off it.

That cricket was slower than most games to cast aside its long-standing structures and spiritual amateurism said something about enduring traditions and something about the lack of activity by rivals. Cricket clung to its old ways with a defiance that combined a healthy scepticism about fads and a deeply rooted love of the game in all its aspects.

As ever the champion team set the tone. If the West Indians could not see any need to change their approach in the 1980s, why should anyone else? The only innovation made by the West Indians was the introduction of a team physiotherapist. Dennis Waight was given the job of stretching the players' muscles every morning the better to reduce injuries, a task he carried out with aplomb. He also helped to discipline the side by ensuring that every player was present and correct every morning, otherwise they faced his wrath and their captain's lashing tongue. It would later emerge that stretching was a waste of time and within a few years it had been abandoned.

The West Indies had the most powerful team despite being the least organised of all the cricket-playing countries. This was all the proof the Luddites needed to confirm their suspicion that cricket did not lend itself to graphs, percentages and theories, save those naturally produced within the ever-ticking brains of the observant player. Australian Luddites feared that over-elaboration off the field was liable to reduce boldness of thought and deed—and that, most definitely, went against the grain.

The revolutions of thought that erupted in Australian cricket in the tail end of the century involved two cricketers best described as contrarian traditionalists. To add to the effect, they were brothers: Ian the provocateur, Greg the visionary. Both argued fiercely and at length—neither is capable of mildness or brevity—that a lot of tosh is talked about the game, especially by non-players. Ian challenged authority in its Melbourne stronghold and Greg used his more respectable position in the game to recommend innovations, themselves the product of his endless quest for a better way. Australia was lucky that two of its most eminent former captains were capable of radical thoughts and actions and that they were sufficiently committed to fight for their beliefs.

In the event, Australia would learn more from its failures in the 1980s than the West Indies from its successes. The West Indies had begun to think that cricketers really did grow on trees (teenagers have the same view of money) and that another crop of champions was bound to ripen at the very time supplies were starting to run low. Too late the region discovered the errors of its ways and ever since their opponents have been exacting their revenge. Those whom the gods wish to destroy they first call invincible.

Smarting from its fall from grace at the end of the Chappell era, and lacking the disadvantages faced by a collection of island states that had turned their backs on federation, Australian cricket was able to act as a single coherent force. As a first step those responsible had to acknowledge that times had changed, the country had changed and that they could not afford to sit back and depend upon the old ways. Most particularly the bush had changed and was no longer as reliable a source of cricketing talent as Barbados. It would take the West Indies longer to realise that its island stronghold was also running out of puff.

Nor was this the only issue to confront those seeking to rebuild Australian cricket. For better or worse the experience of youth, what it is to be young, had changed irrevocably. Unlike their predecessors, teenagers now had money, opinions and independence. Tribal elders could no longer direct them towards their favoured activities. Games had to survive on their merits. Even the most dyed-in-the-wool schoolmasters came to understand that expressive games had to some extent replaced more structured activities, both in the classroom and on the sports field. Youngsters needed to be lured to the game. Traditionally a family affair, cricket faced a particular problem in the breakdown of the relationship between old and young, especially with the rise in divorce rates. From the Graces to the Mohammeds, Khans, Chappells, Waughs and the rest, fathers, sons and brothers have had an uncommonly large part to play in the story of the game. Now the script was being rewritten.

To maintain its popularity, cricket needed to loosen its girdle. Packer had taken care of the entertainment side of things. Night cricket, coloured clothing, jingles and so forth had ensured that cricket no longer had the limited appeal of the chamber orchestra. As far as the marketplace was concerned the game was flourishing. Popularity was not, though, the only issue. Australian cricket needed champions and a winning team. Gone were the days when it was enough to pull on a green cap.

By now Australian sport had accepted that raw talent alone could not match the production lines created in America and Europe as runners, gymnasts, swimmers, cyclists, weight-lifters and so forth were churned out like cars in Detroit. Accordingly, in the early 1980s an Institute of Sport was set up in Canberra, a place where expertise was offered and excellence was expected. The Institute has played its part ever since in raising the tally of medals won by Australian athletes at Olympic Games and other major events. Not that every medallist has passed through Canberra—undue claims are repeatedly made on behalf of academies and such like in an attempt to justify inflated budgets and generous wages paid to those hovering around the fringes of the industry—but its foundation was an indication that Australia had stopped trying to live on its ear.

Cricket was bound to be touched by the rise of seriousness in sport. It is remarkable that Australian cricket flourished for as long as it did because it relied on a succession of extraordinary players emerging from improbable places at just the right time. Australia could not have managed nearly as well without the likes of Don Bradman, Bill O'Reilly, Stan McCabe, Doug Walters and Glenn McGrath, yet these men might easily have passed unnoticed into the night.

That such an array of talented cricketers emerged from the bush speaks volumes about its inhabitants because the complications and perils faced by its inhabitants are not to be underestimated. Even in these days of swift communication and fast transport it is no small thing to carry out any collective enterprise in the outback. Furthermore disaster is only ever a carelessly tossed cigarette butt away. The inhabitants of the outback have a peculiar affinity with the game of bat and ball. By reputation they are a steadfast and sturdy bunch, just the approach needed to survive the slings and arrows of a treacherous game. Moreover, until recent times youngsters were obliged to create their own entertainment because the latest urban craze was not available. Usually they kept it simple, concentrating on the game played by their champions whose deeds could be read in such newspapers as reached the region, or followed on a crackling transistor radio.

In any event, over the years many of Australia's greatest cricketers came from the country. Their achievement in the international arena was all the more notable because many of them were unsophisticated. Often they lacked exposure. Bradman did not encounter a wet wicket until his first Test match whereupon he failed and was dropped in favour of Dr Otto Nothling, a sound all-rounder with a colourful background who was too polite to appeal for leg before in his only appearance, a reserve thought to be unique in the annals of Australian cricket.

Other magnificent players emerged from inaccessible postings such as White Cliffs where, or so Bill O'Reilly stoutly maintained, the crows flew backwards to avoid getting dust into their eyes; Dungog, where Doug Walters opened his innings; and Narromine, a place beyond the black stump where Glenn McGrath bowled his first bouncer. Stan McCabe, too, was a fair dinkum bushie, unlike others so described. Mark Taylor is routinely categorised as a 'bushie', sometimes even a 'typical bushie' when he took guard in Wagga Wagga, a sizeable semi-industrial town not far from Sydney. Crocodile Dundee he is not. Nor is Wollongong, Brett Lee's home town, exactly an outpost, yet he is often described as coming from the bush.

Bradman, McCabe, Walters and others seemed to appear more or less out of the blue. McGrath's discovery was not quite so fortuitous. Indeed it owed much to his performance against a group of travelling players being taken around the bush by Doug Walters by way of giving aspiring inhabitants a chance to strut their stuff. McGrath caught the eye, was invited to try his luck and promptly embarked upon a trip that has become almost as famous as that undertaken by Burke and Wills. After surviving a hazardous journey through the comparative chaos of Sydney traffic behind his indomitable mother (who had not formed a favourable impression of the metropolis), McGrath settled in his caravan and lived on a diet of beans, wickets and hope, a combination that proved potent.

Not that those learning the game in the bush were disadvantaged in every way. They might have lacked spit and polish but from an early age they were used to playing with men. That is the Australian way. Also they were able to play by their own lights. Bradman's unorthodox grip went uncorrected by well-meaning juvenile coaches, O'Reilly was never told to choose between leg-spin and medium-pace, Walters was not instructed to tighten his defence.

Australians liked the idea of young men emerging from some remote corner ready to take on the cricketing world. In some respects they represented a dream captured in the contrasting poems of Henry Lawson and Banjo Paterson. Bradman was not cherished merely because he seemed invincible during the Depression. He was from the bush, 'our kid', our very Australian champion. It was the same with Walters.

Of course the boys from the bush were also a straightforward lot. A mother once brought her son to a posh Sydney school, plonked her feet on the headmaster's table, observed that it was 'ruddy hot', and announced that the school should consider its job complete once the lad knew how to use a knife and fork.

Even now it is usually easy to tell the bushie apart. It is part of the enigma and appeal of Steve Waugh that he resembled a country man yet came from the busy southwestern reach of the biggest city on the continent.

Australia's reliance on the bush could not last. In truth it barely survived the terrible drought of the 1980s that brought so many good men to the doubtful sanctuary of the city. Nor could Australia depend upon urban clubs to continue producing first-class cricketers. For a century, grade clubs had been Australian cricket's backbone as the bush had been its beating heart. But clubs could no more escape the challenges of changing times than anyone or anything else. Wives expected their husbands to become family men and fewer older players were able to meet the growing commitments of night games and increased fixtures as club cricket, too, tried to become more attractive. Nor were they as willing to spend hours travelling to and from a game as authorities tried to overcome geographical and logistical realities. Inevitably the average age of sides dropped, whereupon the educational value of grade cricket was reduced.

Australia's supply lines had not changed for half a century but, with bush and grade cricket under pressure and the national team losing, those responsible for the health of Australian cricket had to think again. Australian cricket had to look elsewhere. It had to start working harder.

It took a certain humility for Australian cricket to admit its weaknesses. After all, the story until now had many high points. Moreover everyone knew that fortunes in sport waxed and waned. Might this not be simply another bad patch? Rejecting all excuses, Australian cricket set out in search of a better way. Naturally it began by examining procedures overseas.

Unfortunately precious little could be gleaned from the experiences of other cricketing nations. Every country has its own evolving way of producing cricketers. In countries where cricket began as a game for the elite, school cricket was crucial, for it was to these private seats of learning that rich parents sent their sons. Playing the game, literally and metaphorically, was regarded as part of the civilising process. That English culture was superior to the local version was seldom questioned within the hallowed walls or on the fields where well-bred youngsters learned to accept the two impostors with equanimity. Of course such a notion could not survive independence movements founded upon the conviction that a nation and its peoples were capable of taking care of themselves.

Until the revolution led by Arjuna Ranatunga, Sri Lanka's best cricketers came from a handful of elite schools in Colombo, including Royal's and St Thomas. The schools did not have facilities to match those to be found at English or South African private schools, but the game was loved and good coaching, discipline and opportunities were available for deserving boys.

Paltry crowds watched the Test matches when eventually they arrived in Sri Lanka, but thousands of spectators turned out for leading school matches. No wonder boys did not want to leave school. They inhabited the fanciful world created in the school stories penned by English novelists a hundred years ago. The rich children were probably the only ones able to read those books because their government's first act upon achieving independence was to abolish the teaching of English on the grounds that it had been available only to the wealthy. Of course the rich promptly hired private teachers, thereby turning themselves into even more of an elite.

Arjuna Ranatunga challenged and changed all of that. Although he, too, was born and raised in Colombo, he was a Buddhist and therefore neither a blue blood nor part of the in-crowd. Undeterred, he fought his way to the top and, once installed, set out to become that most dubious of God's creations, the people's champion. Doubtless it was his way of removing the obstacles that had blocked his path. He was too good a cricketer and too artful a man to be ignored. Nor was he willing to doff his cap to any man. He used changing times and anti-imperial sentiment to widen the game and advance his career. In short he was his country's first cricketing nationalist. Thereafter Sri Lanka looked as much towards its Buddhist schools and its outstations as it did towards its favoured few.

Others followed in Ranatunga's wake. His successor, Sanath Jaya-suriya, attended an unfashionable school located on the southern tip of the island. Muttiah Muralitharan saw the light of day in Kandy and his father, a small businessman, sent him to board at the local Catholic school.

Much the same process, with local variations, occurred in Pakistan and India as the game widened its search for talent. Background, religion, wealth and location no longer counted for nearly as much.

Cricket had made its choice. It did not want to be an elitist game. Everything that has happened in the last 20 years, good and bad, has been the result of that subconscious decision.

Australian officials eager to review their country's production line did not gain much inspiration from South Africa or Zimbabwe, where school sport has been even more important. South Africa's traditionally white sports relied on the schools to instil the standards and attitudes youngsters needed to take the next step. They were the fabled testing ground. Life outside the school gates was altogether more complicated which may explain why many white South Africans are emotionally attached to their seats of learning. Schools offered a security, simplicity and camaraderie not readily available in a changing world.

Since the arrival of democracy, both countries have been trying to transform a game that had been the preserve of the fortunate few into a popular pastime. It has involved more than correcting sporting imbalances. Cricket had not captured the African imagination and thus was poorly placed to prosper once the barriers were removed. In addition, there were formidable logistical and social obstacles to be overcome. After all it is hard to persuade a boy to continue playing a game when his siblings depend on him for food and the nearest water is an hour's walk away.

The West Indies had most in common with Australia because its players proved themselves in the informal cricket academies of parks, streets and club grounds. It also enjoyed the benefit of fiercely contested domestic matches played between proud sovereign nations. Much as the Australians might admire the West Indian team, though, they could not learn anything from the West Indian system because it too closely resembled their own, and that was not working.

The inevitable conclusion was that Australian cricket had to think for itself. If it could not learn from other cricket nations, though, it might be able to learn from other sports. As it happened, the timing could not have been better. Sport's first truly professional age had just begun. Australia would surge to the top of the cricketing ladder because, in its darkest hour, it had the sense to hitch its wagon to a group whose wheels were already moving.

By 1987 the insularity of Australian sport was coming to an end. Money, transport and communications had changed everything.

Perhaps, too, the country was no longer so easily satisfied. Of course, it helped that the teams led by the Chappells kept winning, but when that run came to an end, what then? If Packer and Chappell the elder had provided the stimulus, it fell to Chappell the slightly younger and Allan Border to attend to the practicalities of the matter. It was all very well freeing the antipodean spirit, quite another matter turning that ambition into consistent performance.

Although similar in many respects, not least in their rearing and the penetrative abilities of their brains, the Chappells were blessed with very different temperaments. Partly through an inherent suspicion of officialdom and partly because he thinks the sporting scene is already sufficiently crowded (he has long argued that international teams do not need a coach) Ian has avoided joining the ranks of administrators or instructors. Instead he has worked as a high-profile television commentator and as an accomplished contributor to various English, Indian and Australian newspapers and magazines.

Despite his background, Ian represented the blue-collar section of society against the supposedly crusty establishment. Greg's position was more complex because his unruffled and haughty mien made him an unapproachable figure, besides which he did seem more comfortable among businessmen than tradesmen. But he was no insider either. Perhaps he can most safely be described as a man apart.

Greg was by nature more idealistic and expansionary than his older brother, and not remotely as rebellious. An altogether more stylish batsman, and less inclined to goad, he has taken a more cerebral approach to life. Ian hurled himself directly and relentlessly into the thick of the battle; Greg preferred to ponder his course.

As with the Waughs, the younger brother, or the later developer, was the more withdrawn. Maybe it is the destiny of the first-born or first emerging to blaze a trail and the task of the younger sibling to follow the path as best he can, not as a shadow but as a determinedly distinct personality.

Greg Chappell has also always been a structuralist. Blessed with a mind that is ruthless and analytical and yet also capable of flights of fancy, whether considering his own game or the game as a whole, he has played a significant part in the reshaping of Australian cricket. Throughout, his strong point has been the innovations he recommends. His weakness has been an inability to tell which among them are the most worthwhile. Perhaps, too, he has tended towards impatience when his proposals are left to splutter their way through committees. Accordingly he has been inclined to walk out when there is work left to be done.

In some respects Greg was better placed than Ian to assess the state of the game in his country, having played for both South Australia and Queensland. Moreover he had remained in the game longer and suffered more. Lacking his older brother's thick skin and robust health, he had been vulnerable to sleights, setbacks and the sort of weary disenchantment that lay behind the underarm delivery.

His cricketing experiences were also altogether more varied. By the mid-1970s he had become an integral part of a powerful and populist Australian side that challenged and changed the face of Australian cricket. When Ian found he could no longer put tyro fast bowlers in their place and withdrew from the battlefield, Greg was still at the peak of his powers and therefore denied the luxury of timely retirement. Sustained by the captaincy and the company of members of the old guard such as Marsh and Lillee, he kept playing Test cricket for another six years. It cannot have been easy; he must have felt that he had paid his dues.

Whereas Ian had led the revolution and then passed the flame, Greg was obliged by his age, talent, desire and responsibilities to keep playing. Accordingly he was involved in both the deconstruction of the established order and the gradual reconstruction of the game across the country. History insists that few men are born with the qualities of both the warrior and the organiser. Greg did not quite lead the charge, nor did he exactly preside over the renewal. By contributing to both, though, he did all that can reasonably be expected from one man.

In the vernacular, the second part of Greg Chappell's cricket career was hard yakka. His batting retained its polish, yet there was also an abiding sense of frustration about the man. The slide that followed the end of the World Series inevitably left its imprint upon him. He saw that the uprising had merely been a first step. The opportunity presented by the players' defiance had to be taken or all would be lost.

It was fortunate that the Packer players had not been interested in solely power, money or even protest. Most particularly they believed that cricketers had been exploited for long enough and, not unreasonably, demanded that skills be rewarded. Idealism did not pay the bills and the Australian Cricket Board (ACB) had not accepted any responsibility for the wellbeing of its players, either during their careers or afterwards. In short these men were fighting for something more than their own interests. And Greg Chappell was left with the task of driving home the point.

Australia's unchecked regression during the early 1980s confirmed his conviction that measures had to be taken to put Australian cricket on a more coherent footing and that he ought to involve himself in the process. Accordingly he accepted a position on the ACB where he joined the ranks of those advocating a more calculated approach to the production of players. For a hundred years Australian cricket had grown almost of its own accord, with States added to the first-class competition as seemed appropriate and otherwise left to their own devices.

Greg Chappell joined those proposing a more centralised structure with better-organised youth competitions. They also proposed an Academy, to serve as a finishing school and where the most talented youngsters would learn the process of turning ability into achievement. Of course Chappell was not alone in his belief that the culture of the Australian game had broken down, that young cricketers were not being educated properly within its confines, but he was the most prominent advocate of the case.

It was the proposal to open an Academy that provoked the most consternation because it was an elitist idea that sat ill alongside the proud boast that Australia was the land of the 'fair go'. But Australian cricket did not have a choice other than to take the plunge. Most sports had acknowledged the need to put their houses in order or else to accept the role of minor entertainment destined sooner or later to be surpassed by alternatives spread by the television camera. Australian cricket could no longer sit back and allow events to take their course.

Established in 1987, before long the Academy was creating its own legend. Obviously it helped that players of the calibre of Justin Langer, Damien Martyn, Greg Blewett, Laurie Harper and Shane Warne emerged from a single intake. In those days the Academy was run by a gentle Victorian idealist called Jack Potter who also later ran an icecream kiosk on Glenelg beach. In truth the players were not treated with the delicacy suggested by the notion of an elite squad, nor did they enjoy splendid, purpose-built facilities. Instead, they stayed in dormitories at the University of South Australia, trained early every morning in the gym and practised at the Adelaide Oval. In those days they attended the Academy for an entire year and played cricket for clubs in the city.

As much as anything the Academy was intended to improve the culture of the game by giving it a sharper focus. It was also supposed to persuade talented 18-year-olds that there were many mountains still to climb. Too many of the best youngsters were falling by the wayside. Now they could be brought together, given an opportunity, pitted against each other and called to account daily.

Later the impression would be given that Rod Marsh had run the Academy almost since its inception, but that was far from the truth. Indeed it was a rewriting of history that said more about the mutual loyalties of players from the Chappell era than their devotion to detail.

When the long Australian supremacy of the 1990s began, opponents eager to discover the secrets behind the resurgence of Australian cricket focused on the role played by the Academy and regarded its creation as the decisive moment. But that is to overstate the case. The Academy was merely the icing on the cake. Greg Chappell has long argued that it has played a relatively minor part in the revival, that the Academy itself could not change anything. Unless the game's culture was correct, unless youngsters were properly directed beyond its boundaries, the effects of a period spent among their peers in Adelaide would swiftly fade. But the Academy was a novelty that provoked interest in Australia and overseas. England would establish its own when it realised that its cricketing culture had fallen into decay, and invite Marsh, the Australian ring-master, to take charge.

Australian cricket went much further than merely opening an Academy. Apart from the improvements in youth cricket competitions, increased cooperation between the States and revised coaching standards, the ACB also appointed a coach, a physiotherapist and a reliable management team. Meanwhile the players set up a properly functioning Association.

Of course Australia was not the first country to change the way it thought about a sport. In other athletic activities it languished behind East Germany, China and other nations eager to use sport to build patriotic fervour or else to show their supremacy. It was just that no one else had thought to apply the same principles to cricket.

By attaching itself to the progressive movement that arose in Australian sport in the 1980s, cricket secured an advantage over its rivals. Elsewhere the game retained many of its amateurish and colonial characteristics. Nothing much had changed in England, India, West Indies or South Africa, as regards cricket anyhow. Cricketers were a bit better paid, sometimes wore coloured clothing, but were otherwise hard to distinguish from previous generations. Australia stole a yard and turned it into a mile. Not that the picture looked remotely rosy as Border, Simpson and their unfancied side gathered in India for the start of the 1987 World Cup campaign.

6

CROSSING THE SIMPSON

F ew Australian newspapers considered it worth sending a reporter to cover the 1987 World Cup. ABC Radio, in its infinite wisdom, did not send a commentary team to the event, relying instead upon makeshift arrangements and collaboration with international counterparts with bigger budgets and more faith in their sides. It was a mistake. Admittedly almost everyone expected the Australians to be eliminated in the early rounds but it was a World Cup, only the fourth of its kind. After it was all over, cricket enthusiasts in the Senate would seek an explanation as to why citizens eager to follow the fortunes of their team had been obliged to rely on the booming, old-school intonation of one Henry Blofeld for the latest information. He was supported by the internationalist voice of a certain Roebuck who, as one senator pointed out, at least had an Australian connection. The ABC did not even send a news reporter, relying on an experienced journalist, Mike Coward, to provide the required reports.

Not, by the way, that Roebuck's voice was often heard. Henry Blofeld is a splendid fellow with many fine attributes, among which cannot be included the fondness for the pregnant pause observed in the oeuvre of that other notable cricketing man, Harold Pinter. As climaxes approached, Blofeld became ever more excited and words flew from his mouth like bullets from a machine gun. Now and then, it is true, he did look encouragingly in my direction, but no sooner had my lips began to quiver than another train of thought steamed into Henry's brain and he was off again. It was the fruitiest stuff, and was enjoyed as much from close proximity as around the numerous countries where the broadcasts were heard.

Why had not the ABC sent its own team? The answer was simple. The management of the ABC did not want to commit itself, and a sizeable chunk of its grant, to a tournament being played in a remote land with unreliable services in which Australia had as much chance of winning as Lang Hancock had of securing the leadership of the Greens. Even now, in these days of mass and swift communication, broadcasting from the subcontinent is a fraught business with lines being established at the last possible moment, and after numerous meetings with the local brinksman only to drop out periodically, and usually at the most inconvenient time. On Australia's thrilling tour of India in 2001, commentators were sometimes reduced to describing play on a mobile phone being passed from hand to hand like the conch in *Lord of the Flies*. Hardly surprising then that, 14 years earlier, ABC officials had been reluctant to rely on the efficiency of Telstra's subcontinental counterpart.

ABC Radio was not alone in its pessimism about Australia's prospects, or the likely level of public interest. No Australian television company sent a full-scale team to the subcontinent. As far as the media was concerned the event might as well have been taking place on the moon.

Australia's newspapers were every bit as unimpressed as their colleagues on radio and television. Not that the Australian media group bulges at the best of times. Only two major newspaper groupings exist, a fact which indicates not so much public antipathy towards newsprint as the difficulty of sustaining a national paper in a country with State politics, fanatically followed but contrasting footballing codes and fatally different deadlines.

Both the Murdoch and Fairfax empires considered one reporter sufficient to cover a World Cup in India. News Corporation's man provided copy for different papers, each of which was in different time zones and required different angles. Not much has changed on that front. Only a handful of reporters covered the 2005 Ashes series in England. Add a radio man, two photographers and assorted television crews and the size of the party may have reached double figures. By way of contrast, England has a surfeit of contrasting national newspapers, each with a market of its own, and its touring teams are followed by a pack that invariably passes its half-century and sometimes approaches three figures.

Nor was the Australians' poor form the only reason behind media neglect of the tournament. Australia was still an Anglocentric nation. India was a remote and mysterious land, with curious customs and nasty diseases. On their return, Australian touring teams would regale audiences with amusing tales of rats found in hotel bedrooms, murky water, stomach upsets and the other maladies encountered on the subcontinent. Reputations die hard.

Although it speaks of dullness of the spirit, for many years the view of India as a place to avoid was not entirely unfair. Journeys into the interior often did require a sturdy stomach and an ability to rough it. Some of the aeroplanes appeared to be held together by string. Outstanding work on the ground alone explained the miracle of flight bestowed upon numerous ageing hunks of metal. Some of the roads resembled a dodgem ring. Correction. All of the roads resembled a dodgem ring. Dawn was the best time to travel because India rouses itself slowly and then stays awake deep into the night.

For all these discomforts, though, the reluctance to visit India also points towards a failure of the imagination. In the pink city of Jaipur an elephant pulling a cart was passed by a camel pulling another cart and no one took the slightest notice. Visitors might also be impressed by a people capable of cheerfulness amid grinding poverty.

India is, truly, another country and the Australians needed to adjust to its ways before they could even think of victory.

India is run by its mothers and elders, a combination that conspires to ensure that youthful ways are not allowed to last too long while reinforcing seniority so that talented youngsters eager for opportunity are forced to wait till their turn comes. Not the least contribution of Sambit Bal, the first editor of the Asian version of *Wisden* magazine, has been his encouragement of a stable of gifted young Indian and Pakistani writers, thereby catching them before they were beaten down by a discouraging system.

Australia was, for many decades, an overwhelmingly masculine society. Australian sport can be regarded as the last assertion of the old-fashioned masculinity abandoned elsewhere. By the same token, with his go-karts, scrapes, reluctance to study and suspicion of vegetables, Ginger Meggs can be seen as a final statement of simplicity in youth. It is not inconceivable that the contrast between the spirits of these countries had as big a part to play in the various disputes that periodically arose between their players and Boards as conflicting religions and cultures. It did not help that the Indians thought Australian umpires were incompetent, a favour that was returned. Then there was the tautness of the mats! Not that cricket was ever as scrupulous a game as might be imagined. In his time as a cricket captain, my old headmaster used to walk around dropping pebbles on the pitch.

Previous Australian teams had lacked the spark needed to reach beyond the din and dust that is part of life on the subcontinent. Doubtless the defeats, the dubious umpiring, the upset stomachs and the rest had left their mark. Not that Australians were instinctively hostile to the region or its inhabitants. Some of Australia's most celebrated cricketers have been regular and popular visitors, and their willingness to mix with locals has been much appreciated.

In any event Allan Border and his struggling team arrived in India without much fanfare, let alone accompaniment or expectation. Doubtless the players had heard the infernal tales, cricket having a strong oral tradition. Fortunately, they were a new bunch with nothing to lose and had been blessed with the independence of mind required to decide for themselves about India and whatever they might encounter along the way. In fact they had been selected for this very purpose.

Australian cricket had not been idle in the months before the start of the fourth World Cup. Practices calculated to ensure that better days lay ahead were put in place. Not that the changes had brought immediate results or that the future looked bright even to those closest to the action. Otherwise more reporters would have been sent to cover the proceedings.

Australian cricket had not merely opened an academy and tightened its structures. Rejecting the debilitating notion that success comes in fits and starts, the ACB had produced a strategy designed to raise standards. A process of modernising had begun that was to last several years and to have a profound effect upon the way the game was played and organised across the country. Nor were the changes made within Australian cricket in the period before the fourth World Cup entirely impersonal. Greg Chappell and many others understood the need to strengthen the game's culture and there was no better place to start than at the top. Accordingly, the Board decided that a coach was needed to help the national team, and especially its reluctant and floundering captain. Notwithstanding the objections of dismayed past players, especially the Chappells, Bob Simpson was the man chosen to fill the position.

The Chappells objected to Simpson on several counts. Ian did not think a coach was required regardless of his identity. He said that he had never seen a coach score a run or take a wicket and therefore could not see any point in them. It was a disingenuous argument intended as a protest against the apparent compromising of the captain. Ian Chappell believed that relieving Border of some of his responsibilities set a bad precedent. As far as he was concerned captains ran cricket teams. Since his younger brothers have accepted coaching positions both domestically and internationally, it can be assumed that the Chappell household is not, on this issue anyhow, of a single mind.

Of course Chappell was right to insist upon maintaining the authority and accountability of the captain, but it does not follow that the coach is redundant. Rather, it is a question of assigning duties intelligently, with a coach providing information, organising practices and suggesting strategies. No captain worth a cent would tolerate anyone trying to interfere with his running of the side. Chappell wanted Border to sort out the mess himself and did not think he could be a proper leader otherwise. Perhaps, also, he was objecting as much to the particular as to the general.

That Simpson was not a popular figure among the players of the 1970s added to the contentious nature of his appointment. During the Packer rebellion he had emerged from retirement as the establishment's champion, which did not endear him to those convinced they were fighting the good fight. Much was made of the supposed greed of the rebel players. Ever since, Ian Chappell has been trying to find out how much Simpson was paid to captain the official team. He's convinced he did not come back for honour alone. In any event,

World Series players and commentators who had been made to feel like outcasts now had to watch as the man who had gone out of his way to legitimise the ACB's activities in this fraught period took a senior position with the Australian team. That the rebellion had occurred more than ten years before did not soften the blow.

Moreover there was something chilly about the new coach. That he was universally called 'Simmo' said more about the Australian fondness for abbreviations than about his standing as a fair dinkum bloke. For his part, Simpson regarded Ian Chappell as a 'good hater' and promptly battened down the hatches. From the start he understood that the powers and popularity of a glorious past were pitted against him. It was like watching Darth Vader take on Ned Kelly.

But Simpson was the right man for the job. He had an analytical brain that probed the innards of the game, a trait also evident in Steve Waugh, a young all-rounder who had introduced himself to Australian cricket in the prelude to the World Cup. Simpson sensed weaknesses as a dog does a bone and had the ruthlessness needed to exploit them. To him cricket was not so much a game as a discipline, the solitary purpose of which was to crush the opposition. Pretty or ugly, it was all the same to him. Pragmatism was his watchword. Every step that brought victory closer must be taken, not just in the hours of play but also before and afterwards. It was an unsentimental view whose time had come. Australia had been losing. Idleness had taken a grip. England held the Ashes.

Simpson and Bill Lawry had opened the batting for their country in the 1960s, a time of slow scoring and numerous draws. Simpson was a hard man of the old school, without illusion or sentiment. As a batsman he had started as a dasher and ended up as a ruthless collector of runs. His most famous innings had been played over several days in Manchester. Holding a 1/0 lead in the 1964 Ashes series, Simpson simply ground his opponents into the dust. He was an old-fashioned batsman who moved about in the old way, almost walking into his shots. Nowadays batsmen are more cut and dried in their footwork.

Simpson scored 301 before losing his wicket. Strangely a smile could be seen on his face as the edge was held behind the wicket. He did not often smile on the field. But, then, he had scored a triple century. Ken Barrington saved his side by replying with 256. Hardly any time was left to start the second innings. It was a dull match and a dull series.

Simpson eradicated error from his batting, turned himself into an efficient machine. Talent had taken him only to the edges of success. The game had taught him the importance of rigour. It was a lesson he never forgot. Since he had also been a handy leg-spinner and a magnificent catcher at slip he was well placed to speak to most parts of a team. Moreover he understood how these skills worked, and could teach them.

As coach Simpson's task was to turn a group of like-minded players into a formidable force. Convinced that a team is only as strong as its weakest player, he set out to rid the side of cricketers whose attitudes did not match his expectations, and to find suitable replacements. Simpson could not afford to fail. The shadow of past conflicts was ever-present and his enemies were to be seen and heard everywhere he turned.

Although understandable, his paranoia became a weak point and played a part in his eventual downfall. Simpson was inclined to divide the world between supporters and enemies, and to treat both camps appropriately. Every critical remark was read and taken to heart; often they were regarded as part of a plot. The resemblance with Richard Nixon was uncanny. In both cases there has been a tendency to play the man and not the ball. In both cases there was a sense of struggle with the liberal world, the smart set, and a profound unease with themselves. Simpson, too, was fuelled by early failure and the shattering of youthful dreams. Nor did he like himself much. He knew he was dark, and went with it.

Finding and eliminating the unsettling elements in the side was a straightforward task. Once established, intelligent and humorous players can all too easily fall into the habit of making withering remarks or else amusing themselves in a manner that does not affect their games yet undermines those of colleagues. No team is harder to captain than a university cricket side because it spends so much time together, is usually losing and contains many minds that can see the cost of everything and the value of nothing. And there are few places as naked as a cricket dressing-room.

Allan Border's outfit included several players blessed with sharp tongues and penetrating humour whose approach to the game, whose very lives, hinted at a levity that did not sit well with sustained sporting success. Several seasoned campaigners did not survive the clearances. It was not that they were unpleasant or even bad influences, just that a new side could not be built while old habits remained entrenched. These fellows could not change their ways easily. Once a player has adopted a role in the rooms it is the devil's own work to change.

Simpson wanted men prepared to listen and to work. He was accused of jettisoning those he could not manage. In fact he merely set out to remove shirkers and others he felt were unintentionally undermining the collective will. Border could not have dropped the players because he could not see their faults. On the contrary he enjoyed their irreverent humour and saw in their insouciance a confidence he could not hope to attain. Blessed with a thick skin, as soon as he walked onto the field, he was able to focus his entire personality on his cricket. Others, and especially newcomers, were more affected by atmosphere. In truth it was a simple matter. In order to restore idealism it was necessary to get rid of the cynics.

Reasoning that cricket was not an art but a technique, Simpson's first step was to change the way the players practised. Whereas baseball requires a refinement of natural swings, namely the throw and the swipe, cricket demands mastery of artificial manoeuvres, specifically balls delivered with a straight arm and strokes played with a straight bat. Convinced that these movements must be repeated until they became second nature, Simpson forced his players to treat the nets as a drill ground.

The same applied to fielding. Inflexibility would prove to be his weakness, but attention to detail was Simpson's strongest point. He did not merely encourage close fieldsmen to practise catching for hours upon end; he taught them the best way to catch the ball, by waiting for it with soft hands so that it settled easily. An outstanding slip fieldsman in his time, Simpson knew what he was talking about. His entire philosophy was founded upon respect for the basics of the game. The Chappells had been taught by a tough father. Others relied on trial and error. In Simpson's first few years the Australians continued to drop catches. Before long, though, the slip cordon became as sharp as any the game has known.

Much the same principles were applied to fielding in the deep. The Australian side worked harder than any of its contemporaries on the precision and speed of its interceptions and throws. Before long Border and his men were hitting the stumps, apparently at will. Of course it helped that Simpson had in his charge some unusually committed men. No one can ever have thrown down stumps more often than Border and Steve Waugh. Hardly a shy missed. Here is an insight into sport. These men were not exceptionally talented. Practice played a part in their precision, but there was another thing. Both had the ability to focus on the instant, and an unerring sense of the location of the stumps. Cricket was in their souls, dominated their senses. And both had formidable willpower and an absolute commitment to winning.

Simpson did not work alone. In Laurie Sawle, he had the luxury of a Chairman of selectors as determined as himself to rebuild the values and position of Australian cricket. That Sawle was content to remain in the shadows only added to his contribution.

Sawle was a steady, discreet man who had found his rightful place in the game. A modest player, he had risen through official ranks without effort or ego and was to play a crucial part in the restoration of Australian cricket. Like Simpson he knew what he wanted and in most cases these contrasting characters were of a single mind.

Sawle belonged to another Australian tradition. Other countries tend to promote famous past players. Sawle would be replaced by Trevor Hohns, whose panel included Andrew Hilditch. Eventually Hilditch, a modest cricketer but an intelligent, discreet man with a strong sense of humour, took over. John Buchanan coaches the national team and his equally obscure replacement at Queensland has taken over the West Indian side. Every ball is played on its merits. It is part of the Australian approach that has been ignored.

Cricket teams cannot, though, function properly without an effective captain. None of the improvements detected from 1987 onwards could have occurred without Allan Border, the example he set, the runs he scored and the catches he took.

7

BORDER PATROLS

Allan Border had not wanted to captain his country. He had
not thought that, at a critical time, with the outlook so bleak
that long-suffering journalists had thrown in the towel, he
might be asked to assume the most important job in Australian
cricket. Although happy to serve as a vice-captain, he had not
pictured himself as a serious candidate for higher office. He preferred
to remain one of the boys. Perhaps it was just as well he had not
thought ahead. Since he did not have any expectations, they could
not be disappointed.

Border was and remains a practical man surprised by his achievements but unable to argue with his record. The contrast with Kim
Hughes could hardly have been sharper. Where the newcomer was
cautious, practical, pithy and prickly, his predecessor had been flam-
boyant, loquacious, dramatic, artistic, indulgent and daring. Hughes
played strokes, some of them in the air. Border hit shots, all of them
on the ground.

From the outset Border regarded himself as a battler, a man of
stolen singles and eager cuts, an occupier of the crease, a humble
practitioner, proud of his endurance, unwilling to retreat in the
face of the severest fire but a struggler all the same, a player more

dependent upon determination than any special gift. In hard times he'd retreat even deeper into himself in search of the strength needed to save the day. Although he could not find the words to put the message across, it was a journey he expected others to undertake. Partly because he thought ill of himself, he was inclined to think too well of the men around him. In many respects, though, Border's doggedness was the making of him. As Bob Wyatt pointed out, 'batsmen need to be a little better than they think they are'.

Since time immemorial people and batsmen have fallen into one of two categories—nomad and settler. Nomads pillage, raise merry hell wherever they go, slaughter their enemies, pinch their crops and sometimes their daughters and then move restlessly on to terrorise other victims. Viv Richards, Dean Jones and David Gower were among the nomads, living on their wits, scorning roots, living on the edge.

Border was a settler, one who tends his cattle, encloses his property, grumpily pays his dues and minds his business as he ekes out a harsh living, never giving up, enduring the seasons as they turn. It was this lack of ego that persuaded spectators to join Border in his endeavours.

No sane man could doubt that Border was a great cricketer. A case could be made that he was more even than that. Not that genius is necessarily a higher state. Rather it suggests an ability to make the extraordinary part of daily life. Whereas greatness grapples with structure, genius transcends it. Words, chords, strokes, perceptions enter the brain when they are most needed, and as soon as they appear their rightness is universally understood. It's not that genius lacks discipline, for that is to patronise it, treat it as if immaturity were its bedfellow. Rather it is that genius reaches the limits of contemporary human conception, and then goes a little further. Genius is more haunted than greatness precisely because it dances to a more demanding tune.

Seve Ballesteros was a golfing genius. He could do things others could not even imagine. Nick Faldo was a great player. John McEnroe was a tennis genius whose passions were uncompromisingly engaged. Pete Sampras was a great player. Brian Lara and Shane Warne are manifestly touched by genius. Kim Hughes and David Gower may have been geniuses but neither was a great batsman. Genius goes hand in hand with charisma, that indefinable quality that makes us watch Bogart and Dylan's every move on the stage and screen though they may be merely lighting a cigarette. Viv Richards was touched by genius, Clive Lloyd was a great batsman and leader.

Border was certainly great but he also had some unusual attributes. He had the mentality of the common man, the record of the great cricketer and, sometimes, the deeds though never the aura of the genius. Time upon time his throws broke the wicket. He would intervene in the middle of a match to take a few crucial wickets with his ponderous left-armers. It is hard to recall him dropping a catch. Often he scored centuries on the worst pitches, with innings requiring lightning reflexes as well as the solidity and courage that were his trademarks. He never seemed to misjudge a ball or suffer an injury or run out of mental or physical energy.

It was never prettily done, but it was uncanny. Border could change the course of a match played in the highest company. Perhaps, though, there is indeed something more, namely the ability to make an entire game bend to one's will. Although it caused frustration, it was appropriate that Border did not overreach himself, that his abilities were underestimated. After all, his primary task was to teach his men the importance of the struggle.

Border was not born to lead. On the contrary, it took him an unconscionable time to accept the burden that had fallen upon his shoulders. Only after Australia had secured a narrow victory in the early rounds of the 1987 World Cup did he observe that finally he felt like he was 'the right man to captain the side'. It had taken him three years to reach this conclusion. Not every cricketing country permits its office-holders such a long period of grace. Border was saved both by the esteem in which the position of Australian captain is held and by the lack of alternatives. Rather than sacking him, the ACB concentrated on covering his weaknesses, the better to exploit his strengths. Far and away the most important decision taken in this regenerative period for Australian cricket was to give Border the time and the help he needed to grow into the captaincy.

Border's weaknesses could have crippled his captaincy, but not all of the criticisms levelled at him were entirely fair. Most particularly his native pessimism drew more censure than it deserved. Border's role in the rebuilding of Australian cricket was that of the consolidator, a task he carried out with the utmost distinction. His stubbornness may occasionally have held the players back but more often it pulled them out of another hole. Without his bloody-mindedness, Australia's reconstruction could hardly have succeeded. Border did not merely rebuild a team, he renewed a tradition.

Border was a product of hard times. It's no use expecting men of his sort to dance to the latest tune. They have suffered too many setbacks ever to let go. To encourage Border to take risks was to ask him to become another man. In any case his record survives the closest scrutiny. A leader must be judged not by some fanciful standard but by his starting and finishing points. Border inherited a team in disarray, won a World Cup, left his successor with a powerful and proud side, and gave the next generation an example to follow. It is enough for one man.

A more serious fault was that Border was a poor judge of character. He enjoyed the wit of amusing companions and did not ponder the effect their gibes might have upon team-mates or the team spirit. He suffered, too, from the misapprehension common among those obliged to scrap for every run, that a pretty wrist and genius are bedfellows. Dismissing himself as a grafter, he was unduly impressed by those apparently capable of doing the whole thing on their ear. He was a worker who admired insouciance. He laughed at Greg Ritchie's jokes, admired Wayne Phillips' wit. Later he went on charity walks with Dean Jones. He was not part of any group, could find good points in any man.

Somewhere inside, though, existed a man blessed with a fund of common sense, a man who knew that batting was about scoring runs and bowling was about taking wickets, but this essential soundness did not emerge until he had established his authority. Border was the last of the sceptics about his abilities as a captain. In this regard his honesty was his downfall. He knew that he had an awful lot of fraud in him but he did not realise everyone else was bluffing too. Only when he belatedly came to terms with his position was he able to convey his true self to his charges, who had been waiting for him to assert himself.

Border's first three years as captain of his country were mostly unsuccessful. Defeat followed defeat and in New Zealand in 1985/86 he threatened to resign, saying that the players were not showing any sign of improvement and lacked commitment. As captain he believed he must take responsibility for his side's failures.

Fortunately his senior players talked him out of it and perhaps the threat awoke them to their own responsibilities.

It might not have been obvious to the casual observer, but some progress had been made in the months before the World Cup. By the time the team reached India, the selectors had purged and pruned their side until the beleaguered captain could call upon a sturdy group of players. Geoff 'Swampy' Marsh had been appointed as vice-captain and Border could not have had a more supportive deputy. Blessed with the open and ruddy face of the rural dweller, Marsh was a man to be trusted. He had taken guard on a farm in Wandering, an outpost not quite as remote as it sounded but an ideal place to develop the qualities needed to succeed as an opening batsman and as a loyal second. Mornings spent milking cows are liable to take the edge off a man's ambition. Nor is there anything quite like the birth of a calf or the withering of a promising crop to help a fellow to keep things in perspective.

Marsh knew his limitations and was happy to work within them. Moreover in his case they were not false boundaries created by a reluctance to risk humiliation. He did not covet Border's position, everyone was comfortable with him, so he was well placed to give his captain the support that was manifestly needed. During the course of a productive World Cup campaign, Marsh would tell the indefatigable Martin Blake that he had been mindful of the need to reduce the pressure on his captain and regarded putting some runs on the board as the most eloquent contribution he could make. He explained, 'For a couple of years, if Allan did not score runs then Australia fell in a heap. I just said to myself that someone else has got to take control.'

Marsh was not the only man upon whom Australia's grouchy captain could rely. Another stalwart had emerged from an improbable source, a man sporting a walrus moustache and a barrel of a belly. David Boon had not caught the eye in the 1986/87 Ashes series, largely because he appeared intent on testing the catching abilities of the visiting slip cordon. Fortunately events would justify the selectors' faith in him. Determined to confront and correct his weaknesses, Boon went into the nets, scraped a line indicating off-stump and practised leaving alone the temptations that hitherto had proved his undoing. By the time the Australians reached India he was an established and respected member of the side.

Australia had found its opening pair. Marsh was to average 61 and Boon 55 in their first exposure to World Cup cricket. Marsh generally started slowly and gathered momentum through his innings, remaining calm and scoring mostly though the off-side. Boon stood upright and defiant as he punched down the ground, hooked or worked to leg. Marsh and Boon would become as familiar a part of the cricketing landscape as Mills and Boon were in the realm of romantic fiction. It was a partnership that would remain unbroken until Mark Taylor's emergence from Wagga Wagga. Even then, they would be separated by only one position.

Marsh and Boon were ably supported by the middle order. With the dubious wisdom of hindsight it is surprising that the Australians were regarded as rank outsiders. But, then, they had been in the doldrums for several years and no one knew much about the rookies, except a cricketing community no longer prepared to tolerate the slipshod.

Dean Jones batted at first wicket down. He was everything Border was not—electrifying, energetic, attention-seeking, audacious, hotheaded, unpredictable. At his best he used a flashing blade to cut a swathe through opposing ranks. He was the most brilliant and compelling of batsmen, and ran between wickets like a man who has just clapped eyes on Piers Ackerman. Watching him slide and run was exhilarating. He counts among the great batsmen of the limited-over game, and among the most exciting in any form.

Jones was driven and, ultimately, made vulnerable by his rampant ego. He yearned to be a hero, lived for the roars of the crowd and the challenge of the game, did not so much play the odds as defy them. Unable to accept a bit part and unaware of his own shortcomings, he was destined to dazzle for a few years before crashing to earth. A fine line exists between the distinctive and the distinguished.

Jones was an outstanding 50-over batsman, yet the pinched, pale-faced young man who batted a few places below him in the order would win even more matches for his country. Steve Waugh was already gaining a reputation as a stoical and courageous competitor with an acute sense of timing. Waugh brought to the team an ingredient that had been missing, an instinctive understanding of the inner workings of a cricket match. With every fibre of his body, Waugh wanted to end up on the winning side. As much could have been said about Border and several of his colleagues, but Waugh knew how the feat could be accomplished.

Later in his career, fearful of rejection and anxious to nurse his figures so that they sat impressively in the history books, Waugh would turn himself into a mechanical batsman determined to score runs every time he went to the crease. Hereabouts, he was a match winner, the man to whom the ball was thrown for the critical last few overs, the batsman sent to the crease with runs needed and the clock ticking.

In the mid-1980s Waugh had flattered to deceive and interstate critics were quick to dismiss him as merely another overpraised golden boy from Sydney. Under the impression that I had described the New South Welshman as the best batsman in the world, Bill Lawry was aghast. In fact he was misinformed. Henry Blofeld was the originator of an admittedly premature comment. Ian Chappell denied that Waugh was the best all-rounder in the world, adding with characteristic acerbity that he was not even the best in his own family. Apparently unperturbed by these slights, and by his struggles to establish himself, Waugh took his chance in the 1987 World Cup and never looked back. Of course the barbs were keenly felt. Indeed they were to become the driving force of his career. He would be fighting as much against the black markers as against the opposition. Unsurprisingly he was often more relaxed playing away from home.

This World Cup would reveal Waugh to be one of the canniest of cricketers. He batted eight times, scored the quick runs required and lost his wicket on only three occasions. As far as he could see, heroic self-sacrifice did not advance the cause. Instead of thrashing around like a hooked fish, he studied the field, figured the odds, worked out the requirements, completed these calculations in an instant and then went about his business in the unemotional way that was to become his trademark.

From the start it was obvious that Waugh was a remarkable cricketer. Despite his unfashionably slight build, he could hit the ball with withering power and often into unexpected places. Most particularly he was able to crack almost any delivery over mid-wicket with control and uncommon force. Unless an off-spinner is bowling, the boundary forward of square leg is the hardest part of the field to protect. Michael Bevan's limited-over career was founded upon this realisation, and his ability to exploit it.

Although impressive, Waugh's batting was not yet his most important asset. His nerveless bowling affected the outcome of several matches, including Australia's memorable first encounter of the World Cup, with India. By rights it ought not to have been possible for a medium-paced trundler who did not move the ball much in either direction to bowl so effectively, late in the innings against capable opponents. Waugh, though, was not inhibited by his lack of pace, bounce or swing. Rather he bowled as might an inquisitor, constantly asking the right question, relentlessly punishing a weakness.

Waugh was effective because he challenged conventional thought. In the previous decade it had become orthodoxy that bowlers must deliver straight yorkers in the last few overs, to prevent batsmen lofting the ball while also reducing the range of shots they could play. In theory they would be limited to driving towards fieldsmen placed deep behind the bowler. As time went by batsmen became accustomed to this strategy and devised their individual responses, including leaving their stumps to create room for their shots. It is not easy to deliver a succession of pinpoint yorkers late in the innings. An imprecise yorker is an inviting full-toss or half-volley. In Gujranwala, the last ten overs of the English and West Indian innings between them produced 186 runs. A new tactic was required.

Waugh had to think beyond the square. He knew that he lacked the height and pace needed to york opponents. Nor were the Indian pitches, baked and brown, well-disposed towards his style of bowling. In India a paceman must either swing the ball or pack his bags. Undeterred, Waugh was eager to play a role late in the innings. Apart from anything else it would make him harder to leave out, might make him indispensable. Cricketers are always more insecure than they care to admit. Many players spend their entire careers looking over their shoulders.

Realising his limitations, Waugh concentrated on the weapons he did possess. Straight skidders could be hard to put away, provided they were not sent down at a predictable pace. Surprise and deception would become his tools of the trade.

It worked. In Australia's first match, against the host nation, Waugh settled the issue with a straight ball that removed Maninder Singh with India two runs shy of victory. Repeatedly thereafter

Waugh would deliver the telling spell. By some sixth sense he could predict batsmen's intentions. He preyed upon their anxieties, and pretended he had none of his own. All told he would take 11 wickets at an average of 26. No less significantly he would concede only 4.5 runs an over. Considering he was bowling the last few overs, this was an economical return. Simon O'Donnell was the most miserly of the Australians, averaging 4.3 an over in the middle of the innings.

Not that Waugh led the attack, a task that fell upon the red head and youthful shoulders of Craig McDermott. The Queenslander rose to the occasion by taking more wickets than anyone else, 18 at an average of 18.9. Taking into account the heat and pitches, it was a fine effort. McDermott relied on his strong shoulders and outswingers supported by a well-disguised off-cutter. Some held reservations about the size of his heart, and he was inclined to return home early from tours and also to frustrate captains when he remained. He was a vulnerable man. Like Andrew Caddick he was constantly ringing home. Afterwards he would build an independent life, outside the game, and now he sits alongside Graham McKenzie in the list of Australian bowlers yet to be properly recognised.

Bruce Reid, Tim May, O'Donnell and Border bowled the rest of the overs while Mike Veletta added his lustre to the batting.

Australia's campaign began with its thrilling victory over the host nation at Chepauk Stadium in Madras, a ground built alongside an inhospitable river which was at its most pungent during the tied Test played at this same venue, a match memorable for Dean Jones' double century, India's inspired chase, Greg Matthews' tireless bowling, the brilliance of Sunil Gavaskar and Kapil Dev and the umpiring howler that settled the match in the final over.

Marsh (110) and Boon (49) added 110 for the first wicket, a partnership that allowed later batsmen to cut loose. Chasing 271, India reached 3/207 and needed to collect 65 runs from the last 95 balls. McDermott changed the mood of the match and raised the Australians' confidence with a burst of four wickets. The hosts needed a further eight runs from the final over, with two wickets remaining. Two were needed off the last two balls, whereupon Waugh produced his coup de grâce.

Border and his men were both surprised and delighted to have beaten the hosts in the opening encounter. Crammed into a small dressing-room, the Australians had a party described by no less a judge than Dean Jones as the best he had attended. Players, reporters, diplomats and supporters packed into the room to join the merriment. The most telling comment on the game came from Border. 'I think we have turned the corner in one-day cricket,' he said. 'I think that from now on we are going to be very, very hard to beat.'

Australia then won another close match in their qualifying group, beating New Zealand by three runs after the Kiwis had needed to score seven runs in the last over with wickets in hand. Instead Waugh took two wickets, including Martin Crowe's. Perhaps the outcome reflected the difference between the two men. At the crunch, Crowe fell back while his sometime Somerset colleague pressed ahead. Much the same happened in the sides' subsequent encounter, as Crowe was unluckily run out at the crucial moment.

Their place in the semi-finals secure, the Australians lost their second match against India and flew to Pakistan to contend for a place in the final. By now, Border's men had surpassed the expectations of even their most loyal supporters. It would emerge later that their own outlook was not nearly as pessimistic. Encouraged by some of the younger players unused to defeat, they had banded together to place a sizeable bet on themselves at the generous odds offered by the bookies.

Australia rose to the occasion at Gaddafi Stadium, Lahore, thereby silencing a crowd that had come to celebrate their team's march towards the final in Calcutta, and to bid farewell to Imran Khan, their captain, who was due to retire at the end of the competition.

Australia's batsmen took the score to 267 and the bowlers responded with early wickets. Pakistan's batting leant heavily upon Javed Miandad, the game's most artful dodger. Javed had taken the team into the semi-finals with a typically opportunistic innings against Sri Lanka. Batting in the manner of a man haggling in a Cairo market, smiling, arguing, calculating, the charming rogue had scored a century. Now, though, he failed and not even Imran's defiant 58, to add to his three wickets, could save the day. Imran's palmist had predicted immortal fame for his man. Defeat made him appear a charlatan. But Imran kept playing and four years later would lift the World Cup trophy.

Naturally Border's men were 'ecstatic'. Nor did their mood deteriorate when England unexpectedly beat India, as Graham Gooch and

Mike Gatting swept the home spinners to distraction. The old enemies would meet in the final. Outside the cricketing enclave, the world went along. The stock market had crashed, a bomb blast in Northern Ireland had killed ten people, scores of nurses in Melbourne had been sacked after a dispute with the State government.

All cricketing roads, though, led to Eden Gardens, Calcutta. The great Pakistani batsman Zaheer Abbas, the 'Asian Bradman', had dismissed most of the Australians as 'club players'. Subcontinental newspapers had been unable to spell their names. But Border's men were on the verge of a mighty achievement. Win or lose, Australian cricket was on its way back.

England stood between Border and glory. Although strong in most positions, it was not quite the side that had trounced the Australians in 1985 and 1986/87. For a start, David Gower was not playing. Burdened with a wonky shoulder that prevented him throwing, and tiring of the company of the roundheads running the team, he had announced that he did not intend to tour again. Mickey Stewart, the England coach, expressed the conventional regrets but in truth the two men were as far apart as sand and clay. An impression has been given that all was well with English cricket until the 1990s. In fact the decline began earlier, a case conclusively made by Scyld Berry in *The Cricketer*. Stewart had been appointed to check the deterioration, a task beyond his modest capabilities. As far as English cricket was concerned, the Age of the Stewarts was a disaster.

Nor did Ian Botham report for duty in India, although England did have its other 'Gs': Gooch and Gatting. Moreover the side had survived a tough group, overcoming the mercurial West Indies and Sri Lanka on its way to the latter stages of the tournament. This was the last World Cup to include only the eight strongest sides in the world. Viv Richards and his players had tried hard to arrest the decline already evident in West Indian cricket. Richards had become even more volcanic, occasional eruptions interrupting long periods of imperious conduct as emotions found their articulation in sudden fury. His successors would be blamed for the fall of cricket in the Caribbean but the Antiguan's volatility was a contributing factor. By the end of the tournament it was clear that the game's domination by Richards and Botham was over, and that the time of Steve Waugh and Australia had arrived.

Richards' team lacked the balance provided by a genuine all-rounder and displayed undue faith in defunct tactics towards the end of the innings. In their first encounter with England Allan Lamb scored 22 runs off Courtney Walsh's last two overs to win the match, but it wasn't until their second meeting with England that the West Indies were eliminated.

And so, as Frankie Howerd used to put it, it came to pass that England and Australia met in the final of a superbly organised, entertaining and competitive World Cup, the first staged in the subcontinent and one of the best ever held anywhere.

Despite its absentees, England had a competent side. The Australians had improved in leaps and bounds. Simpson's relentless concentration on the basics of the game had been rewarded with more alert fielding and more aggressive running between wickets. So far, Border himself had not scored many runs but, as Majid Khan observed, 'So far is not the end.'

Eden Gardens awaited. Nothing in cricket compares with a Cup final played on this teeming, heaving, excitable ground, an arena that seems to live and die with every ball, a stadium packed to the rafters with little dark faces that resemble a hundred thousand sultanas. The heat may be unbearable, bodies may be tightly packed, the police may threaten with their lathis, 20 000 extra tickets may have been sold on the black market, officials may not have seen fit to provide any refreshments or rest rooms, but still the ground pulsates throughout the day. Not even a vibrant night at the MCG or an historic occasion at Lord's can match the atmosphere of Eden Gardens when its soul has been awakened.

Border won the toss and, despite the dew and the cacophony and the nerves, decided to bat. Roughly 80 000 spectators had been packed into the ground and, partly because their group had been playing in India, partly because they were the underdogs and partly because they were not the colonial power, or at all snooty, most of them were cheering for the Australians. As usual Boon and Marsh gave their team a steady start whereupon the rest contributed handily, especially Mike Veletta, a grafter in Shield cricket but an alert and clever improviser in the abbreviated form of the game.

Reminding all and sundry of the dangers of over-categorisation, the West Australian scored 45 in the liveliest offering of the contest.

Boon's combative 75 gave the innings its backbone and secured for the Tasmanian the nomination as Man of the Match. Australia's total of 5/253 was challenging as opposed to daunting. Neil Foster had bowled the tightest spell of the English bowlers.

England had never won a World Cup. Nor, though, had it ever enjoyed the luxury of playing away from home. No team has ever taken the trophy in its own backyard. Presumably the pressure proves overwhelming. When Bill Athey began the chase with his customary skill it seemed that the Poms must prevail. Yet as their own greatest poet had pointed out, 'there's many a slip twixt cup and lip'.

Steve Waugh hardly had time to take guard before the Australian innings was over. Naturally he yearned to make his mark on this greatest of all cricketing days. Moreover all-rounders are not so easily denied. He still had the chance of taking a few wickets with his 'up and downers' or maybe turning the match on its head with a sudden run-out. Meanwhile Jones prowled in the covers, Border urged his men onwards and O'Donnell plugged away with his honest mediums. O'Donnell was an accurate bowler and a strong hitter of the ball whose performances in 50-over cricket touched such a nerve that long after he had departed spectators longed for another of his kind. In truth he was an occasional as opposed to a regular contributor but he is fondly remembered and highly regarded by supporters. Crowds love the bloke willing to have a go.

In the end Waugh did make a vital intervention. By removing Allan Lamb and Phil DeFreitas in quick succession, he stalled the England innings just as it was entering the final lap. Border, though, had already taken the most important wicket. Batting with his customary bustling belligerence, Gatting had reached 41 in 45 deliveries. If the bowling was not exactly at his mercy, the match was in his hands. But Gatting had a flaw in his character, a thick-headedness that held him back and prevented him building upon his early success as captain of his country. After all, he began by holding the Ashes in Australia in 1986/87 and thereafter did not preside over a single victory.

Gatting was an accomplished player of the reverse sweep. He had not quite invented the stroke. Not everything started yesterday. In the 1970s Mushtaq Mohammad played the stroke for Northamptonshire and Pakistan. Despite his cherubic countenance, the most cheerful of the Mohammad cricketing clan also possessed a beautifully controlled and devilish flipper. Hitherto Gatting had been the most precise and habitual player of the unorthodox stroke. Now he faced Border's first delivery on a surface offering slow turn. Young cricketers are taught not to attempt anything untoward against the opening offering of a new bowler. Better to become accustomed to flight and pitch. Moreover the field had been set with two men backward of point. The reverse sweep was plainly a bad risk, a dangerous shot against a new bowler that at best could produce a single run.

Undeterred, the England captain gambled, and lost. A simple catch was held at short third man. Australia celebrated. Gatting was deservedly castigated. There is nothing wrong with taking risks. There is nothing right about boneheaded recklessness. Waugh stepped in with his two wickets for five runs. Supporters became more hopeful. Australia might not have been watching but it was listening and suddenly it was winning.

Meanwhile Blofeld was waxing lyrical in the small, hot and appropriately named broadcasting box. A huge crowd was becoming ever more deafening as its favourite edged towards victory. Finally the deed was done, whereupon the Cup was presented and held aloft, and cars were driven around the boundary's edge, displaying the trophy and the victors. It was a warm, vibrant, noisy, excited, exhilarating evening and it was exactly the fillip Australian cricket needed to confirm its renaissance. Thereafter Australia would be, indeed, very, very hard to beat, in any form of the game.

Allan Border's comment upon winning the fourth World Cup was as self-defining as it was honest and unpretentious. 'I'm ecstatic, just over the moon,' he told Blake. 'It's like a dream come true.' Before long he was being carried around the ground on the shoulders of his players, a hard-bitten professional whose time had finally come. He had scored a few runs, taken a crucial wicket and kept his nerve as the match reached its wrenching climax.

The triumph was as personal as it was passionate. Raised in a period of sustained success, contemporary Australians may find it hard to understand the strength of the emotions involved. And the strongest of them was surely relief. After several years of struggle, years that seemed to move along in painful slow motion, Australian cricket could start looking forwards.

AUSTRALIA V ENGLAND, WORLD CUP FINAL
8 NOVEMBER 1987, EDEN GARDENS, CALCUTTA, INDIA

Toss: **Australia**
Result: **Australia won by 7 runs**
Man of the match: **D.C. Boon**

Australia		R	BF	4	6
D.C. Boon	c Downton b Hemmings	75	125	7	0
G.R. Marsh	b Foster	24	49	3	0
D.M. Jones	c Athey b Hemmings	33	57	1	1
C.J. McDermott	b Gooch	14	8	2	0
A.R. Border (c)	run out	31	31	3	0
M.R.J. Veletta	not out	45	31	6	0
S.R. Waugh	not out	5	4	0	0
S.P. O'Donnell					
G.C. Dyer (k)					
T.B.A. May					
B.A. Reid					
Extras	(b 1, lb 13, w 5, nb 7)	26			
Total	**5 wickets**	**253**			
	50.0 overs at 5.06 rpo				

FoW

1–75	Marsh	2–151	Jones
3–166	McDermott	4–168	Boon
5–241	Border		

Bowling	O	M	R	W
P.A.J. DeFreitas	6	1	34	0
G.C. Small	6	0	33	0
N.A. Foster	10	0	38	1
E.E. Hemmings	10	1	48	2
J.E. Emburey	10	0	44	0
G.A. Gooch	8	1	42	1

England		R	BF	4	6
G.A. Gooch	lbw b O'Donnell	35	57	4	0
R.T. Robinson	lbw b McDermott	0	1	0	0
C.W.J. Athey	run out	58	103	2	0
M.W. Gatting (c)	c Dyer b Border	41	45	3	1
A.J. Lamb	b Waugh	45	45	4	0
P.R. Downton (k)	c O'Donnell b Border	9	8	1	0
J.E. Emburey	run out	10	16	0	0
P.A.J. DeFreitas	c Reid b Waugh	17	10	2	1
N.A. Foster	not out	7	6	0	0
G.C. Small	not out	3	3	0	0
E.E. Hemmings					
Extras	(b 1, lb 14, w 2, nb 4)	21			
Total	**8 wickets**	**246**			
	50.0 overs at 4.92 rpo				

FoW

1–1	Robinson	2–66	Gooch
3–135	Gatting	4–170	Athey
5–188	Downton	6–218	Lamb
7–220	Emburey	8–235	DeFreitas

Bowling	O	M	R	W
C.J. McDermott	10	1	51	1
B.A. Reid	10	0	43	0
S.R. Waugh	9	0	37	2
S.P. O'Donnell	10	1	35	1
T.B.A. May	4	0	27	0
A.R. Border	7	0	38	2

8

PUT IN THEIR PLACE

Despite their triumph, Allan Border's Australians did not immediately thereafter dominate the game. Apart from anything else, the title of World Champions bestowed upon them was misleading. No one familiar with the strengths and weaknesses of the various contenders regarded Australia as *primus inter pares*. After several lean years, Border and his men had won a single competition. Admittedly it had been the most important meeting of the great cricketing nations that the game had yet seen fit to arrange, a tournament that carried more weight than any other cricketing encounter. Still, it was an isolated case. Some thought it a fluke.

Moreover it had been a one-day tournament. Cricket is not like other sports. A boxing champion may be challenged and toppled in a night. Soccer World Cups satisfactorily determine relative strength because they are proper matches played over the full 90 minutes. Acknowledging their legitimacy, nations take years to prepare for them, an approach that reinforces their importance. Likewise England's victory in the 2003 Rugby World Cup was significant. Regardless of subsequent events, it meant they would be recognised as champions for the next four years. Everyone understood the rules.

The length of Test matches prevents cricket from organising a full-scale tournament. This means that determining the true champion of the game requires a scrutiny of results over a few series. As it happens, for the last quarter of a century the outcome has been clear-cut. Doubtless the position will not always be as simple, but the game can manage perfectly well without a title holder. It is unlikely that teams hereafter will ever dictate terms for as long as the West Indians did through the 1970s and 1980s, and the Australians since then.

Border's team was merely champion of the shorter and less significant version of the game, a version created to ensure that cricket remained in the forefront of the sporting debate, at any rate in the lands where it had taken hold. Like music, movies, books, fashion houses and so forth, cricket had to move with the times. Fifty-over cricket was the result.

Inevitably, the game was eventually obliged to go further in search of popularity, introducing 20-over matches by way of attracting the attention of a public impatient for stimulation and unwilling to wait upon the slow unravelling of events or the gradual realisation of character. It is merely another stop along the way. The remarkable thing is not that shorter matches have been introduced, but that the longer version endures.

Twenty-over cricket—comedy cricket as it has been called by some enthusiasts—has been a success wherever it has been tried, in England and South Africa, in Brisbane and North Sydney. Eventually, there will be an international competition, yet the winners will no more be regarded as champions of the game at large than a superb player of speed chess is regarded as a grand master.

Border's men were not yet the rightful rulers of their game. That the leading nations and top players had taken part added to the tournament's legitimacy but did not render obsolete the game's true testing ground. Border's team had played wonderfully well under intense pressure. Their hard work had been rewarded and the side was playing with skill and commitment. But it was not yet even a contender for the world title let alone its holder.

The Australians had a long way to go before they could even match the West Indians in Test cricket. For the time being the attack lacked a cutting edge. Traditionally Australia had relied on fast bowling and wrist-spin, and both were in short supply. Border's team depended upon the efforts of the tried and trusted, to which had been added the promise of McDermott, Jones and Waugh. (That the Waugh household had more to offer was not yet widely known.)

Nor had any of the players yet made a conclusive case for inclusion in the ranks of the game's immortals. Australia could not sit back and wait for the emergence of those blessed with a special gift, nor could it assume that emerging players would rise regardless. Scoring runs and sinking putts for a sustained period requires a certain state of mind, an ambition, a desire that is not compromised by fame or fortune, the yearning that still makes Tiger Woods and Vijay Singh walk out onto the practice range in rain and wind. When Singh first played in Sydney as an unknown he was to be found out on the course at all hours. As darkness fell a local journalist tried to track him down and was advised to head for the 15th green. Greatness and ordinariness are not as far apart as they seem. Although it is hard for the unexceptional to rise to greatness, it is all too easy for the supremely talented to sink into the commonplace.

Australian cricket needed to find young players capable of achieving greatness and, on finding them, had to create around them a culture calculated to ensure that their gifts were not wasted. Astute selection and unwavering commitment were the keys. From this point on, Australian cricket would never forget its identity or lose sight of its aim. Most particularly it recognised the need to restore the centrality of footwork and fast bowling, athletic fielding and wrist-spin. Brazil has had great defenders in its soccer team, but never a great defensive team. Australia must attack. Success demands unfailing determination and a lot of hard work. Players and teams must be willing to push themselves to their limits.

Although progress had been made, Australian cricket could not yet rest upon its laurels. If nothing else, the recent struggles had served as a reminder that a sporting body must conduct itself with restless energy. It is not a comfortable place to visit. Indeed it is notoriously hard to find. Anything less and the soul dies. As Bob Dylan sang so many years ago, a man is either 'busy bein' born or busy dyin''.

In hindsight it may seem that winning the World Cup was merely part of an inevitable and inexorable restoration. After all, Australians were tough blokes with leathery skins born in an uncomplicated country, raised on firm pitches and dedicated to games of any sort, especially cricket. Doubtless the bad spell would have ended sooner or later. But those involved deserve credit for refusing to bide their time, for demanding that weaknesses be confronted and corrected without delay, for producing and executing a plan.

Australia would not dominate the world scene until a fast bowler had been found in Narromine and a spinner on Brighton beach. Without these extraordinary cricketers, Glenn McGrath and Shane Warne, Australia might have been hard to beat but would not have achieved its current prominence. In the end cricket is a battle between bat and ball, batsman and bowler. It was precisely because the Australian game was working on the right lines that these players' abilities were recognised and developed.

But that was in the future. For the time being there was a lot of work to be done. Although not the force of old, the West Indies remained the team to beat. And England held the Ashes.

Australia faced the West Indies three more times in Border's remaining years. In 1988/89 Richards' team toured down under and secured a conclusive victory by three matches to one. As usual Australia prevailed in Sydney but by then the series was over. To watch Richards' team during this period was to witness a formidable and proud outfit committed to playing uncompromising cricket. That it was already fraying at the edges, that Richards lacked the wherewithal to carry the team with him, was not immediately obvious.

Richards walked to the crease with the swagger of the unquestioned and led with the ruthlessness of the dictator. He led by sheer force of character. It was his glory and eventually his undoing. But what a sight he was on the field, chewing gum, blasting the bowlers, leaving the crease with head held high, pouncing in the field, imperiously disdaining the struggle in Sydney. Richards' moods varied from humorous cajoling to strong-minded intolerance. Eldine Baptiste remembers going to his rooms once, seeking advice, wanting succour and being told to remember his name and honour it. He left with hope renewed and tears in his eyes. Richards could be mean or majestic, he could make or break men. Carl Hooper never met his requirements. Observers said he was too hard on the youngster. Or was Hooper too soft?

What a side Richards had at his disposal, a wonderful opening pair in Desmond Haynes and Gordon Greenidge, a gifted keeper in Jeffrey Dujon, sleek, athletic and supremely skilled fast bowlers in Malcolm Marshall, Courtney Walsh, a destroyer in Curtly Ambrose, plus Richie Richardson's scintillating work on the back foot! No wonder they took some beating.

Throughout the 1988/89 series, Border would feel let down by the pitches and by the ACB's refusal to change the order in which matches were played. Some consideration was given to playing the first Test in Sydney, where the Australians had managed to win even in 1984/85, but a concert had been arranged next door to the SCG and the ACB was not prepared to risk a conflict, not least in the car parks. In the event the Tests were arranged in the usual order, with the first three played on the fastest pitches. West Indies won the lot.

Australian cricket's reluctance to take short cuts indicated its determination to restore high standards. Victories on doctored surfaces serve only as a smokescreen. Once the smoke has cleared, their hollowness is revealed. A match may have been won but nothing has changed.

Of course, captains cannot be expected to think about much beyond the next ball, the next day and the next match. Border was a players' player, involved in every ball, relieved in victory, raging against defeat, fighting against everything that blocked his path including umpires, selectors, opponents, reporters and commentators. Certainly he was single-minded and, sometimes, bad-tempered. He was not hosting a tea party. The idea that captains must be polite to their players belongs to the current generation of huddles and 'man management'. Border's players did not expect sensitivity from their captain. Commitment was the only requirement, and those who give most of themselves are bound now and then to become frustrated.

Border once cussed McDermott in Taunton, threatening to send him home, and a hullabaloo followed. Warne was wrongly accused of chiding a team-mate on the field in Hobart and another controversy ensued. It is hard to believe that cricketers took either episode seriously, or not those who had played under Brian Close anyhow!

If Border was disappointed by his Board's inflexibility with the order of matches, he was enraged by the pitches provided. The worst would be at the MCG, where a brutal match would be played out on an unreliable surface. Although a brown and slow pitch was produced for the first Test at The Gabba it did not subdue an attack featuring Malcolm Marshall, supported by the raw pace of Patrick Patterson and a couple of newcomers by the names of Courtney Walsh and Curtly Ambrose. Patterson was the most menacing, rawest and least-skilled of the West Indian pacemen. His colleagues were not merely fast; they were masters of their craft. They could bowl outswingers and leg-cutters, could change their line and movement for each batsman and maintain a rhythm and a discipline that made them dangerous hour after hour, day after day. They bowled with the control and subtlety of outstanding medium-pacers and at the pace of a howling gale. It was not a bad combination. And there were three of them in the team, sometimes four. Small wonder the West Indies thought it could afford to include a wild man like Patterson.

Richards was able to set aggressive fields precisely because his main bowlers were extremely accurate. The West Indies might have played exciting cricket. They also played the odds. Fields could be set for edges and back for shots because nothing else was offered. Not that this Test was overtly violent. Rather, the threat hung in the air. Australia's batsmen may have been pushed back by pace and hostility but more often than not they were beaten by superbly conceived deliveries that arrived as part of a relentless and precise onslaught. Solitary deliveries don't take many wickets. They need to be part of a collection. And the bowler needs to be good enough that fieldsmen can be kept close to the bat till the chance finally comes along.

By the end of the first day Australia's worst fears had been confirmed as they subsided to 167 all out. By his estimation, Border 'copped a roughie' in the first innings. By everyone's estimation his side was battered. Steve Waugh batted at fourth wicket down and reached 4 before falling leg before to Marshall.

Although unproductive at the batting crease, Waugh roused himself to greet the visiting captain with three successive bumpers, thereby showing that he could not be cowed. He confirmed as much in the second innings. Promoted to second drop after an injury had inconvenienced his captain, and batting with stubborn relish, Waugh reached 90, enough to make his mark but not sufficient to stop his side sliding towards defeat by nine wickets.

Dropped catches cost the Australians dear in the second Test, on a grassy pitch in Perth. As has often been observed, struggling teams drop catches and their throws miss the stumps. Nervousness is the only possible explanation. Constant exposure to the furnace of competition is the only solution. Nowadays it is assumed that a young fieldsman makes mistakes because he is fearful of the wrath of his elders. Perhaps, though, it is necessary to go through the fire to reach true excellence. Regular and effective practice and sound techniques are also needed.

Geoff Lawson's broken jaw was the most memorable event of the Perth Test, a cruel blow suffered as he ducked into a bumper towards the end of a torrid third day upon which, assisted by 49 sundries, Australia came within range of their opponents' 449. Lawson was carried from the field, taken to hospital, wired and returned saying he'd bat in an emergency. When Lawson was felled, shortly before stumps, Border declared, whereupon Merv Hughes unleashed an assault that had seemed beyond him and any other Australian bowler. Hughes' ferocious response to his mate's injury would rouse an entire cricket community.

Hitherto the Australians had seemed a worthy but intense bunch. Perhaps they did need a roughneck to awaken their spirits. Until this spell, an effort sustained throughout the fourth day, there did not seem to be any particular reason to take the burly man with the Victorian whiskers seriously. Showing immense strength of body and character, Hughes took 8/87 in 37 overs of unrelenting fury. His contribution to the revival ought not to be overlooked. Australian cricket needed a hero, a character and an extrovert in the mould of Chappell's larrikins. Hughes could not have arrived at a better time. Curiously he tiptoed to the crease as if treading on eggs before unleashing his fusillade. Nor did he hesitate to express his opinions. An unusual blend of cumbersome and fluent, rugged and subtle, Hughes was a much better cricketer than he seemed. In his case, familiarity bred respect.

Despite Hughes' honourable valour, Australia was trounced again, losing by 169 runs. Nor did Melbourne bring any respite. A rotten pitch had been prepared, bouncy and uneven, the sort of surface these opponents were as well placed to exploit as any side in the history of the game.

And exploit it they did. Melbourne was a debacle and afterwards Border was beside himself with rage. It was not much fun facing the West Indian bombardment on any surface, but no fun whatsoever to confront them on a fast, kicking pitch. Naturally the West Indians appreciated the hospitality. Batting looked dangerous enough in the stands. Ball after ball thudded into the batsmen's ribs or flew past their noses. Never the most tolerant of leaders, Border seethed.

Changes were made for Sydney. A new man was chosen to open the innings, with David Boon pushed down to first drop as a way of countering the pace attack. Mark Taylor was the fellow's name and reports indicated that he came from Wagga Wagga. Of all the selections made during this period of reconstruction, this would be one of the most significant. Taylor brought calmness and capability to the team. Also, he was a left-hander whose inclusion brought balance to the batting order as well as the dressing-room. That he could catch mosquitoes at slip added to his attractions. He was a comfortable, unthreatening man lacking both the laziness of the recent past and the zeal sometimes evident in reformers. No one can remember any of his innings. Everyone can remember his bad patches. Yet he scored a stack of runs and would lead Australia with distinction.

Australia prevailed in Sydney but it wasn't much of a match. The West Indians were inclined to regard spinning pitches as part of a conspiracy to undermine them and careless, arrogant cricket was the result. After Desmond Haynes had brought his side back into the match with a skilful second innings, Richards threw his wicket away and the match swiftly followed. Border's seven-wicket haul in the first innings was the highlight of an unsatisfactory contest. As usual the drama took place on a Friday afternoon, and left all and sundry in the press box scrapping their leads and scrambling for their record books. A cub reporter came along that day and was unable to write a word. He had expected silence and time to compose, not the madhouse of a Friday evening with some wretch changing the story an hour before deadline.

The Australians were well beaten. The emergence of Taylor and Hughes was a consolation, although the beefy paceman had only taken one more extremely expensive wicket since his marathon effort in Perth. Australia was improving but was not yet ready to take over.

Australia and the West Indies met again in the Caribbean in 1990/91, a series that confirmed that Border's side was second-best. Australia lost the series 2/1, not a bad outcome in some respects because England was suffering repeated whitewashes at the hands of the same opponents. It was a bad-tempered series spoilt by unpleasantness between the sides as the ageing West Indians resisted the visitors' desperate challenge. In a masterful report in *Wisden*, Tony Cosier regretted that such a promising contest should be 'ruined by the obvious acrimony between the teams', which 'manifested itself time and again'. He added that 'it seemed appropriate' that the Sir Frank Worrell Trophy was nowhere to be seen at the presentation ceremony since the presence of a trophy remembering the most sporting of leaders and the greatest of Test series would have been 'incongruous'.

That the series was full of rancour indicated both the intensity of the Australians and the fury of a home side anxious to prolong its domination and the careers of its senior players. At the final press conference of the campaign Viv Richards launched a vitriolic attack on the visiting coach, Bob Simpson, indicating in his angrily inarticulate way that he was not his cup of tea. Mike Whitney's imitation of the enraged West Indian captain's address at that conference would become the focal point of his after-dinner speeches. In truth neither the home captain nor the visiting coach emerged from the series with his reputation enhanced. Richards batted poorly and was clearly near the end of an illustrious career. Simpson was held responsible for the cautious tactics used throughout the series by the Australians.

As Cosier summed up, 'the main difference between the teams was in attitude. The Australians consistently erred on the side of caution; the West Indies, especially in adversity, chose the option of counter-attacking.' He pinpointed the second Test match as the turning point of the series. After the first Test at Sabina Park in Kingston, Jamaica, had been spoilt by rain, Australia had seemed to take the initiative by winning the one-day series 4/1. This was the first such defeat suffered by the hosts on their own soil. Nevertheless the West Indies were the aggressors in mind and deed during the crucial second engagement in Georgetown, Guyana.

Australia chose a defensive team, long in batting and thin in bowling. At various points in the series Steve Waugh and Greg

Matthews batted at 7 with Ian Healy to follow. Australia lacked the confidence and conviction needed to attack. Trying to shore up the batting is a mistake most captains make at some point in their career. It is a result of worrying about possible setbacks but it shows a negative mindset. Almost without exception the wiser course is to choose the six best batsmen and the four best bowlers and to let the rest take care of itself. Good teams contain good cricketers.

The contrasting approaches of the sides were revealed on the first two days in Georgetown. After the Australians had fought their way to 348 in 116 overs on Bourda's true pitch with its fast outfield, the West Indian second-wicket pair tore the Australian bowling apart to add 297 in 70 overs. It did not help the visitors' cause that Dean Jones was run out in the second innings while leaving the field after being bowled by a no-ball. Unfortunately neither the umpire nor the captains realised that a batsman cannot be run out off an illegitimate delivery unless he is trying to take a run. As it happened, I was familiar with the law, not because the situation had arisen in 15 years as a professional cricketer but as a result of an umpiring course run while coaching school cricket in Sydney.

It was not easy for the touring selectors to field an attacking side. Whichever team was chosen, the bowling was weak and the tail was long. Craig McDermott would take 24 wickets at an average of 23 in the series but lacked support. Worse, the bowlers were unable to contribute with the bat. In 27 combined innings the Australian lower order scored only 68 runs. In 28 combined innings their West Indian counterparts amassed 337 runs. It is a truism that strong teams hold their catches, hit the stumps with their throws and enjoy late rallies. Weak sides drop sitters, miss run-outs and suffer complete collapses. Perhaps it is simply the power of positive thinking. Powerful sides expect things to go well and have faith in each other. Battling outfits live on their nerves and constantly fear the worst. Patently Australia had not yet broken out of this cycle.

Defeat at Bourda was followed by a wet draw in Port-of-Spain, Trinidad, where the outfield spent most of its time under water. The West Indies secured their second, decisive victory in the fourth Test at Kensington Oval, in Bridgetown, Barbados. After a low-scoring first innings, the home batsmen took charge of the match, as Gordon Greenidge renewed his flagging fortunes with a double century and

Richie Richardson confirmed that he, at least, was at the height of his powers with another thrilling effort that ended one run shy of a century.

Only in the last match, by which time it was too late, was any attempt made to strengthen the Australian bowling. Dismayed but not broken, the Australians played their boldest side in the last match in St John's, Antigua, and promptly prevailed by 157 runs as Viv Richards fell for 0 and 2. To be fair the West Indians were inclined to relax once the issue had been settled. Mark Taylor and Mark Waugh scored centuries and McDermott and Hughes took wickets. Peter Taylor picked up a couple of scalps with his dropping off-breaks. He had been another of the selectors' unforeseen nominations. Indeed his inclusion in the side to play England in Sydney the previous year had been so unexpected that newspapers bellowed 'Peter Who?' and journalists speculated that the selectors had meant to name Mark Taylor, only to be the victims of an administrative blunder. Probably it was nonsense. In the event Taylor, a farmer from the outback, would bowl his spinners skilfully for several seasons, particularly in one-day cricket, and eventually would become a thoughtful selector.

Among the Australians, Geoff Marsh and Dean Jones were the main failures with the bat, though Border himself only passed 50 once. Greg Matthews, Terry Alderman and Bruce Reid also performed below expectations. On the other hand Mark Waugh revealed that a steely resolve lay beneath his velvet touch. Introduced in Adelaide a year before, and burdened with the somewhat unkind nickname of 'Afghanistan' (the forgotten war), Waugh the slightly younger had started his career with a smooth century and continued the good work to become Australia's most effective batsman in the Caribbean. That Waugh held his place in the side so much longer than Dean Jones was due to his adroit catching at slip and the ease with which he fitted into the team. Jones and Matthews required higher maintenance.

Mark Taylor also batted well and, despite the defeat, the gap between the two sides did appear to be closing. By now, too, confidence was rising among the Australians. Already the Ashes had been won, the batting was gaining strength and the team was clearly moving in the right direction. Two primary tasks remained. Australia needed to find a wrist-spinner to bring variety to its attack and

Border's men needed to believe they could overcome the West Indies. As it turned out, the two would be achieved at roughly the same time.

In 1992/93 the West Indies returned to Australia. It was Border's eighth series against these opponents and he was, understandably, desperate to secure his first victory. In the first Test at The Gabba, the Australian captain was fined half his match fee after complaining about the rejection of numerous legitimate appeals for leg before wicket as the visitors fought for survival on the final afternoon. Only 12 such decisions would be given in five matches so the umpires were, at least, consistent. Match referees had been introduced so the Australian captain was called to account. As usual Border was right, the umpires had been timid, but champions tend to get the rub of the green.

The Australian selectors had started the campaign controversially by dropping Dean Jones, a well-loved and exhilarating batsman. Their explanation was that he had not been scoring enough runs when it mattered. Although a glorious batsman in full flight, and a cricketer of mighty deeds, especially in one-day cricket, Jones had become a mixed blessing. Many observers regarded his rejection as a defeat for individuality and many did not forgive the selectors for omitting him ahead of his time. Jones never played Test cricket again. He had a wonderful career and, with more discretion on and off the field, might have lasted longer. But discretion was not his way.

Damien Martyn took the Victorian's place, and would manage to score more runs than Mark Taylor or Steve Waugh, which was not as hard as it ought to have been.

It was a time of change. Dean Jones was not the only Victorian left out of the team for the Brisbane Test. Shane Warne's omission came into sharper focus as the hosts tried to take the last few wickets on the fifth day. He had first appeared as a rotund performer inclined to float his deliveries towards the off-stump, but Warne's cricket had matured beyond expectations. Already he was starting to show the intensity and accuracy that later would be his hallmarks.

No less importantly, Warne's attention had been drawn to the attractions of the famed 'blind spot', whose exploitation was subsequently to count among his strengths. In short he had learnt to curl the ball through the air so that it landed on leg-stump, or thereabouts, before spinning across the bat. If only he had played at The

Gabba, if only Australia had dared. But the scars were deep. Border needed him as he tried to prize out those last few wickets. Instead he was left cursing the umpires and ruing his luck.

The Gabba Test ended with Australia two wickets shy of victory, but the sight of the World Champions struggling to save the match suggested that without Viv Richards, Gordon Greenidge, Malcolm Marshall and Jeffrey Dujon, they were ripe for the plucking. Some thought them overripe and urged their men to go for the jugular.

As much seemed to be confirmed when the teams met again in the Boxing Day Test. Centuries from Border and Mark Waugh contributed to the visitors needing to score an improbable 359 to win on another dubious Melbourne pitch. At 1/143 on the final morning, with Richardson and Phil Simmons in full cry, there did seem to be a chance of an upset. Then came a piece of bowling so unexpected and so brilliant that even now it lingers in the mind, a delivery that deserves a mention if not in the same sentence as the celebrated 'ball of the century', then at any rate in the same paragraph.

Reinstated for his home Test, Warne was wheeling away to the West Indian captain. Richardson, impressed neither by pace nor spin and his intent clear, was driving and cutting in that coruscating Caribbean way. No indication had been given that the Victorian had anything up his sleeve. Border looked rattled. His worries deepened as his spinner sent down another long-hop and he prepared to curse the punishment that seemed bound to follow. Richardson had spotted the errant delivery and leant back to cut.

But it was neither a leg-break nor a long-hop. Rather it was a perfectly pitched and cunningly disguised flipper. Had Warne bowled one previously? If so, no one had noticed, least of all the captain of the visiting side. Alarm bells ought to have started ringing in the batsman's ears when the ball failed to drop as anticipated, instead continuing to cut through the air like a scream. Richardson, though, did not sense danger. Apart from anything else the bowler looked gormless. He was blond, round, obscure and apparently untouched by guile.

Not until the ball completed its sinuous slide and started to skid off the pitch did the mighty West Indian realise the extent of his predicament. Alas, the flipper is the most unforgiving of deliveries.

Too late, Richardson tried to rearrange his response but, in truth, he hardly played a shot at all as the ball burst through and broke his stumps. Did Warne punch the air? Memory insists that he did, but may have been too long immersed in journalistic licence. At any rate it was a moment of triumph that won the match. Plain as day, the balance of power had changed.

Shaken, the West Indians lost their last eight wickets for 76 runs. In only his fifth Test match, Warne finished the innings with 7/52. Australia was one up with three to play. Had Warne played in Brisbane it might have been 2/0. But there was no point looking back. Still, the thought surely must have gnawed away in the mind of the home captain.

When hostilities resumed in Sydney, another emerging cricketer, one destined to provide rich entertainment and cause headaches to friend and foe alike, took the chance to introduce himself, a twinkle-footed, sweet-faced cavalier whose growing reputation had not yet been reinforced by achievement in the antipodes. That he wore the maroon cap of the West Indies would somewhat restore the balance of power between champion and contender.

Watching Brian Lara bat has been a delight to put alongside African sunsets, dry white wine, eating a ripe mango, catching a wave, reading P.G. Wodehouse and listening to Mozart and Bob Dylan. In short the Trinidadian satisfies the senses. Even the most jaded cricketing palate of an ancient reporter condemned to decades of fretting about twelfth men and cloak-and-dagger Indian politics feels his guard slipping as the left-hander constructs a humble defensive stroke. Having reluctantly accepted that the ball cannot be put away with the certainty demanded by his circumstances, Lara does not lower himself merely to interrupting the ball's progress. Rather he constructs an ornate and yet impenetrable blockade that serves its purpose without giving too much ground to the prosaic. Never has 'Thou shalt not pass' been so prettily done.

Surrender is complete as soon as the twinkling southpaw unleashes one of those cover drives in which conjuring hands and flashing arms are thrown at the ball with apparent abandon and yet without any loss of control. At once 'Shot!' escapes from a veritable collection of press-box mouths. Suddenly everyone remembers the things that brought them to the game all those years ago, the childish delight at a moment's glory, the game's infinite and mostly unexpressed possibilities. Some incumbents may have played a stroke almost as good in 1998, or 1963, the year of The Beatles' first LP. Naturally the unforgettable and sustaining moment has lingered in the mind. Mediocrity is not incapable of swooping upon revelation. It's just that the moment is always lost, like a butterfly that can be contained only by death.

Others may please the mind—Rahul Dravid with his academic rigour, Geoff Boycott with his craft and graft, or Steve Waugh with his unconquerable will. Some may impress the soul—Inzamam-ul-Haq with his sleepy magnificence, Virender Sehwag with his naked audacity, Gundappa Vishwanath with his schoolboy cheek. Was not Vishy forever pinching an apple? Sachin Tendulkar can send the spirit soaring with a single straight drive, so Indian of conception, so Roman of execution. None, though, can summon the level of artistry reached by Lara at his most compelling.

Not that style alone is sufficient to impress anyone save those prone to parading in slacks on seafronts, with a handkerchief delicately placed in a top pocket and a tolerant smile permanently attached to their faces; the sort of imbeciles convinced that wisdom can be found in a book of quotes. Without runs, Lara is a child of batting, an adolescent toying with a gift, a juvenile preferring protest to power. Like an inspiring sculpture, painting or speech, sporting performance depends on the properly constructed thought.

Lara's batting can contain flamboyance and flourish, but these alone would satisfy only the most frivolous mind. Any fool can wave his bat around like an excitable traffic cop. Indeed many fools do. Nor is it enough to score nice thirties, or to be described as 'gifted', or to be modest or even sporting. None of it compares with the construction of a substantial body of work. None of it can sit beside the power of the performance. Does Shakespeare's reputation rest on one play? Did Tagore write but a single story?

Without runs, Lara's frills are the merest frippery. Without hundreds, his style is irrelevant. Without intelligence, his batting is empty. Without records, his genius must be denied. Fitfulness placates only the army of apologists.

Lara has put the runs on the board. Sydney was merely the start of it. Not that his contribution has been any more flawless than his character. Indeed the pair have been interwoven. The reason is simple. To a greater and lesser degree, mere mortals are at the mercy of a notoriously fickle game. They may follow all the procedures required, listen to all the leading coaches, watch footage of every opponent, imagine every ball, eat the appropriate food, build muscles, develop stamina and still they may come a cropper. It only takes a single ball.

When Lara commits himself body and brain, he hardly ever fails. Twice he has taken the leap demanded by his talent, the plunge into the deep waters of his gift, where the pearls can be found. In the first part of his career he produced the batting of a young genius, unfurling a succession of beautiful, destructive and timely innings. Nor was he content with hundreds. Massive scores were compiled. Already it was clear that appearances were misleading. Lara might smile and celebrate, might party and parade, but he was no lightweight. He craved attention, yearned for conquest. From the start he knew he was blessed, and thought as only the blessed may think.

From the beginning he was, in full flow, the most glorious of sights. In a single over he might shimmer down the pitch to stroke a spinner through the covers, kneel to sweep square or fine, step out to lift a six with a sudden explosion of power and tap a single into a gap so that the assault could be continued. Every limb seemed to be working in perfect harmony. He made the unusual swings and movements required by batting appear as natural as the flapping of a bird's wing.

Lara's innings at the SCG in 1992/93 was the start of all that and the excitement lasted several years. Then came a period of self-indulgence and, eventually, self-recrimination. Genius cannot afford to listen to cautionary tales or else it will remain forever caged. A hundred times, sage words are ignored. Not until Sir Garfield Sobers, another genius, came upon him did the Trinidadian cease squandering his talent.

If anything, Lara's second fruitful period was to be more satisfying than his opening onslaught. Maturity has much to commend it. His strokeplay retained its beauty, yet his batting gained an authority lacking in the days of brilliance. Previously inclined to launch an exhilarating attack from the first ball, now he took his time, had a look at the bowling, built stronger foundations. Sooner or later genius has to realise that organisation is not an enemy but an ally.

Has any cricketer given supporters of the game more pleasure? David Gower was an excellent stylist yet frustrating because he was incomplete. Lara has overcome sharp spin in Colombo and aggressive fast bowlers in Australia, has played Test cricket's most massive innings and been responsible for the game's most memorable fifth-day chase. He has also been around for a long time. Longevity has its place.

Yet it is his artistry that will be remembered longest, the thrilling drives that always seem to split the field, the calculated assaults, the ineffable combination of eye, feet, shoulder, arm and wrist that set him apart. Remember how he became Test cricket's highest scorer? Glenn McGrath sent down another probing delivery at off-stump. Lara stepped across his crease and tapped it with a cross bat to fine leg with the ease of a mother taking the top off a child's breakfast egg and the anticipation of the supremely gifted sportsman. The nerve of the man! It was not merely beautiful. It was downright unfair.

As Lara walked to the crease at the SCG, the visitors' cause seemed lost. Australia had scored 9/503 on a slow pitch and the West Indians had suffered two early casualties. Lara proceeded to produce as dazzling an innings as the game has known. In part the dazzle was caused by the element of surprise. Few had thought to see anyone dispatch the respected Australian attack with such élan, let alone a Trinidadian short of form and playing for an embattled side. Lara unleashed an explosion of strokes, dispatching the ball to the boundary apparently at will, and usually with a flash of arm and wrist. It was a bravura display, the 'innings of a lifetime', ironically only one of many he would play. It was an unclouded innings, simple in its construction, bold in its execution.

Hindsight has not diminished the performance. It might have been Garry Sobers out there. At times Lara might have been playing with children in a backyard, he seemed so carefree. Hindsight revealed that it is never quite as simple as that. Lara was not a circus act. He was a man with a life to lead and a talent to understand. In some respects it is easier for those blessed with limited resources. They must just work hard and every day can look themselves in the mirror.

Lara's magnificent innings of 277 saved the match and restored confidence among his comrades. Richardson, too, scored a hundred. Hope had been restored. His fast bowlers were looking forwards to the final Test in Perth, a ground where the West Indians were seldom challenged let alone beaten. Clearly the Adelaide Test was going to decide the series. Adrift 1/0, Richardson and his players were determined to make a strong stand. Border, too, understood the significance of the contest. It had been a long wait.

Few matches have been as unrelentingly tense, as physically demanding, as the fourth Test match of the 1992/93 series. An awful lot was at stake. An astonishing contest produced the narrowest victory margin in 116 years of Test cricket. Not that it is possible to get closer than a single, miserable, half-forgotten, underestimated, often-neglected run, the margin that separated the victors, as they charged around the field, from the vanquished, their heads bowed in a torment of self-reproach.

Unusually wet weather before and during the match made the Adelaide pitch fresher than usual. Pace and spinners alike enjoyed themselves as embattled batsmen fought for whatever scraps could be taken from a normally well-stocked table. The drama began before the first ball as Martyn incurred an injury and was forced to withdraw, whereupon his stablemate, Justin Langer, rushed across the country to make his first appearance. It was to be a baptism of fire.

After winning the toss, the West Indies scored 252 and Australia replied with 213. Already Boon had been forced to retire hurt and Langer had been cracked on the helmet, one of many blows he was to endure. Returning to form, and enjoying better luck than previously, Curtly Ambrose was magnificent, taking six wickets with deliveries that seemed to plummet from the skies before erupting out of the pitch. Before the match was over, his tally would rise by four more, as the enigmatic Antiguan finally made his mark.

Richardson's beautifully crafted 72 took his team into a powerful position but his tailenders threw it all away as the last five wickets fell for 32 runs. In his first Test appearance for four years, and in front of his home crowd, Tim May claimed 5/9. Nor was his work complete.

Needing 186 to win the series and the title, the Australians sank to 8/102 as Ambrose, Walsh and Bishop cut swathes through their ranks. All seemed lost as May walked out to join Langer in front of a fourth-day crowd resigned to defeat.

But the match had not yet completed its course. Putting their heads down with admirable resolution, the ninth-wicket pair inched their team closer to the target. Normally the most relaxed of grounds, the Adelaide Oval was agog. A depressed Australia dressing-room began to sense a glimmer of hope. It was not as if the batsmen seemed to be in any particular trouble. Cricket is puzzling that way. Batting can appear well-nigh impossible and then a couple of fellows take root and suddenly it is hard to see when another wicket will fall.

Watching in the rooms must have been an agony. It was not much fun in the press box. No one could write a thing. Waste of time. Journalists like clear-cut finishes, especially as deadlines approach. Seasoned reporters tell novices only ever to use 'what you've got'. In other words never throw forwards, never anticipate.

Everything seemed to rest upon the shoulders of the doughty newcomer from Western Australia. At the time the adjective was apt but it would become a limitation. Later Langer would understand the need to move beyond his adjective—everybody has one—and to explore his wider personality. He learnt to release the feisty aggressor who also lived within. (A decade later I would write that Langer's attempt to widen his character had improved his game whereas Hayden's similar attempt had harmed his batting, and was surprised to receive an email from a senior Australian player saying that the point had been well made. Soon afterwards Hayden went back to his basics.)

Langer took his team halfway to the target, adding 42 with May, a supposedly timid partner, before he was taken behind the wicket. Forty-two still needed as the supposedly even more timid McDermott walked to the crease. Like 'ragged', timid is one of those euphemisms used by commentators to camouflage a harder point. Obviously it is intended to convey that the player is thought to be scared stiff of anything faster than medium-pace.

McDermott was assumed to be in a funk, so journalists starting writing their reports. He could not possibly last five minutes. Yet the momentum was with Australia and still the runs kept coming, first like water seeping through a crack and then in a rush as the crack widened. At last the Australians came within striking distance of victory, two runs away, a mere trifle, an unconsidered push to leg or a hurried second off an edge.

But the last run is the hardest to collect. Inevitably something changes within, as one side abruptly looks the spectre of defeat in the eye and the other awaits unexpected, massive, inspiring victory. There is a tightening as the moment of victory approaches, a defiance as defeat looms. When intellectuals dismiss sport as the preserve of muddied oafs and flannelled fools they are failing to grasp not merely its beauty of expression and cohesion but also its struggles of the mind.

Courtney Walsh was bowling. Would Australia win match, series and world title? The West Indies had played its last card. Hadn't they? Walsh tried a bumper. McDermott tried to parry the ball and it flew through to Junior Murray behind the stumps. Along the way it had brushed something. But what?

Darrell Hair was the presiding umpire. An unusual man, an old-fashioned Australian, fond of a punt, blessed with strong opinions, larger and louder than life, he was not everyone's glass of beer. Some thought him headstrong. Few doubted his ability as an umpire. Now he had his finest hour. Convinced that the ball had brushed McDermott's glove, a conclusion reached after a few moments of reflection that seemed like hours, he raised the index finger of his right hand. Walsh was charging around the ground already like a man possessed, his eyes ablaze, his colleagues in hot pursuit. The Australians were devastated. So near and so far. It might have been better to lose by 50 than to come within a whisker of victory. It would have been easier to recover.

Border took it hardest. Adelaide was never easy for him. The Australian captain had to rebuild his own, and his team's, confidence in the brief respite between Tests. Now came one of those incidents that from time to time crop up in sport as unforeseen forces impose themselves upon the usual flow of events. Every activity has its undercurrents.

Unhappy with the performance of its curator, the West Australia Cricket Association had decided to dispense with his services, a decision that had not gone down especially well. Moreover the gentleman concerned was of New Zealand origin. As has been observed from time to time, some members of New Zealand's diverse and mostly amiable population have taken against their genial neighbours to the northwest. Somehow these otherwise mild citizens have detected in the ranks of their fellow antipodeans a strain of arrogance, even self-obsession.

Whether or not the gentleman preparing the pitch for the decisive engagement of a ferocious series adhered to this school of thought cannot be said, his innermost thoughts never having been revealed. Was it his intent to secure revenge upon his employers? Perhaps it was simply that his mowers had broken down, and that a search of the metropolis had brought neither spare parts nor replacements. Whatever the cause, the pitch presented for the final Test could have kept a pack of horses fed for a month. Since this book hopes to attract the attention of youth, the Australian captain's comments upon inspecting the grassy field posing as a wicket will not be recorded verbatim. Suffice it to say that Border was not best pleased.

Nothing in the two-and-a-bit days it took the visitors to trounce their surprisingly obliging hosts improved his state of mind, and certainly not the pair of ducks recorded against his name. Scarcely able to believe his luck, Ambrose took 7/25 in Australia's brief first innings. In their slightly longer second effort, Bishop took 6/40. In between, the West Indies passed 300, thereby securing an innings victory. It was all over before lunch on the third morning. Picture the scene, imagine the wickets, feel the despond in Australian stomachs, and the lingering sense of betrayal.

Opinion was divided as to whether these events contained more sorrow or farce. At any event, both elements could be found in the vividness of the cricket, the abrupt dashing of Australian hopes, the glower on Border's face, the rejoicing of Ambrose and the celebrations of champions who had escaped the noose in Adelaide and now sat resplendent on their throne. Still the master of all they surveyed.

Border left Perth in a filthy mood, only too aware that his last chance of achieving supremacy had gone. He had run his race, had taken Australian cricket as far as he could, which was much further than anyone had expected. As much as an opponent fighting hard against the dying of its light, he had been beaten by a brushed glove and a grumpy Kiwi. But, then, every captain leaves something on the table. Perhaps it is just as well.

After 1987, these were the only series lost under Border's captaincy. That the gap between Australia and the West Indies narrowed was poor consolation. Not until a new leader had been appointed would the old champion be beaten. Not without reason, Border would be criticised for failing to recognise that Richardson's team was vulnerable, for failing to turn defence into attack. Certainly he was constantly fighting rearguard actions. Doubtless his hesitancy stemmed from past experiences. It is harder for older players to realise that a respected opponent has lost his edge. Nursing bruises from past encounters, they may need confirmation that a blow has landed before moving in for the kill, and by then it can be too late. A new man will take every opponent as he finds them.

AUSTRALIA V WEST INDIES, FOURTH TEST

23–26 JANUARY 1993, ADELAIDE OVAL, SOUTH AUSTRALIA

Toss: West Indies
Result: West Indies won by 1 run
Man of the match: C.E.L. Ambrose

West Indies (1st Innings)		R	BF	4	6
D.L. Haynes	st Healy b May	45	95	6	0
P.V. Simmons	c Hughes b S.R. Waugh	46	90	8	0
R.B. Richardson (c)	lbw b Hughes	2	15	0	0
B.C. Lara	c Healy b McDermott	52	76	6	0
K.L.T. Arthurton	c S.R. Waugh b May	0	4	0	0
C.L. Hooper	c Healy b Hughes	2	9	0	0
J.R. Murray (k)	not out	49	80	7	0
I.R. Bishop	c M.E. Waugh b Hughes	13	19	2	0
C.E.L. Ambrose	c Healy b Hughes	0	2	0	0
K.C.G. Benjamin	b M.E. Waugh	15	23	2	0
C.A. Walsh	lbw b Hughes	5	5	0	0
Extras	(lb 11, nb 12)	23			
Total	**All out**	**252**			
	67.3 overs at 3.73 rpo				

FoW				
	1–84	Simmons	2–99	Richardson
	3–129	Haynes	4–130	Arthurton
	5–134	Hooper	6–189	Lara
	7–206	Bishop	8–206	Ambrose
	9–247	Benjamin	10–252	Walsh

Bowling	O	M	R	W
C.J. McDermott	16	1	85	1
M.G. Hughes	21.3	3	64	5
S.R. Waugh	13	4	37	1
T.B.A. May	14	1	41	2
S.K. Warne	2	0	11	0
M.E. Waugh	1	0	3	1

Australia (1st Innings)		R	BF	4	6
M.A. Taylor	c Hooper b Bishop	1	4	0	0
D.C. Boon	not out	39	136	4	0
J.L. Langer	c Murray b Benjamin	20	79	2	0
M.E. Waugh	c Simmons b Ambrose	0	2	0	0
S.R. Waugh	c Murray b Ambrose	42	78	5	0
A.R. Border (c)	c Hooper b Ambrose	19	52	2	0
I.A. Healy (k)	c Hooper b Ambrose	0	3	0	0
M.G. Hughes	c Murray b Hooper	43	66	3	1
S.K. Warne	lbw b Hooper	0	3	0	0
T.B.A. May	c Murray b Ambrose	6	33	0	0
C.J. McDermott	b Ambrose	14	18	1	0
Extras	(b 7, lb 3, nb 19)	29			
Total	**All out**	**213**			
	75.2 overs at 2.83 rpo				

FoW				
	1–1	Taylor	2–16	M.E. Waugh
	3–46	Langer	4–108	Border
	5–108	Healy	6–112	S.R. Waugh
	7–181	Hughes	8–181	Warne
	9–197	May	10–213	McDermott

Bowling	O	M	R	W
C.E.L. Ambrose	28.2	6	74	6
I.R. Bishop	18	3	48	1
K.C.G. Benjamin	6	0	22	1
C.A. Walsh	10	3	34	0
C.L. Hooper	13	4	25	2

West Indies (2nd Innings)		R	BF	4	6
D.L. Haynes	c Healy b McDermott	11	14	2	0
P.V. Simmons	b McDermott	10	20	0	0
R.B. Richardson (c)	c Healy b Warne	72	106	6	2
B.C. Lara	c S.R. Waugh b Hughes	7	11	1	0
K.L.T. Arthurton	c Healy b McDermott	0	8	0	0
C.L. Hooper	c Hughes b May	25	63	2	0
J.R. Murray (k)	c M.E. Waugh b May	0	10	0	0
I.R. Bishop	c M.E. Waugh b May	6	21	0	0
C.E.L. Ambrose	st Healy b May	1	4	0	0
K.C.G. Benjamin	c Warne b May	0	6	0	0
C.A. Walsh	not out	0	0	0	0
Extras	(lb 2, nb 12)	14			
Total	**All out**	**146**			
	41.5 overs at 3.49 rpo				

FoW

	1–14	Haynes	2–49	Simmons
	3–63	Lara	4–65	Arthurton
	5–124	Hooper	6–137	Murray
	7–145	Richardson	8–146	Ambrose
	9–146	Benjamin	10–146	Bishop

Bowling	O	M	R	W
C.J. McDermott	11	0	66	3
M.G. Hughes	13	1	43	1
S.R. Waugh	5	1	8	0
T.B.A. May	6.5	3	9	5
S.K. Warne	6	2	18	1

Australia (2nd Innings)		R	BF	4	6
D.C. Boon	lbw b Ambrose	0	17	0	0
M.A. Taylor	c Murray b Benjamin	7	42	0	0
J.L. Langer	c Murray b Bishop	54	146	4	0
M.E. Waugh	c Hooper b Walsh	26	38	4	0
S.R. Waugh	c Arthurton b Ambrose	4	11	0	0
A.R. Border (c)	c Haynes b Ambrose	1	17	0	0
I.A. Healy (k)	b Walsh	0	1	0	0
M.G. Hughes	lbw b Ambrose	1	3	0	0
S.K. Warne	lbw b Bishop	9	60	0	0
T.B.A. May	not out	42	99	4	0
C.J. McDermott	c Murray b Walsh	18	57	0	0
Extras	(b 1, lb 8, nb 13)	22			
Total	**All out**	**184**			
	79.0 overs at 2.33 rpo				

FoW

	1–5	Boon	2–16	Taylor
	3–54	M.E. Waugh	4–64	S.R. Waugh
	5–72	Border	6–73	Healy
	7–74	Hughes	8–102	Warne
	9–144	Langer	10–184	McDermott

Bowling	O	M	R	W
C.E.L. Ambrose	26	5	46	4
I.R. Bishop	17	3	41	2
K.C.G. Benjamin	12	2	32	1
C.A. Walsh	19	4	44	3
C.L. Hooper	5	1	12	0

9

PUMMELLING
THE POMS

England awaited the Australians' arrival in 1989 with supreme but ill-placed confidence. English cricket had long since fallen into a decline it scarcely realised had begun. Results had remained satisfactory thanks to remnants of the old school, to opponents' below-par performances and to the emergence of an extraordinary cricketer raised in an unpromising semi-industrial town in the more neglected parts of Somerset, a spirited, headstrong youth by the name of Ian Botham.

Any country can at any moment unearth a brilliant cricketer whose exceptional abilities create excitement across the land. Botham was a roughneck who took the game to the masses, a blue-collar cricketer who performed comic strip feats. Ultimately he would become a comic book character, even in his own mind, and suffered more than most from the exposure of his flaws and the intrusion of reality. His triumphs, regular in the early years, astonishing in 1981/82 and sporadic thereafter, cozened England into supposing that all was well. Not until his withdrawal were the cracks noticed, and even then it would take years for them to be filled.

English cricket's problems were to be found in its traditions. Professional cricket had long been an honourable but poorly paid craft with its own code. By the 1980s it was starting to feel the influence of a much wider world, a world of celebrities, stars, advertisements and rewards. Botham had become the country's first celebrity cricketer since W.G. Grace. In some respects the game had been dragged from its poverty and privacy and thrust into a more commercial world.

In the 1980s, however, cricketers were being paid wages more appropriate to the 1950s. Soccer had long since broken the bounds of financial restraint, yet great cricketers such as Botham and Richards were paid relative pittances by their counties and countries. They bestrode the game but were not reaping the rewards. A craft had been replaced by an entertainment yet the old thinking endured behind the scenes. There was an emptiness in the soul of the English game and not until an accommodation was found between old truths and modern ways would the English game recover its sense of purpose.

Nevertheless, in 1989 the hosts were expected to retain the Ashes with ease. Border's team contained many players unfamiliar with local conditions. It was, though, a side that had squared up to the West Indians, a side that had won a World Cup. Studying the names it is hard to understand the disdain with which the tourists were greeted. Not that outfits subsequently arriving in Perth have been treated with any more respect.

Australia's bowling had fallen into the hands of Geoff Lawson, Terry Alderman, Merv Hughes and Tim May. In hindsight it is not a bad attack and Alderman especially remained dangerous on English pitches. Had the West Australian been available in 1985 that debâcle might have been avoided. Instead he had chosen to join the rebels in South Africa. Throughout the 1989 tour, Alderman's swingers and cutters would torture the English batsmen, particularly Graham Gooch whose technique did not survive the examination. Alderman was assisted by the willingness of English umpires to give leg-before decisions on the front foot. Alderman matched Shane Warne's ability to take wickets with straight deliveries. He'd send down a series of outswingers until he sensed that his opponent was lining them up whereupon he'd deliver a faster straight ball. Lawson was experienced, skilful and blessed with a high arm and a long memory. Hughes had the strength and heart of an ox and May was the cleverest spinner Australia had fielded since Ashley Mallet.

A new wicket-keeper had been found in Ian Healy, a man plucked from the Queensland reserve team, baptised in Pakistan and then sent to England. Greg Chappell had watched him during a rare appearance in Shield cricket and liked the cut of his jib. As usual the Australian selectors had the courage to back their hunches. They regarded Healy as a dedicated cricketer likely to improve with opportunity, and did not feel the same about the incumbent, Tim Zoehrer.

Some critics felt that, properly handled, Zoehrer had much to offer. But Australia had moved past man management and all that rot. The selectors wanted players who could take care of themselves, who could run their own lives. Those lacking drive and discipline were pushed away. Later those demanding more attention than they deserved would also be replaced. It was ruthless. Simpson, Sawle and company were not running a health clinic but an international cricket team.

The selectors' judgement was vindicated and 14 years later Healy had the honour, keenly felt, of being nominated by a large and distinguished selection panel as Australia's greatest ever gloveman.

Australia's batting had been strengthened by the inclusion at the top of the order of Mark Taylor, an unfussy left-hander with an uncomplicated game who brought an air of maturity to the team. Border, Boon and Marsh and those contrasting but hungry middle-order men, Dean Jones and Steve Waugh, completed the line-up. It was a powerful side yet almost everyone was predicting heavy defeat.

The odds lengthened further when the Australians lost their opening match in Worcester. A draw followed at Somerset where the tourists only managed to take three wickets on the final day. Border was looking grim, yet Border had changed. In 1985 he had been happy to exchange jokes with opponents. He had even played a season for Essex. Now he refused to talk with the opposition, and was altogether more demanding on the field. His team also adopted a meaner approach. They had come to win, not to make friends.

Everyone went to Leeds for the first Test expecting another home victory. Instead England was overpowered. Australia scored 7/601 in its first innings and 3/230 in its second, declaring on both occasions. Mark Taylor and Steve Waugh scored substantial centuries in that first marathon. Botham was not playing. England's swing bowlers had a miserable time but Alderman took ten wickets as his side romped home by 210 runs.

AUSTRALIA V ENGLAND, FIRST ASHES TEST
8–13 JUNE 1989, HEADINGLEY, LEEDS, UK

Toss:	**England**
Result:	**Australia won by 210 runs**
Man of the match:	**T.M. Alderman**

Australia (1st Innings)		R	BF	4	6
G.R. Marsh	lbw b DeFreitas	16	63	1	0
M.A. Taylor	lbw b Foster	136	315	16	0
D.C. Boon	c Russell b Foster	9	24	1	0
A.R. Border (c)	c Foster b DeFreitas	66	118	9	1
D.M. Jones	c Russell b Newport	79	172	7	0
S.R. Waugh	not out	177	242	24	0
I.A. Healy (k)	c & b Newport	16	31	2	0
M.G. Hughes	c Russell b Foster	71	105	6	2
G.F. Lawson	not out	10	13	1	0
G.D. Campbell					
T.M. Alderman					
Extras	(lb 13, w 1, nb 7)	21			
Total	**7 wickets declared**	**601**			
	178.3 overs at 3.37 rpo				

FoW				
	1–44	Marsh	2–57	Boon
	3–174	Border	4–273	Taylor
	5–411	Jones	6–441	Healy
	7–588	Hughes		

Bowling	O	M	R	W
P.A.J. DeFreitas	45.3	8	140	2
N.A. Foster	46	14	109	3
P.J. Newport	39	5	153	2
D.R. Pringle	33	5	123	0
G.A. Gooch	9	1	31	0
K.J. Barnett	6	0	32	0

England (1st Innings)		R	BF	4	6
G.A. Gooch	lbw b Alderman	13	46	2	0
B.C. Broad	b Hughes	37	74	5	0
K.J. Barnett	lbw b Alderman	80	118	10	0
A.J. Lamb	c Boon b Alderman	125	204	24	0
D.I. Gower (c)	c Healy b Lawson	26	39	5	0
R.A. Smith	lbw b Alderman	66	132	8	0
D.R. Pringle	lbw b Campbell	6	15	1	0
P.J. Newport	c Boon b Lawson	36	73	3	0
R.C. Russell (k)	c Marsh b Lawson	15	33	3	0
P.A.J. DeFreitas	lbw b Alderman	1	6	0	0
N.A. Foster	not out	2	5	0	0
Extras	(b 5, lb 7, w 1, nb 10)	23			
Total	**All out**	**430**			
	121.5 overs at 3.53 rpo				

FoW				
	1–35	Gooch	2–81	Broad
	3–195	Barnett	4–243	Gower
	5–323	Lamb	6–338	Pringle
	7–392	Smith	8–421	Newport
	9–424	DeFreitas	10–430	Russell

Bowling	O	M	R	W
T.M. Alderman	37	7	107	5
G.F. Lawson	34.5	6	105	3
G.D. Campbell	14	0	82	1
M.G. Hughes	28	7	92	1
S.R. Waugh	6	2	27	0
A.R. Border	2	1	5	0

Australia (2nd Innings)		R	BF	4	6
G.R. Marsh	c Russell b Foster	6	22	0	0
M.A. Taylor	c Broad b Pringle	60	112	8	0
D.C. Boon	lbw b DeFreitas	43	95	6	0
A.R. Border (c)	not out	60	76	8	0
D.M. Jones	not out	40	34	3	0
S.R. Waugh					
I.A. Healy (k)					
M.G. Hughes					
G.F. Lawson					
G.D. Campbell					
T.M. Alderman					
Extras	(b 2, lb 5, w 9, nb 5)	21			
Total	**3 wickets declared**	**230**			
	54.5 overs at 4.19 rpo				

FoW

	1–14	Marsh	2–97	Taylor
	3–129	Boon		

Bowling

	O	M	R	W
N.A. Foster	19	4	65	1
P.A.J. DeFreitas	18	2	76	1
D.R. Pringle	12.5	1	60	1
P.J. Newport	5	2	22	0

England (2nd Innings)

		R	BF	4	6
G.A. Gooch	lbw b Hughes	68	118	10	0
B.C. Broad	lbw b Alderman	7	12	1	0
K.J. Barnett	c Taylor b Alderman	34	46	7	0
A.J. Lamb	c Boon b Alderman	4	6	1	0
D.I. Gower (c)	c Healy b Lawson	34	44	6	0
R.A. Smith	c Border b Lawson	0	3	0	0
D.R. Pringle	c Border b Alderman	0	27	0	0
P.J. Newport	c Marsh b Alderman	8	27	1	0
R.C. Russell (k)	c Healy b Hughes	2	22	0	0
P.A.J. DeFreitas	b Hughes	21	18	3	0
N.A. Foster	not out	1	16	0	0
Extras	(b 4, lb 3, nb 5)	12			
Total	**All out**	**191**			
	55.2 overs at 3.45 rpo				

FoW

	1–17	Broad	2–67	Barnett
	3–77	Lamb	4–134	Gower
	5–134	Smith	6–153	Gooch
	7–153	Pringle	8–166	Russell
	9–170	Newport	10–191	DeFreitas

Bowling

	O	M	R	W
T.M. Alderman	20	7	44	5
G.F. Lawson	11	2	58	2
G.D. Campbell	10	0	42	0
M.G. Hughes	9.2	2	36	3
A.R. Border	5	3	4	0

Worse was to follow for David Gower's side in the second match at Lord's. Although Gower and Robin Smith were scoring runs, the rest were struggling, Gooch was having a horrible time and the bowling was threadbare. Australia reached 528 and lost only four wickets, securing the 118 runs needed to take a 2/0 lead. Alderman took nine wickets. By now Gooch's answerphone carried the message 'Graham is out, LBW bowled Alderman'. Or so impish reporters contended.

By now the hosts had begun to realise the extent of their troubles. They were dipping into the magic hat called county cricket to pull out such unlikely Test performers as Phil Newport, Paul Jarvis and Kim Barnett. All the follies of the recent past had returned to haunt them. Botham was back for Birmingham but his slow mediums did not worry the visitors. Jones contributed 157 and Hohns offered 40 as their team reached 424. Rain meant that Australians continued batting into the fourth day but the match was drawn. By now Tim Curtis and Chris Tavare had been called up.

Standing two up with two to play, Australia arrived in Manchester confident they had England's measure. Geoff Lawson took six wickets with his tortured bounce and movement and deserved his nomination as Man of the Match. He had bowled well throughout the campaign and, with Hughes and Alderman, formed a potent pace attack. Having suffered in 1981 and 1985, he relished this turnaround. Lawson would retire with 180 Test wickets to his name. At the time only six Australians had taken more. Alderman claimed five scalps in the second innings and by the fifth afternoon the Australians were knocking off the 78 runs needed for victory and the Ashes. Boon played the winning shot, the balcony erupted and the celebrations began: 3/0.

Nothing changed at Trent Bridge. Geoff Marsh (138) and Mark Taylor (219) batted the entire first day (0/301 at stumps), Australia passed 600, Botham was injured and unable to bat, Alderman took more wickets, Eddie Hemmings and Nick Cook joined the side, England followed on and lost by an innings and 180 runs: 4/0.

By now the hosts had reason to regret that six matches had been arranged for the 1989 Ashes series. The side now included John Stephenson, Gladstone Small, Alan Igglesden and Mike Atherton. Martin Moxon had come and gone. Dean Jones scored 122, Australia reached 468 but the match was spoilt by rain and England escaped.

Had the weather been kinder Australia must have won all six Tests. England was in absolute disarray. The incompetence on and off the field was alarming.

England ventured down under in the northern winter of 1990/91 determined to bring back the Ashes. On paper, the England line-up did not seem to offer any particular reason to fear for the future of English cricket. Unfortunately bad habits had become ingrained and although the names remained the same, attitudes had deteriorated. During the course of an unhappy tour, players would be punished for returning late to their hotel in the middle of a Test match after visiting a casino (to make matters worse their companions were Kerry Packer and Tony Greig). Allan Lamb, one of the culprits, lost his wicket in the first over next morning.

David Gower and John Morris were fined for trying to brighten up a practice match staged in a hot bush town in deepest Queensland by buzzing the ground in a Tigermoth hired for the purpose. It was intended as a light-hearted romp but was interpreted as an attempt to undermine the captain's authority. England had fallen into the hands of Graham Gooch, Mickey Stewart and Peter Lush, one of the most uninspired groups ever to take charge of anything, let alone a bunch of ageing sportsmen visiting a sunny foreign land.

Never had the contention that English cricket has always been a battle between roundheads and cavaliers seemed truer than during the course of this gloomy expedition. Not that England had much luck, losing Graham Gooch, their captain and best batsman, Allan Lamb and Angus Fraser to untimely injuries. England was only once able to field its best side.

By way of contrast, the Australians played with a single mind and called on only 14 players. Allan Border and his players did not waste time and energy on internal matters and concentrated on trouncing the opposition, a task they accomplished by three victories to nil. Australia owed a good deal to its fast bowlers—Bruce Reid, restored to the ranks after 18 months on the sidelines nursing an injury, and Craig McDermott, who did not take the field until the fourth Test and promptly took 18 wickets in two matches.

Australia's batting was oddly unproductive, with none of three senior batsmen, Mark Taylor, Steve Waugh and Dean Jones, averaging over 24 in the series. Against a stronger, more focused opponent, this might have been critical. Fortunately Boon, Matthews, Marsh and Border could be depended upon. In the event Waugh lost his place to his twin brother, a fact confirmed at the family breakfast table. Mark Waugh marked his debut with a sublime hundred in Adelaide, an innings containing a wide range of gracefully played strokes. Perhaps Australia was also torn between the roundhead and cavalier. Certainly the Waugh household seemed to be.

Spin remained Australia's weak point. In five matches its slower bowlers claimed eight scalps between them, Greg Matthews contributed seven at an average of 60, and Border collected Wayne Larkins' wicket in Sydney. It was around this time that the first whispers were heard about a lad in Melbourne who could spin the ball on a billiard table. Rod Hogg had provoked mirth by predicting the youngster would take 500 wickets in Test cricket. Even a news-paper as liberal as *The Truth* could not tolerate nonsense of that sort and the former fast bowler was given his marching orders. Techni-cally, the paper was right. Warne has not taken 500 wickets. He has taken 600 and the number is rising.

Despite their cuffing, England still had little reason to fear the onset of a decade of suffering. Hope springs eternal. By the time the Australians arrived in 1993, the lingering effects of the rebel tours to South Africa had passed. Everyone was available. Had the hosts realised that over the next ten years they'd be battered and belaboured by Australia's 'three Ws', they might not have felt as opti-mistic about their prospects. In hindsight England was living on borrowed time and Australia was approaching its zenith.

Warne was taken to England for the 1993 visit. No one expected much from him. Hitherto he had taken 31 Test wickets at an average of 30 apiece. The West Indians and panicking Sri Lankans had fallen foul of him, but it was a long time since a leg-spinner had succeeded in England, especially in the first half of the 'summer'. Yet Warne's wickets were not without significance and his statistics had been affected by a profligate first appearance against India at the SCG. Since then he had bowled out the West Indians on the final day of the Boxing Day Test and taken three wickets as the Sri Lankans pursued a modest target on the last afternoon in Colombo. In short he had played crucial parts in two victories. Here was a young man with a sense of occasion.

Warne was not expected to play in the first Test at Old Trafford, although as far as spinners were concerned, Manchester was the most helpful pitch in the country. England played two spinners, Peter Such and Phil Tufnell. Tim May was the visitors' senior spinner. But the Australians had tired of finger-spin, besides which the selectors knew that these opponents were as familiar with wrist-spin as they were with droughts. Accordingly the youthful, smiling, calculating, endlessly cheeky leggie was thrown to the sheep.

England won the toss and surprised most observers by choosing to bowl on a pitch with a greenish tinge. Mark Taylor scored a century, and Michael Slater contributed 58 on his first appearance for his country. Australia slipped from 2/183 to 289 all out and England had moved along capably to 1/80 with Graham Gooch and Mike Gatting at the crease when the ball was tossed to the upstart tweaker. Most spectators and viewers started watching more closely. Here was a young, blond leg-spinner bowling to two of England's most withering batsmen, a pair capable of seizing upon any nervousness in their opponent. If nothing else, it was going to be interesting.

Even now the moment lingers in the mind. In one sense it happened quickly: a delivery, a wicket, a shock, a departure. In another sense it was frozen in time. I can remember watching that ball as it made its way down the pitch, an apparently amiable missile destined to be dispatched summarily. Watching on television, and not unaware of Warne's powers, I had time to think that his first ball had been a waste and to mutter sage words about 'callow youth' and 'improving once the butterflies had settled down'. Nor did the ball look any better as it headed further down the wicket. Indeed it faded even more to leg, and four byes seemed to be the likeliest result. Was there time for so many thoughts? Can an angel dance on a pinhead? I remember thinking all of them, quite distinctly. A lot can be packed into a second.

Then the ball began to change course. Nor was it a mild alteration, a minor adjustment of the sort within the powers of many bowlers. Rather, the delivery swerved to leg and then, suddenly, quite suddenly, it revealed its devilry. There was an explosion, a moment of violence that had about it the terrible beauty of nature at its most raw. Far from passing harmlessly down the leg-side, or wrapping into Gatting's voluminous front pad, the ball turned viciously, almost at right angles, ripped across the batsman and took the off-bail.

In 115 years of trying, no bowler in Ashes history had struck the stumps with his first offering. Warne had not merely broken that record, he had sent down the finest, most startling first delivery the game has ever known. It was like the opening chord of 'Satisfaction'. Cricket was fortunate in its victim. Gatting has one of those faces that convey emotion even as they try to retain their secrets. At first he was merely bemused. In an instant bafflement became bewilderment and then, as Ian Healy raised his arms, other feelings found their places. Gatting was first thunderstruck, then devastated. His was the look, captured in photographs, seen on a soldier's face as a bullet strikes. Only then could the Londoner start to drag himself from the arena. As he left he shook his head and looked back, as if seeking confirmation that it had not all been a dream.

Warne had worked the first of his wonders. It is part of the secret of great sportsmen that they hide their humanity, disguise their concerns, become indomitable. Victory does not take them by surprise. Triumphs are celebrated without any hint that they might be flukes. Champions take to the field clad in armour, impervious to bullets. Warne rejoiced but did not give much away, managed to appear less astonished than his colleagues, let alone his opponents, as they watched the replays on television. He recovered quickly enough to take another wicket a few balls later as Robin Smith was held at slip.

England collapsed, as Warne and Merv Hughes took four wickets apiece. In the second innings, Ian Healy became only the second Australian wicket-keeper to score a Test hundred—Rod Marsh had become the first in the Centenary Test match in 1977—whereupon the two Victorian bowlers repeated their first-innings performance and Australian won by 179 runs.

Australia won again on a spinners' pitch at Lord's—Mark Waugh took the new ball for the tourists and McDermott collapsed in the dressing-room with a twisted bowel that required surgery. He took no further part in the series. By the third Test, Gooch had dropped himself down the list in an attempt to prop up a middle order that was floundering against Warne, and both the home captain and Graham Thorpe scored second-innings centuries before Australia was invited to chase 371 in 77 overs. Early wickets were lost, leaving Steve Waugh and Brendon Julian to bat out the last session, a task accomplished with considerable ease, and the third Test was drawn.

England had not found a match-winning spinner or a fast bowler of character and penetration. Martin McCague and Mark Ilott took the new ball.

Normal service was resumed at Leeds as the Australians piled on the runs against an inept attack, Border scoring 200 not out. England had relied on the ball swinging at Headingley. Sometimes it does, and sometimes it does not. Everything depends on the weather. Alas, the sun shone. Paul Reiffel took eight wickets, and Hughes, Warne and May did the rest. All too easily, Australia had held the Ashes.

Australia won again at Edgbaston to take a 4/0 lead. By now Gooch had resigned and Michael Atherton was captaining the home side. England made five changes for the sixth and final Test at The Oval and secured an encouraging win by 161 runs as Angus Fraser took eight wickets and Devon Malcolm made the visitors hop about. But it was all the merest consolation. At least England had ended the series stronger than it began, with an intelligent captain, emerging players of promise in Nasser Hussain and Thorpe, and a threatening new ball attack in Fraser and Malcolm. On the other hand they had also encountered Warne and must have suspected that he was going to be around to torment them for quite some time.

Atherton faced a daunting task as he brought England down under in the summer of 1994/95. In 118 years and 242 days only four England captains had recaptured the Ashes in Australia. In 1903/04, Plum Warner had a secret weapon called Bertie Bosanquet who sent down googlies, which some didn't think quite fair. In 1920/21, Johnny 'Won't Hit Today' Douglas also had a dangerous bowler in S.F. Barnes, arguably the grumpiest paceman ever to put on a pair of boots (and the competition has been hot). In 1932/33, Douglas Jardine had Harold Larwood and Bodyline. In 1971/72 Ray Illingworth brought John Snow and the tenacity needed to overcome umpires who did not give them a single leg-before decision in the entire series.

Atherton's resources were altogether more modest. The first Test was bound to be crucial. Australia won the toss and batted first at Brisbane. Michael Slater scored 176 and his team led by 269, as the visitors batted poorly. Now came a surprising moment. In his first Ashes Test as captain, and with his opponents at his mercy, Mark Taylor opted not to enforce the follow-on. It was a singularly brave and independent decision. After an hour's play on the third morning, Taylor's fresh bowlers had dismissed England for 167. Later, research would be produced which revealed that batting again is a more reliable path to victory but it must depend on the circumstances. If nothing else, Taylor had confirmed that he had been the right choice to lead the side. Here was a calm, thoughtful man with the courage of his own convictions.

Australia batted badly in its second innings and at stumps on the fourth day England stood at 2/211, only 297 runs shy of victory. Warne was clearly the main threat, but he had bowled a lot of overs. All winter his opponents had thought about him, talked about him, pondered ways of playing him and it had all led to this moment. Not the least remarkable part of Warne's record is that it has been achieved in the age of television, in the era of analysis and replays. But, then, Warne's entire career has been a television show.

Warne dominated the final day, taking eight wickets for 71 runs in 50 overs. All eight executions had about them an elegance that hid their sporting cruelty. Warne has much of the bull-fighter in him. He sliced through the Poms not so much like a knife through butter as a saw through wood, a gradual splintering and then, at last, the final cut. Australia won by 184 runs.

On the first morning of the ensuing Boxing Day Test in Melbourne, Taylor's side nearly surrendered its advantage. In a trice Slater had embarked upon a madcap run and David Boon, usually the most dependable of batsmen, had stepped down the pitch without taking his brains with him. Boxing Day is never the easiest day upon which to build a Test innings.

As had become his custom, Steve Waugh restored the side's sanity with an unbeaten 94 whereupon Warne went to work on his home patch, taking 6/64 to give his side a precious lead. Determined not to die in their beds, as had been the case in Brisbane, the Englishmen charged straight at the enemy guns, with a fusillade of adventurous strokes. Boon promptly redeemed his reputation with a century in the second innings and the local leg-spinner, Craig McDermott, and Damien Fleming did the rest as England collapsed to 92 all out and lost by 295 runs.

Fleming was a fine swing bowler dogged by injury. Australia was lucky to have bowlers of the calibre of Fleming and Reiffel in reserve.

Both relied on late movement to take wickets, Fleming working through the air and Reiffel off the pitch, approaches that reflected both their actions and their temperaments. Swing bowlers are more inclined to be open and gregarious, whereas seam merchants, like off-spinners, are generally canny customers.

England needed to win in Sydney and started well. Atherton and John Crawley added 174 for the fifth wicket, a partnership that made up for the continuing failures of the old guard. Australia is not a hospitable environment for ageing batsmen. England reached 309 and then came an astonishing period of play. Darren Gough had been his team's driving force throughout the tour. Impassioned, energetic and warm, he had clouted his opponents around and bowled with all his heart and most of his head. Now he took 6/49 as the Australians were skittled for 116. Malcolm and Fraser also bowled well. This was as handy a pace attack as England had fielded in 15 years.

England needed to drive home its superiority but the scoring was slower than Atherton had hoped. He collected 67 from 166 balls and then became frustrated as Graeme Hick advanced slowly to 98, also in 166 balls. For several years Hick had been fighting to come to terms with others' expectations of him and a hundred against Australia was important to him. He pottered around in the nineties and Atherton declared. It was a fateful mistake that would affect both their relationship and the mood of the team. Communications had broken down, and they would take a lot of mending. Dressing-rooms are strange and emotional places.

Australia began its pursuit of 449 brilliantly, with both openers smashing the ball around. The largest crowd seen at a fifth day of a Sydney Test since 1962/63 was agog. Then the wickets started to tumble and it was left to the lower orders to organise the rescue mission as England crowded the bat and twilight fell across the ground. Much to the relief of the Australians in a fascinated audience, though to the dismay of the Barmy Army, May and Warne batted through the last hour to leave their side seven down at stumps. Fraser took five wickets but Tufnell took none. Warne was the difference between the sides. By now, too, Tufnell had become a figure of fun owing to his poor work in the outfield and media representation of him as a cricketing version of Albert Steptoe. Possibly the cheers were not good for him, encouraging the more wayward elements in his character. In any event he would never trouble the Australians again.

Two down with two matches left to play, England could not recover the Ashes. By now England seemed so down and out that one half expected George Orwell to turn up and start writing about it. Nothing much was expected from the trip to Adelaide. Undeterred and showing unexpected resolution, England pleased their raucous followers and surprised all and sundry with a notable rally. Gatting started the fightback with a hundred and Phil DeFreitas' swashbuckling 88 from 95 balls in the second innings gave the hosts another challenging last-day target of 263 in 70 overs. The Australians chased with gusto, only to be dispatched for 156 by Malcolm and Chris Lewis. Among the home players, only Greg Blewett caught the eye, with a spirited and unbeaten century on debut, a fine effort from a cricketer who had seemed destined to live in the shadows cast by better favoured and apparently more gifted contemporaries.

England played the stronger cricket and won fair and square. Had the Ashes still been at stake the hosts might have abandoned the chase earlier but that did not detract from their opponents' performance. Rather, it indicated that the Australians were vulnerable on the final day.

Reality returned to English cricket in the fifth and last Test in Perth as Slater scored a hundred and Steve Waugh 99 not out in the first innings, and Blewett another hundred in the second. Although Thorpe and Ramprakash batted capably for the visitors in their first outing, England needed to score 453 in the final innings of the campaign and fell short by 329 runs as McDermott and McGrath took nine wickets between them.

England had been trounced 3/1. Not for the first or last time in meetings between the sides, the result could have been closer but could also have been worse. Overall Australia was superior with bat and ball, and also caught better in the slips. England had been good in parts but lacked both the depth and the aggression needed to regain the Ashes.

Hostilities resumed in England in 1997. Australia had continued to build around its core of strong players. Whether Mark Taylor still belonged in that core was a matter of widespread debate. Australians had long disapproved of the English practice of naming a captain and then selecting the side, preferring their own more egalitarian method of choosing the best 11 players and then nominating one of them to lead the way.

Of course it was no longer quite as simple as that, and hadn't been since the advent of professional captains in England after the Second World War. Although a few Oxbridge graduates had subsequently led the side only Mike Brearley had lasted long, and he was chosen in an attempt to release the talent of the country's greatest cricketer. The Welsh charmer Tony Lewis and the upright Scotsman Mike Denness both failed to make much of an impression. England has mostly tried to find and support a leader worth his place in the side. Chris Cowdrey was an exception but the experiment did not last long. Apart from anything else England could not afford to carry a player.

The Australian position was not as clear-cut as observers liked to pretend. Bill O'Reilly voiced one point of view by saying that as far as he was concerned all captains did was to toss the coin in the morning and, in some cases, buy a round of drinks in the evening. But then, as a fiery, flame-haired, Irish Catholic leg-spinner, he was unlikely to kowtow to authority or Anglo-Saxon orthodoxy. Ian Chappell defended captains and the captaincy from the interference of coaches and anything else likely to compromise the leader.

At the start of his captaincy, Taylor had established himself as the senior voice in the dressing-room by supporting the replacement of Bob Simpson with Geoff Marsh, a more obliging character. Given plenty of licence by Border, Simpson had become a driving force in the team. Taylor was more self-confident than his predecessor, and found in Marsh a man willing to concentrate on organising practices and helping individuals. Simpson had spent part of his stint on the selection committee. Marsh preferred to keep in the background. Taylor had found his man.

The pressure on Taylor mounted as he dropped himself from the one-day team for the matches played before the Tests started. His struggles meant that Australia started the series without the intensity detected in previous series. Taylor's position was becoming almost untenable. Ian Chappell, especially, was calling for his head. To his credit, Taylor remained the same man through thick and thin, approachable, honest, never taking criticisms personally.

England had its best chance of winning an Ashes series since 1986/87. Australia's great men needed to summon their resolve or the day was lost. Taylor himself showed his mettle in the first Test in Birmingham. Had he failed in both innings he might have stepped down. Instead he rallied with a hundred in the second innings, a contribution that prolonged his career without saving the match. Australia lost by nine wickets. Against expectations Australia had fallen behind. Could England deliver the killer blow?

Despite McGrath's 8/38 at Lord's, the match was left drawn as rain fell across London. No one has used the Lord's slope better than McGrath. Whenever he bowled from the Pavilion End, which was always, batsmen had to calculate the degree of his break-backs. Often they got it wrong. Taylor's attack included McGrath, Gillespie, Warne and Kasprowicz. Two tours and eight years later the same quartet would still be charging to the bowling crease.

Matthew Elliott contributed a fine hundred at Lord's and would be the team's heaviest scorer in the series. Elliott had replaced Michael Slater at the top of the order. Among the regulars, only Paul Reiffel had a higher batting average in the series than the strained left-hander. Having rejected all the inhibiting nonsense about left elbows, Reiffel had developed into a capable lower-order batsman. Apart from these Victorians, Ricky Ponting alone averaged over 40 in the series, and he did not secure a place till Michael Bevan had failed in three successive matches (43 runs in five innings).

Considering their undoubted abilities, it must seem odd that Slater and Bevan had lost their places. Both had strong populist support, not least because they provided rich entertainment. Both were wonderful batsmen. Slater could produce an assault from the first ball of a series that would affect the mood for the rest of the campaign. More than any other Australian batsman of the era he created excitement in the stands. Whereas Steve Waugh set out to conquer himself, Slater seemed the most natural of men and players. Upon reaching three figures he'd jump for joy and kiss his helmet. Yet it was never quite as simple as that, or not after boyhood anyhow. Slater was not without his demons. Supporters lived on their nerves whenever he was batting. Friends simply hoped the derring-do could be contained.

Curiously Slater and Waugh did have one thing in common. Both kept losing their wickets in the nineties. Slater's excitement got the better of him. Waugh's sense of his place in history undid him.

Bevan was a minor genius touched by ghosts from his formative years, anxieties that unsettled him, made him a disconcerting companion. Yet he was also the most nimble and feline of batsmen. From a distance it seemed that the strength of the inner man demanded a countering assertion of aggressive masculinity. The edginess detected in early years spent wrestling with his astonishing creativity was manifested in various celebrated 'Bev attacks' wherein rooms, bats and other conveniences felt the full force of his wrath. In his early years, Bevan was also suspected of that greatest of Australian crimes, fallibility against fast bowling. Mud sticks.

Torn between a desire to defend and attack the short stuff, the left-hander was inclined to attempt something in between. His mind seemed to be frozen by indecision. Much to Bevan's frustration, the reputation became his shadow. Bevan would mature into a superb batsman obliged to strut his stuff in 50-over matches and otherwise to content himself with thousands of runs collected in domestic matches. He was never quite able to relax. Yet he made a mighty contribution and turned the one-day arena into his own. His ability to flick the ball through or over the leg-side will linger in the mind.

Nor was Elliott destined to enjoy a long run in the side. He was, and remains, a skilful batsman uneasy with the nakedness of international cricket. Unless he felt on top of his game, he found the exposure painful. In the West Indies he had sought and depended upon the reassurance of his room-mate, Shane Warne. At times he'd wake up in the middle of the night complaining of a bad back and saying he could not play.

Every cricketer recognises this terrible, sometimes crippling fear of failure. Sooner or later a man must move past it, must accept himself and his circumstances. Success in another field helps to promote a sense of worth. Somehow Elliott could not find his way out. Scoring runs remained his be-all and end-all, and that is a fearful load for any man to take to the crease in any match, let alone the public grilling that is Test cricket. Elliott looked like Bill Lawry and batted like Bill Lawry, but lacked the great man's pigeons and home life.

At his best Elliott was outstanding. He could step onto the front foot to drive on the rise, or lean back to pull a barely distinguishable delivery. His judgement of length was immaculate. He might have been better understood in England, where agony is more or less compulsory. Nor ought his career be regarded as a failure. On the contrary, he had many fine days. Any man who has scored a Test century at Lord's and a one-day hundred in a domestic final on the same ground has left his mark upon the game.

All three Australians were superb batsmen in their contrasting ways. All three were high maintenance. Simply, a cricket team does not have time for all that. It is an efficient fighting force representing the cream of the nation's cricketers, not a healing group.

The third Test, at Old Trafford, was going to be crucial to the outcome of the 1997 campaign. A damp, green wicket had been prepared and the captain winning the toss was expected to bowl. Taylor called correctly and took the first innings. He had noticed the dustiness of the footmarks on nearby pitches and guessed that the pitch was powdery under its watery cloak. He did not think England would enjoy facing Shane Warne in the fourth innings. Considering his predicament and the state of the series it was a courageous decision. Ricky Ponting would be much less astute when his turn came at Edgbaston in 2005.

No one had been more frustrated about Taylor's position in the side than Steve Waugh, his vice-captain and expected successor. No one did more than Waugh to turn Taylor's bold decision into a masterstroke. Not since Allan Border's epic performance against the full might of the West Indies pace quartet in Trinidad in 1983/84 had an Australian batsman put together two innings to compare with those constructed by Waugh in the 1997 Manchester Test.

Marching to the crease in that business-like, splay-footed way, Waugh first took the score from the perils of 3/42 to the comparative comfort of 235 all out. Australia secured a lead of 73, whereupon the New South Welshman gave another masterly display and, assisted by the lower order, took the match beyond the reach of a stunned opponent. Exhausted by his effort, Waugh did not score many more runs in the series, and ended with an average of 39. Gillespie, McGrath and Warne took the wickets needed to win the match and square the ledger, a feat they would repeat on many subsequent occasions.

England had missed its chance. Although Australia's senior batsmen failed again in Leeds, a fifth-wicket partnership of 268 between Elliott (199) and a recalled Ponting (127) gave them the runs needed to secure an innings victory. The Australians completed their comeback at Trent Bridge and, too late, were narrowly defeated in the sixth Test at The Oval as they failed to chase 124 on a deteriorating pitch.

Taylor's team left England with the Ashes, a strong attack, a fine young emerging batsman in Ponting and the world at its feet. Taylor himself was the only problem. He had scored steadily, but unremarkably, after the hundred at Edgbaston and ended the series with an average of 32. It was respectable but insufficient to suggest that he had another surge in him. Few doubted that he had played his last Ashes series.

The Australian selectors are known for responding to the first signs of deterioration and acting accordingly. As Laurie Sawle and his successor as Chairman of selectors, Trevor Hohns, often pointed out their remit is to consider the future of Australian cricket as well as the present. Of course they did not respond to every bad patch but sought confirmation that the decline was permanent. Generally it was a middle-aged player's footwork or, rather, the lack of it, that gave the game away.

During his last summer, Geoff Marsh kept edging the ball onto his stumps, an indication that he had moved too slowly into position and did not have enough time to construct his stroke properly. It was the same with David Boon and, now, Taylor. Yet this time the selectors' axe did not fall. Instead a highly regarded captain was given extra opportunities to prove that he had more to offer, a luxury that later would be extended to Steve Waugh. Partly this hesitation was a mark of respect both for the position of the Australian captain and also for the incumbent as a distinguished servant. Meanwhile, gifted but less easily accommodated players were pushed away. Australian cricket has a strong sense of the collective and hostility towards the factionalism that had been such a problem in the early 1980s.

In the event Taylor survived to lead his team into the next Ashes series. Although he continued to captain and catch well in 1998/99, his batting fell back once more and he passed 50 only twice in ten innings, ending with an average of 22. Despite their captain's struggles, Australia retained the Ashes 3/1. As was usual at the end of the 1990s, the Waugh twins scored most of the runs and McGrath and a leg-spinner took most of the wickets. But Warne was not that spinner. His body had started to complain about the endless punishment to which it was daily being subjected and he missed most of the series. Few expected the Victorian to recapture his former glories.

Stuart MacGill took his place and promptly claimed 27 wickets in his faster, flatter style, a tally that confirmed both his own skills and the cluelessness of the English batsmen against well-delivered wrist-spin. In every way MacGill was different from Warne. He was a maverick, an outsider, at times even an awkward customer. He was more intelligent than Warne but much less cunning. He could not match the Victorian's astonishing match-playing abilities, or his genuine all-round skills. He lacked Warne's ability to think batsmen out and could not make the ball drift to leg before fizzing across the right-hander. That being said, he could spin the ball hard and could take wickets with bad balls. Unless Warne was at the peak of his powers, subcontinental batsmen were more worried about his understudy. Fully fit, Warne was beyond compare.

MacGill continued to take such chances as came his way, and often outbowled Warne when they played together without ever suggesting that he could match his subtleties or close down his end on an unsympathetic surface. He had the wit to turn his role as Warne's constant reserve into a humorous party piece, not least as a way of answering the questions and passing the time. Apart from shooting Warne, there was not much else he could do. He was an old-fashioned leg-spinner, a regular wicket-taker more interested in the last line of his analysis than the second last.

Taylor's last Ashes series was odd and unsatisfying. After taking a 2/0 lead into the Festival Test matches, the Australians should have won 4/0. Certainly they had reason to curse themselves for losing at the MCG where Steve Waugh scored 122 not out in the first innings and an unbeaten 30 in the second, yet still finished on the losing side as Dean Headley took four wickets in two overs and the Australians collapsed from 4/130 to 162 all out, 12 runs shy of victory. Waugh bore the brunt of the blame. After taking his team within a few blows of victory, and with two wickets in hand and the ground in a ferment, he took a single off the first ball of an over, whereupon his remaining partners, MacGill and McGrath, departed in the space of three deliveries. Distant critics roared their disapproval and vowed not to support any Australian side led by such a selfish player. Past cricketers also muttered about Waugh thinking only about his average. In the pavilion Mark Waugh was especially outspoken about his twin brother's tactics.

The suggestion that Waugh was thinking about himself seemed harsh. He had added 88 with MacGill in the first innings, 21 in the second with Matthew Nicholson, a tall debutant from Sydney who was destined to lose his nerve and his place. Moreover, to blame Waugh excused the true villains of the piece, the other senior batsmen. Australia had no business being in such a perilous position. In his defence, Waugh had followed his usual habit by trusting his partners, a custom that had worked so well over the years. He had also been offered the light and had turned it down because the match was reaching its climax and the crowd deserved a result.

Later lower-order partnerships between Mike Hussey and various tailenders would show Waugh in a less sympathetic light. Several times in 2005/06, Hussey engineered large late-wicket partnerships by dint of seeking boundaries and pinching singles, thereby showing an adaptability not always evident in Waugh's work at the crease.

Upon reflection, Steve Waugh conceded that he ought to have protected his partners that evening in Melbourne. Not that it is easy to abandon successful practices under pressure. Moreover the session had already lasted four hours and the crowd was in a hubbub. Waugh had much upon his mind.

Not that it mattered. The Australians won easily in Sydney where MacGill took 12 wickets, ten more than Warne who was fit to play his first match of the campaign. Once more English hopes had been crushed.

The Ashes campaign was not the only cricketing topic to provoke debate as the summer of 1998/99 went along. Between the second and third Test matches, Malcolm Conn, cricket correspondent for

The Australian newspaper, published his revelation about the relationship that had arisen a few years before between an Indian bookmaker and two Australian players, Shane Warne and Mark Waugh.

When the story broke, a 'mutual friend' said that Waugh had years before talked openly about encountering a bloke from the subcontinent eager to give him cash for snippets of information unrelated to the performance of the team. He reported that Waugh had dismissed his contact as a mug, regarded the offer as a stroke of luck and thought the relationship harmless.

Although no evidence was produced that Waugh had been seriously compromised, his arrangement with 'John' did last a considerable time, longer than did Warne's exposure.

Waugh's willingness to accept packages of money from an unchecked source indicated a lack of judgement but also told of a young man still trying to escape from the shadows cast by his twin brother. An essentially gentle, introverted fellow, Waugh had been more hurt than he ever showed by the acclaim, opportunities and wealth that came his brother's way. Once he asked a reporter seeking an interview for a fee and upon his request being rejected muttered, 'Yeah, that'd be right.' Perhaps the attraction of the easy money was that, for once, he was able to put one across the world. Not that it turned out that way.

From the moment the story appeared, Warne and Waugh were subjected to fierce abuse and intense scrutiny. They gave a press conference admitting that they had been foolish but denying any involvement in the fixing of matches. Unfortunately the public and parts of the media were not prepared to make distinctions and a tendency arose to bracket the Australians with Hansie Cronje and various subcontinentals. Neither man was allowed to answer questions at the conference. Officials reputedly feared that Waugh would break down under hostile questioning.

Waugh was booed for the rest of the summer but survived. Warne bounced back. Those involved around the fringes escaped with their reputations intact. Some deserved censure. Taylor had appeared before a legally constructed hearing into corruption in Pakistani cricket run by a properly appointed judge and did not mention that some of his players had been compromised. Admittedly the question was not asked. Nor did the ACB insist that the full facts be put before such an august body. When they were first informed about money being received from dubious sources, officials contented themselves with imposing a fine roughly the equivalent of the bribes. An opportunity to nip the scandal in the bud was missed.

In any event, at the end of the summer Australia had, once again, retained the Ashes but might easily have taken the spoils 5/0. After all, the victories were decisive, the defeat in Melbourne was narrow and the match in Brisbane drawn when a ferocious storm descended upon The Gabba with the Englishmen fighting for survival. Yet the cricket did not come to life. No one could blame the visiting supporters for the unsatisfactory nature of the summer. A large group of Englishmen, calling themselves the Barmy Army, followed their team around and took delight in reminding their hosts that they remained subjects of the Queen and that three local dollars were needed to purchase a single pound note.

England had been pushed back. Taylor's cricket career was almost over. Another man had taken charge of the 50-over team, a stone-faced fellow by the name of Steve Waugh. England would not get any gifts from him, or any encouragement in their quest to recover the urn.

10

SUBDUING THE AFRICANS

To reach the summit, the Australians not only had to recapture the Ashes, but also meet and defeat the South Africans, beat the West Indians and overcome their subcontinental block. The South Africans were not the easiest of propositions because they were hungry, disciplined and back. Moreover they had won 4/0 the last time around, in 1969/70. Admittedly Bill Lawry's side had arrived hotfoot from India and had been beaten as much in the board room at Jolimont Street as on the field in Africa. Still, it was remembered, rankled and remained unavenged.

South Africa returned from its long period of isolation in 1991. By then Nelson Mandela and his fellow political prisoners had been released from Robben Island and the ban on the ANC had been lifted. But the referendum about the proposed constitution had not yet taken place and the first free elections were three years away. Accordingly, debate raged about the wisdom of welcoming back Keppler Wessels' side before the process had been completed. Liberals argued that the team still represented the old ways and ought not to be accepted. Protests were promised at the World Cup to be held in Australia and New Zealand in 1992.

Of course the protesters were wrong, as was confirmed by Steve

Tshwete during a conversation in a taxi ferrying the former political prisoner back to the city centre in Sydney. When the issue of the protests was raised, the former activist and prospective Minister of Sport observed that the time for that had passed and it was a matter of moving forward. He spoke with the authority of those who have sacrificed much in a cause. He had spent half his adult life in prison in pursuit of the emancipation of blacks in his country, so his opinion carried more weight than those whose activities were restricted to a heroic refusal to buy wine from the Cape region.

South Africa's return to the fray was more successful than had been anticipated. After all, most of the great men had long since retired and some of their replacements, especially the bowlers, had failed to make a mark even in county cricket. There was a curiously fraught quality about the South Africans. They seemed constantly to be on the verge of mighty deeds only for something to go horribly wrong, or someone to drop a sitter, or get run out, or for an opponent to surpass himself. Perhaps they wanted to rise a little too much, and too quickly. Some of the players had been waiting a long time and now were representing a changed country. They found the outside world a different place. Sport has a way of sensing hidden vulnerability and exposing raw nerves.

South Africa's first encounter with the Australians occurred in the 1992 World Cup and it took only a single ball for long-suppressed emotions to resurface. That first ball at the SCG was a warning, a clear edge from Geoff Marsh heard and seen by everyone present except the umpire. Even Marsh looked embarrassed. Allan Donald was inconsolable. In various guises this sense of injustice, this inner grievance, would hold back the Proteas as they tried to bring down the Australians. At the critical moment something always went wrong. Why? In the answer lies sport's most profound trait. It knows a man better than he knows himself. There is no hiding place on the field. Of course it was not a one-off. It was the same with Herschelle Gibbs' notorious dropped catch in Leeds. It wasn't the miss that beat the South Africans, but that instant when all and sundry sighed, 'Here we go again.' However, South Africa did manage to win by nine wickets.

South Africa continued to fight hard in the 1992 competition only to be frustrated by an untimely shower and some curious rules that left them needing to score 22 not in 13 balls, as before the interruption, or 7 balls, as originally appeared on the screen, but a single ball. Unsurprisingly the players were aghast and supporters were outraged by this twist of fate. England, the victors of that encounter, reached the final. The South Africans might have lost that match anyhow, but they were not beaten fair and square. And it had happened in Australia, with rules devised by an Australian.

Between them, the rejected appeal and the strange rain rule reinforced African misgivings about the Australians. White South Africans have mixed feelings about their 'cousins across the water'. On the one hand, Australians are regarded as arrogant and unprincipled louts, an attitude often heard on radio and sometimes in sports grounds. On the other, many think that Australians and South Africans have much in common, regarding them as brothers-in-arms with similar histories, weather, economies, landscapes and attitudes.

Australians are not comfortable with either the welcome mat or the loaded gun. Naturally they are not prepared to admit to arrogance, an accusation usually made by distant observers convinced that a country can be judged by its newspapers and sporting strategies. In fact Australians are assertive as opposed to confident. Determined to get on with life, anxious to be noticed, scared of isolation, reluctant to indulge in introspection, Australians can be a trifle loud at first acquaintance. Closer inspection reveals a nation desperate to make a mark and a people more hospitable than might be guessed from their opening gambits.

If anything, Australians are even more wary of the notion that the Anglo-Saxon members of the two communities are hard to tell apart. At first glance the idea seems not unreasonable because both nations relish sunshine and the outdoor life, and inhabit harsh terrain governed by a climate inclined towards extremes. Farming and mining are burned in their collective souls. And then there is the question of the indigenous tribes.

But the comparison is superficial, the traditions are far apart, as can be told from the contrasting nature of education in the two countries. White South Africa is a hierarchical, conservative and profoundly undemocratic place. Boys at leading South African schools and universities are trained to show respect for their elders and to accept rigorous discipline. Those joining senior teams are routinely subjected to an initiation that usually includes painful physical chastisement. First-year students at Afrikaner universities can expect to be belted by their seniors with a cricket bat or a sandshoe filled with stones. At one highly regarded seat of learning, first-year students are not allowed to look third years in the eye and must learn to tell them apart by their shoes. And they cannot walk on the grass.

Education was crucial for white South Africans because it reinforced a sense of hierarchy. White Africa could not allow movement between classes, ages or colours because it would herald the destruction of its way of life. For reasons that reached beyond an enduring opinion that *Lord of the Flies* was right, obedience and discipline had to be instilled at an early age.

Draconian as these educational practices may sound, an overwhelming majority of white South Africans support them. Indeed the regret most commonly heard among those attending junior and senior schools is that they have become lax. Africa is a harsh continent and youngsters do not expect to be pampered. Unsurprisingly, boys from African schools tend to be tougher and better trained than their English counterparts. Four members of the current successful Hampshire team were schooled in Africa.

Australia's history is altogether more egalitarian. The line between blue- and white-collar workers is less distinct, movement between races and colours is much easier and the divide between adults and youth is altogether less rigid. Politicians, schoolmasters, bishops and even parents, let alone boys in higher forms, are not respected *ex officio*. They must earn their stripes. Authority figures are rudely treated down under, though authority itself is accepted.

Not that white Australia was an egalitarian country from the outset. Not until the economic boom that began in the 1850s did the divide between gentleman and tradesman start to close. As pay and property prices rose so it became harder to distinguish between them. Spreading wealth meant that labourers and tradesmen could vote, stand for Parliament and in most other respects take their places in society. If Australia was not egalitarian from the outset, it became so through economic development.

White South Africa stood resolute against change. Australia was catapulted along a course that led to universal emancipation. And yet in many ways Australia is the more authoritarian country. South Africans are often taken aback by the way life is regulated down under, with its seatbelts, enforced speed limits, road-worthiness tests, crash helmets for bicycles, jaywalking and the rest of it (and that is just the roads).

Border and company knew that the South Africans had a proud tradition to restore and that they would be hard to subdue. And so it proved. South Africa's first tour to Australia for 30 years took place in 1993/94. Only three Test matches were played because the privilege of playing five had been reserved for West Indies and England, an arrangement that owed more to continuity, tradition, popularity and financial rewards than cricketing strength.

Keppler Wessels captained the touring team. At the same time he seemed to represent past and present, mercenary and loyalist. Raised in the heart of Afrikanerdom in the Orange Free State capital of Bloemfontein, and a product of its greatest school, Grey College, he had become a professional cricketer and played all around the world. Along the way he had turned into an Australian and played Test cricket for his new country. He has always denied playing any part in raising the rebel side that toured South Africa in 1985, a tour that tore the guts out of his adopted country's cricket.

Now he was South African again and leading the side. Wessels was respected as a tough, cramped batsman more interested in runs than appearances. His team was entirely white and supposedly chosen on its merits. Was he part of the problem or part of the solution? He did seem to represent the old ways yet Grey College was bilingual; its headmaster moved between English and Afrikaans regularly, and often mid-sentence. Also, Wessels' son was playing cricket in Port Elizabeth, where the family had settled. Could the new South Africa, and its cricket team, find a way to combine the rigour represented by Wessels with the wider requirements of an emerging nation? Therein lay the challenge. Even now it is too early to attempt an answer. Meanwhile Wessels could fight the last few campaigns of his sporting career confident that, for the time being, his homeland thought only about winning.

Alas his team's eagerly awaited reappearance at the Boxing Day Test of 1993 was spoilt by rain. Fortunately the Sydney Test that followed counts among the most compelling ever played on that ground as the visitors summoned every ounce of their celebrated resolve to defend a paltry score in the fourth innings. In the last morning session the alarmed hosts tried to scrape and scrounge their way to a modest target of 117. Every ball contained immense possibilities yet almost all entered the scorebooks as mere dots.

The Australians hardly dared to play a shot. The South Africans refused to give anything away. Fanie de Villiers and Allan Donald bowled tirelessly on a grudging surface. Hansie Cronje, leading the side in the absence of his injured captain, turned upon a rand and threw down the stumps to execute a crucial run-out. To add to the effect, bushfires were raging outside the city, the weather was fiendishly hot and the air was full of burnt relics that dropped without prejudice on gardens and ovals.

Finally Glenn McGrath pushed back a return catch and the deed was done. De Villiers hurled the ball into the air and his comrades celebrated a great victory. Every touring player had served with distinction. South Africa's intensity had been unwavering. Yet the Afrikaners in the team had stood out. They have always counted among the toughest of tribes, and those present were in their element.

Although Border lost his wicket in that critical fourth innings for the paltry score of seven, Damien Martyn was blamed for the defeat. He had passed 50 in the first innings and in the chase held on for 106 minutes until, as *Wisden* reported, 'his nerve failed', whereupon he drove a catch to cover. Martyn was dropped and endured several instructive years in the wilderness before forcing his way back into the side. In truth it was not one errant shot that brought him down so much as its cause, the arrogance of youth. Arguably Border was as much to blame for not taking the initiative.

Australia rallied to square the series in an Adelaide Test notable for the batting of Steve Waugh, returning to the fray after a hamstring injury, and de Villiers' defiance on the last day as, ignoring his broken thumb, the night watchman held his ground for 198 minutes. It was not enough. South Africa had missed the opportunity to subdue their most feared opponent and time was running out. More complicated days lay ahead. Men whose careers start late in the day are haunted by time.

No sooner had the series been completed than the sides repaired to Africa to continue their robust confrontation. Since time did not permit a full-scale tour of either country, their summers being concurrent, the next best choice seemed to be consecutive three-match series. In the event this campaign, too, was left undecided as South Africa decisively won the first match, thanks to Cronje and the pace bowlers, whereupon Australia just as conclusively took the second match thanks to Boon and a startling all-round contribution from Steve Waugh, who followed his 86 by taking 5/28. Waugh's figures contradicted notions that South Africa could outplay these opponents on pitches designed for pace bowling. Strong teams and thinking cricketers are not so easily overcome. Again the suspicion arose that South Africa had taken a lead and then tried to consolidate, an attitude that builds insecurity.

Unfortunately the decider, played in Durban, fizzled out as Wessels failed to press home an advantage secured on the first day whereupon Slater, Border and Mark Waugh guided their team to safety. South Africa's team contained neither a spinner nor a non-white, situations that manifestly could not last. Moreover the grounds were mostly empty. Many challenges lay ahead.

That the two series were drawn said something about the captains involved. Neither man was prepared to give a proverbial inch. Both were stubborn to a fault. Both were raised to stand firm in the face of adversity. Both seemed to anticipate that adversity lurked around the next corner. Both inspired admiration and loyalty in their men. Both were brave, defiant and led from the front. Both belonged in the trenches. Neither was inclined to blow the bugle.

He did not know it at the time, but Border's second innings in Durban would be his last in Test cricket. Although he was loath to admit it, his time was up. He had served his purpose. Border's task had been to restore standards in Australian cricket. By force of character and unfailing commitment, he had succeeded. Along the way he had won a World Cup and taken his team to second place in the rankings. It had been a magnificent contribution. Now, though, Australian cricket was ready for the next step and Mark Taylor would lead the Australians into their next series against the South Africans.

By 1996/97 Wessels had retired but the core of the home team had not changed—Donald, Pollock, Cronje, Richardson, Rhodes. A new champion, though, had emerged in Jacques Kallis, his country's first great player of the democratic era.

As far as most followers of the game were concerned, this series pitted against each other the two best cricket teams in the world. Australia started well by demolishing their hosts in the first match, winning by an innings and 196 runs after Steve Waugh and Blewett had batted through the entire third day, taking the score from 4/191 to 4/479. Warne and Michael Bevan both took wickets in the second innings to supplement those claimed by McGrath and Gillespie on the first day. At this point, Taylor was packing his side with batting and using Bevan as second spinner in a four-man attack supported by Blewett and the Waughs. Taylor has been portrayed as a relentlessly attacking captain but, like any shrewd leader, he played the odds.

The South Africans fought back valiantly. Port Elizabeth provided a nail-biter. After three days which were dominated by the bowlers, the Australians found themselves needing to score 270 to win the series. South Africa's first-innings tally of 209 had been the highest total mustered by either side in the match. Alas South Africa had lost the services of Shaun Pollock to a torn hamstring. Battle royal was joined as the Australians chased their target. Not did they poke around as might have been the case under a previous leader. Taylor argued that batsmen, like bowlers, have a natural rhythm, a tempo that suits them. He told his men to play their normal games and to think only about the next ball and not distant targets.

Wickets fell regularly but they did not fall in clumps, and by stumps on the third day the visitors had reached 3/145. Next day it was a close-run thing. Mark Waugh held the key. Over the years he had been suspected of a certain insouciance, a lightness, a vagueness that made him seem an unlikely champion of lost causes. Although he had often batted sublimely he had not quite put his mark on a match so that it went into history as belonging to him.

Waugh-the-slightly-younger set out on this final day with an intent that had seemed to be missing on previous occasions. Perhaps it was the fact of the chase, the existence of the target that inspired the gambler in him. Moreover the Waughs have always known how to win cricket matches. It is a family trait, not the preserve of the oldest son.

Although wickets continued to fall, Waugh held firm. Throughout he batted fluently and doggedly, playing graceful strokes but retaining the concentration that so often deserted him. Waugh did not have the killer instinct. When he had put his opponents on the ground he often relented with the air of a man who had no cruelty in him, a man who lived for the moment and was not concerned about the rainy days that might lie ahead.

Hard as they tried, the South Africans could not break the Australian second drop. Waugh had chosen a fine time to play his most famous innings. He took his side to the verge of victory, before departing on 116. It was left to Healy to score the last few runs, a task he accomplished with a clattered six over mid-wicket off the bowling of a despairing home captain. Years later Cronje's decision to bowl himself at the critical moment and his error in placing an off-side field and then sending down a loose leg-side delivery would provoke suspicions a dead man could not allay.

Healy was coming to the end of his Test career. A fellow called Adam Gilchrist had replaced him in the 50-over side. Gilchrist had been forced to cross the Nullarbor in search of a chance in first-class cricket. He had also been advised to concentrate on his batting. Everyone makes mistakes. Dropped after this series, Healy was denied the chance to play a farewell match on his home patch, a match that would have been the 100th Test of his career. Australia's selectors are about as sentimental as puff adders.

Australia lost the third Test match of the 1996/97 tour, a defeat put down to undue relaxation after the spoils had been secured. Not until Steve Waugh took over the captaincy would the team maintain its rage in dead rubbers. But the South Africans deserved credit for winning by eight wickets, thereby ending the series on a high note.

Unsurprisingly the Australians were expected to beat their opponents when the teams met again on Australian soil nine months later. By then another talented cricketer had been added to the South African side. Herschelle Gibbs was a fair-skinned young man craftily defined as coloured by Dr Ali Bacher, a man well aware of the political nuances of his changing homeland. Otherwise the team remained resolutely white. Cronje's outfit also retained its other celebrated quality: it was hard to beat.

Kallis saved his side in the Melbourne Test match with a century that confirmed his maturing into a skilful and tenacious cricketer. Confident in their abilities, the Australians liked to set their opponents stiff targets on the final day, trusting Warne and McGrath to take the required wickets. Curiously, McGrath had the better fourth innings record. Often Taylor did not enforce the follow-on in order to give his important bowlers time to rest and the pitch time to deteriorate. Helped by luck and assisted by his captain, Kallis thwarted the Australians by sustaining his team through most of the 124 overs left in the match. It was a superbly crafted and defiant defensive innings.

South Africa was comprehensively outplayed in the second Test in Sydney and beaten by an innings. Between them, Australia's three Ws, Warne and the Waugh twins, took most of the wickets and scored most of the runs. Warne had so tormented Daryll Cullinan, the visitors' most gifted batsman, that he had repeatedly lost his wicket in moments of madness, and had by now lost his place in the side. By and large Warne picked his victims well. One of his strengths was his ability to sense and expose bluster. A consummate thespian himself, he could detect bluff in his opponents. McGrath was also prepared to select a target but in his case it was not personal. Rather, he chose batsmen according to their importance and their technique and pitted himself against them. Champions need danger. They need to face extinction, need to renew the challenge.

The SCG Test was memorable for a ferocious confrontation between Donald and the Waughs, a heavyweight contest that bristled with raw aggression. The twins had outstared Ambrose in the West Indies. They survived Donald's supreme onslaught in Sydney though the 'streak of white lightning' did later return to remove the more wizened brother. Another tale might have been told had Cronje given his fast bowler the support that was manifestly needed. Instead he failed to place a man at short leg even as the fusillade became a veritable bombardment. Seizing the moment has not been a South African strength. Maybe the belief in method is too deep rooted.

Mark Waugh and Cronje were also the central figures in Adelaide as the visitors tried with every power at their disposal to secure a drawn series. Donald and McGrath could not play and both were missed in a hard-fought match that began with the tourists passing 500 without anyone reaching three figures and ended with Waugh saving his side with an unbeaten century. In between Taylor carried his bat through his team's first innings.

Once again, the South Africans were left to curse a small moment that had huge consequences. On that tense final day, Mark Waugh disturbed his bails after completing a leg-glance. Cronje and his cohorts appealed furiously and were aghast when, after a long delay, the third umpire rejected their entreaties. In fact law 35 had been correctly applied. In any case the South Africans had only themselves to blame. Ten catches were missed, several of them by Adam Bacher at short leg. In his frustration, Cronje damaged the door to the umpire's room with a stump.

Not that Cronje immediately admitted responsibility for his actions. Once again this revelation was ignored because it did not fit the image of the man. Seldom in sporting history has any man been as poorly judged or as many facts blithely ignored. This was a man who was caught on camera treading on the ball in a break in play during a one-day match in Sydney. Everyone said it was out of character.

Cronje's resignation as captain brought to an end the era of robust and united simplicity. Now another South Africa had to try to find strength in complexity, unity in distraction. The old guard had gone. It was bound to be some time before the South Africans became as formidable as they had been in the nineties, with its numerous close shaves, its nodding acquaintance with greatness. Eventually they found a cheerful, balanced and wise elder in Vince van der Bijl, a solid citizen in Gary Kirsten and a highly motivated young captain in Graeme Smith and had the sense to put them in charge. The next step was to build around the various qualities offered by young Afrikaners, coloureds and blacks, the very challenge faced by the new nation at large.

11

REACHING THE SUMMIT

By the middle of the 1990s, the Australians had held the South Africans and overwhelmed the English. They still had to beat the subcontinentals in their own backyard and end the long supremacy of the West Indies. The Australians now were regarded as a competitive as opposed to a dominant side. A lot of work was still to be done before any legitimate claim to ascendancy could be entertained.

An opportunity to bring down the curtain upon the long and impressive West Indian reign came when Mark Taylor took his side across the globe as spring arrived in the northern hemisphere in 1994/95. As Steve Waugh mentions in his memoirs, the Australians arrived in the Caribbean wearing new striped blazers. More importantly they had a new captain, a man not used to losing to these opponents, a man prepared to consider them objectively with a view to finding faults. Looking like a wharfie, moving like a carthorse, thinking like a statesman, Taylor was a fine leader. Previous teams had approached series against the West Indies with a heavy tread. This time, far from wearing the weariness of a long season, Taylor's men were full of energy and resolve. In many respects it was the same mood shown by Border's side throughout the 1987 World Cup.

The West Indians had not lost a series since 1980, and when the Australians lost the one-day series 4/1 the hosts' record appeared safe. Worse, the main Australian pace bowlers, Damien Fleming (injured shoulder) and Craig McDermott (torn ankle ligaments) had been forced to go home. McDermott did not hide his fear of fast bowling and colleagues joked that he must have searched for the hole in which he hurt his foot! The task of supporting Glenn McGrath and Shane Warne was given to the unlikely pairing of Brendon Julian and Paul Reiffel.

To arrive in Barbados hereabouts was to anticipate meeting a touring party down in the dumps. Not a bit of it. To bump into the remaining players was to be told that the West Indies were vulnerable. Neither opener could bat, or so the visitors reckoned, Curtly Ambrose had slowed down, Brian Lara was weak outside off-stump, Richie Richardson had gone gaga, Carl Hooper was feeble and neither Benjamin was up to it. Taylor and his senior players had done their best work. Half the fight had been won. The battle of the mind was over.

Taylor and his players made one critical decision before the first Test match, to be played in the local stronghold of Bridgetown. Rather than trying to absorb their opponents' blows, they'd seize the initiative. In short they intended to attack their hosts at their supposedly strongest point. They meant to bowl bumpers at Walsh and Ambrose. Far from suing for peace as they were expected to do, they were going to declare war.

Much to his credit McGrath, the poorest batsman in the touring party and a man scarcely able to protect himself, led the charge. McGrath has seldom served his side better. It was a telling contribution that delivered a clear message to the champions. Australia was not afraid.

Hereabouts, the West Indies were a curious team, sometimes angry, sometimes laid-back, sometimes proud, sometimes apparently unconcerned. Observers could be forgiven for thinking that they wanted to succeed without seeming to try too hard. Certainly they lacked the focus that Clive Lloyd, aided by his outstanding henchmen, had brought to the team. The mountainous anger, the boggling ambition, the supreme athleticism that had been the features of the side in the previous decade had been replaced by a mixture of nonchalance, incompetence, periodic inspiration and surliness.

Lloyd had been the West Indians' disciplinarian. Woe betide a player late for a commitment or otherwise stepping out of line. One night he saw a senior player chatting up a woman in a corner of the hotel bar. Realising that the female concerned was the wife of the team's bus driver, he marched across to the player and ordered him to go to bed, an instruction that was instantaneously obeyed. Rejoining his party, Lloyd remarked that the driver had looked after the players.

For the time being Richie Richardson, more amiable Bajan than edgy Antiguan, was trying to counter the indulgences and arrogance that eventually would bring West Indian cricket to its knees. He was supported by some staunch characters, notably the Jamaicans, Jimmy Adams and Courtney Walsh, and the widely respected Trinidadian, Ian Bishop, a man already emerging as the best of his generation.

Although these players offered valuable support, Richardson's inheritance was not as strong as it might have seemed. A proud tradition had fallen into bad habits, suppressed rivalries had surfaced, and the selectors seemed unable to find any great players except a wayward genius from Port-of-Spain. Yet expectations remained high. The West Indians were champions of the world and it was going to last a hundred years. Some considered it a birthright. No one had told the more dimwitted players that there is only ever the struggle. Richardson was popular but he was also carrying a considerable burden.

Moreover the West Indies had been unable to find replacements for their great opening pair, Gordon Greenidge and Desmond Haynes, whose contribution to the success of the side was often overlooked. Haynes was at odds with his Board, by no means the last dispute to affect a team that now, more than ever, needed all hands on deck.

No sooner had the series begun than the optimism of the visitors was boosted. In a trice their hosts subsided to 3/11 against a supposedly lame pace attack. Carl Hooper and Lara responded with a thrilling counterattack that lasted until the underachieving right-hander hooked a catch. Soon afterwards Lara was controversially held at gully by Steve Waugh. Relying on the fielder's word, the left-hander departed without further ado. Replays cast doubt on the legitimacy of the catch. In the next morning's papers, Viv Richards fulminated over the Australians' supposed cheating and added that they had been playing by their own lights ever since he could remember.

From the press box, the thought did occur the ball might have been grassed. However it was not clear-cut. Even the replays were a blur of hand, loose ball and turf. Although a third umpire could not have given it out that did not mean the catch was not taken.

After dismissing the West Indies for 189, Australia won by ten wickets. After the early onslaught, McGrath and Warne took most of the wickets while Steve Waugh, Taylor and Ian Healy scored most of the runs. McGrath's bumpers had the local tailenders leaping about. They were both an act of courage and an affront.

Perhaps, too, the manner in which Michael Slater and his captain scored their runs told a tale. Scintillating drives were mixed with pulls that said, 'Aren't you blokes supposed to be fast?' Slater set the tone with a characteristically uninhibited effort. Thinking before you act is the approach recommended by sages, schoolmasters, courts and books. Yet it has never held any appeal for Slater. He hooked almost onto the grandstand roof and stepped down the pitch to thrash deliveries back past the bowler. As one ball sped away to the boundary Slater fell head over heels. A wise captain releases his players from the fear of failure, thereby using their talents to the utmost. Taylor's players were not chastised when they erred.

A typically rain-affected draw in Antigua followed and then the teams met in Port-of-Spain, where they were presented with a surface as damp, green and menacing as a crocodile. Hitherto Ambrose had only taken three wickets. Apparently he had a sore shoulder but he was also a notoriously slow starter. A rotten match was over in three days with the hosts winning by nine wickets as they threw the bat at everything in pursuit of 98. The Australians were bowled out for 128 and 105. About the only highlight of the batting was the furious exchange between Steve Waugh and Ambrose that contained a few choice words from the Australian and many glares and ferocious bumpers from the taciturn but aroused Antiguan.

Accordingly the teams repaired to Jamaica for the decider. After winning the toss for a fourth consecutive time, the West Indians wasted a batsman's pitch by scoring only 265. In reply Australia staggered to 3/73. Then came the most exhilarating partnership of the series, a combination between the Waugh twins that brought 231 runs and effectively broke the West Indies. Hitherto Australia's batting had been a weak point because no hundreds had been scored. Now both Waughs reached three figures and then rubbed it in. Mark reached 126 before tapping a catch to short leg. Steve occupied the crease for ten hours and reached 200 before edging a lifter to slip. It was a titanic effort. Finally Steve Waugh had produced an innings more satisfying even than his two centuries for Somerset, dazzling innings played against Walsh and Sylvester Clarke in which he touched heights previously unscaled in his Test game.

Australia led by 266. The rest was easy. The West Indies were beaten by an innings and handed over both the Frank Worrell trophy and the title of World Champions. An extraordinary supremacy was over. The West Indians had dominated the game for 18 years. Although the Australians could hardly hope to last as long or to produce such a flawless record, they intended to have a crack at it. From the outset they understood that it is one thing to reach the top, another to stay there. They had dared to believe and the daring had been the secret. They had stormed the castle and taken it. Now it was a matter of refortifying the walls so that ambitious challengers could be put in their place.

After securing victory in the Caribbean, the Australians were in no mood to throw it all away when battle resumed on their own patch in the last weeks of 1996. After all, they'd suffered too many heavy defeats. Nor did they want to give these opponents the slightest encouragement. The West Indies arrived with some great players and even greater problems. Walsh had been promoted to the captaincy and although Lara, Ambrose, Adams and Bishop remained, his team had many weak points. Try as they might, the selectors had still been unable to find either a reliable pair to take the shine off the ball or a gloveman capable of supporting the bowlers and contributing with the bat. Moreover Lara had entered the long bad patch that would hurt his reputation as a man and as a player, a period he would regret later in his career as his thoughts turned towards his legacy.

Long and unproductive tails had by now become a feature of West Indian cricket. More often than not, five out was all out. Although the bowlers protested that it was up to the batsmen to score the runs, the fact remained that their incompetence with the bat meant that their team took to the field under a severe disadvantage. The West Indies could hardly hope to recover from a setback. Matches were either won from the front, or lost. Naturally the batsmen felt under extreme pressure. It did not help that the West Indian fielding was poor. Moreover the failure of the lower orders to apply themselves to their batting displayed contempt for a game that had served them so well.

Tactically, too, the visitors were outclassed. Taylor had the imagination, experience and confidence needed in a captain. Walsh was feeling his way and the West Indians had a long tradition of depending more upon strategy and talent than tactical acumen. Walsh had under his command a strong pace attack, a lively middle order and not much else. To make matters worse, Ambrose took only three wickets in the first two Tests and missed the fourth, while Lara did not put up a three-figure score until the final match in Perth.

Considering these facts, it might be thought that the Australians romped home. They did nothing of the sort. The Australian selectors started the series by springing a surprise. Michael Slater was dropped. The immediate reason given for his omission was a reckless shot played in a one-off Test match in Delhi, a flash at a wide delivery that brought the penance of a superb catch at slip. As usual the problem lay deeper, in the loss of self-control that lay behind the reckless stroke. Slater had advanced as far as he had precisely because he had followed his instincts. But instinct can be a fickle friend. It relies on a properly functioning brain. Along the way, somewhere, Slater had stopped hearing the alarm bells and Matthew Elliott took his place.

Australia's batting was unreliable and Taylor himself was the worst offender, averaging 17. He had spent part of his winter under the surgeon's knife, so his bad trot was excused. His captaincy was widely admired, especially his achievement in bringing out the best from Michael Bevan.

Bevan had a wonderful time that seemed a prelude to great days that never came. He averaged 55 with the bat and 17 with the ball. Considering his supposed vulnerability to short-pitched bowling, it was a notable performance. Previously the left-hander had seemed troubled by rising deliveries. Now he worked them away with a feline touch. It is hard to remember him subsequently betraying any uncertainty against bumpers. He could hardly have scored so many runs in county and Shield cricket had such a fundamental weakness been present.

Perhaps the real problem lay in his mind. It could be significant that Bevan was at his most productive with the bat when he was also taking wickets. He felt central to the cause, felt that he belonged. It is important to some men, but often a luxury in the hectic, self-centred world of international sport.

Thanks to a blistering attacking century from Ian Healy and a fine innings from Ponting, promoted into Boon's position at first wicket down, Australia won the first Test in Brisbane by 123 runs. A few days later the sides met again in Sydney. Matthew Elliott was felled by injury, which gave Matthew Hayden his chance in the third Test. The Queenslander became the only Australian batsman to score a hundred in the series and the hosts won by 124 runs. Next Ambrose took nine wickets for 72 runs in the Melbourne Test to bring the series back to life. Bevan replied with 10/113 in Adelaide, where the unlikely trinity of Blewett, Bevan and Hayden scored most of the runs. Australia had taken an unassailable 3/1 lead.

As might have been predicted, Ambrose returned to form in Perth and shared the wickets with Bishop and Walsh as the West Indies won by ten wickets. Bevan scored an unbeaten 87 in Australia's first innings but it was not enough to get the monkey off his back.

The West Indies had been subdued for a second time. In truth they had been flattered by the narrow margin of defeat. When it mattered, Australia was much the better side. One of the telling factors had been McGrath's deconstruction of Lara's batting, and a return engagement was eagerly awaited.

AUSTRALIA V WEST INDIES, FOURTH TEST

29 APRIL-3 MAY 1995, SABINA PARK, KINGSTON, JAMAICA

Toss: West Indies
Result: Australia won by an innings and 53 runs
Man of the match: S.R. Waugh

West Indies (1st Innings)		R	BF	4	6
S.C. Williams	c Blewett b Reiffel	0	2	0	0
R.B. Richardson (c)	lbw b Reiffel	100	222	12	1
B.C. Lara	c Healy b Warne	65	78	9	0
J.C. Adams	c Slater b Julian	20	33	4	0
C.L. Hooper	c M.E. Waugh b Julian	23	69	3	0
K.L.T. Arthurton	c Healy b McGrath	16	39	1	1
C.O. Browne (k)	c Boon b Warne	1	21	0	0
W.K.M. Benjamin	lbw b S.R. Waugh	7	24	1	0
C.E.L. Ambrose	not out	6	17	1	0
C.A. Walsh	c Boon b S.R. Waugh	2	5	0	0
K.C.G. Benjamin	c Healy b Reiffel	5	17	1	0
Extras	(b 1, lb 9, w 1, nb 9)	20			
Total	**All out**	**265**			
	85.4 overs at 3.09 rpo				

FoW				
	1–0	Williams	2–103	Lara
	3–131	Adams	4–188	Hooper
	5–220	Arthurton	6–243	Browne
	7–250	W.K.M. Benjamin	8–251	Richardson
	9–254	Walsh	10–265	K.C.G. Benjamin

Bowling	O	M	R	W
P.R. Reiffel	13.4	2	48	3
B.P. Julian	12	3	31	2
G.D. McGrath	20	4	79	1
S.K. Warne	25	6	72	2
S.R. Waugh	11	5	14	2
M.E. Waugh	4	1	11	0

Australia (1st Innings)		R	BF	4	6
M.A. Taylor (c)	c Adams b Walsh	8	18	0	0
M.J. Slater	c Lara b Walsh	27	65	2	0
D.C. Boon	c Browne b Ambrose	17	31	3	0
M.E. Waugh	c Adams b Hooper	126	192	12	0
S.R. Waugh	c Lara b K.C.G. Benjamin	200	425	17	1
G.S. Blewett	c W.K.M. Benjamin b Arthurton	69	130	9	0
I.A. Healy (k)	c Lara b W.K.M. Benjamin	6	19	0	0
B.P. Julian	c Adams b Walsh	8	27	0	0
P.R. Reiffel	b K.C.G. Benjamin	23	81	2	0
S.K. Warne	c Lara b K.C.G. Benjamin	0	2	0	0
G.D. McGrath	not out	3	7	0	0
Extras	(b 11, lb 6, w 1, nb 26)	44			
Total	**All out**	**531**			
	160.5 overs at 3.30 rpo				

FoW				
	1–17	Taylor	2–50	Boon
	3–73	Slater	4–304	M.E. Waugh
	5–417	Blewett	6–433	Healy
	7–449	Julian	8–522	Reiffel
	9–522	Warne	10–531	S.R. Waugh

Bowling	O	M	R	W
C.E.L. Ambrose	21	4	76	1
C.A. Walsh	33	6	103	3
K.C.G. Benjamin	23.5	0	106	3
W.K.M. Benjamin	24	3	80	1
C.L. Hooper	43	9	94	1
J.C. Adams	11	0	38	0
K.L.T. Arthurton	5	1	17	1

West Indies (2nd Innings)		R	BF	4	6
S.C. Williams	b Reiffel	20	38	1	0
R.B. Richardson (c)	c & b Reiffel	14	14	1	1
B.C. Lara	lbw b Reiffel	0	6	0	0
J.C. Adams	c S.R. Waugh b McGrath	18	63	3	0
W.K.M. Benjamin	lbw b Reiffel	51	118	5	0
C.L. Hooper	run out	13	47	2	0
K.L.T. Arthurton	lbw b Warne	14	26	1	1
C.O. Browne (k)	not out	31	66	4	0
C.E.L. Ambrose	st Healy b Warne	5	8	1	0
C.A. Walsh	c Blewett b Warne	14	34	1	0
K.C.G. Benjamin	c Taylor b Warne	6	9	1	0
Extras	(b 13, lb 8, nb 6)	27			
Total	**All out**	**213**			
	69.4 overs at 3.06 rpo				

FoW

1–37	Richardson	2–37	Lara
3–46	Williams	4–98	Adams
5–134	W.K.M. Benjamin	6–140	Hooper
7–166	Arthurton	8–172	Ambrose
9–204	Walsh	10–213	K.C.G. Benjamin

Bowling	O	M	R	W
P.R. Reiffel	18	5	47	4
B.P. Julian	10	2	37	0
S.K. Warne	23.4	8	70	4
M.E. Waugh	1	0	1	0
G.D. McGrath	13	2	28	1
S.R. Waugh	4	0	9	0

12

GREAT DAYS INDEED

By the time the teams met again the Australians had a new captain. Despite the arguments put forward by the guardians of the Australian inheritance represented by the 1970s group, Steve Waugh's long vice-captaincy had come to an end. In the first few months of 1999 he took his side to the Caribbean. It proved to be a great series, among the finest ever played. It was also the start of an extraordinary year of Test match cricket. As will be related in the next chapter, the one-day experiences were almost as good!

Waugh was under scrutiny in the Caribbean. He could not lose his position—Australia does not appoint or sack its captain willy-nilly—but he needed to prove that an essentially introverted man could take a team along with him. If he failed, the rise of Australian cricket was bound to falter. Critics had yearned for a more instinctive leader, a Warne or a Ponting. In the event, Warne would take only two wickets in the series, and the Tasmanian did not secure a place in the side until the third Test.

Having come out on top in recent series, the Australians were expected to win again in the Caribbean. But their hosts had always been hard to beat on their own patch, besides which the visitors were handicapped by the physical condition of their leading spin bowler, whose bones were starting to complain about their lot in life.

It proved to be an epic series as one of the game's geniuses pitted himself almost single-handedly against the strongest side in the world. Lucky is the supporter who lives to witness a more varied, inspired, destructive and brilliant display of batsmanship than Lara produced in those weeks of March and April 1999. Other compelling series have been played—Australia's meetings with India in 2001 and England in 2005 were in some respects even better than this campaign because entire teams were in compelling conflict—but not since the Don was in his pomp can a single batsman have had such an impact on a series.

Waugh passed his first test with flying colours, by drawing from his team a committed, ruthless performance in the opening match in Trinidad. As Dave Joseph and Lara began to pile on the runs in the first innings, Waugh had seemed perturbed, just for a moment. For an instant, supporters yearned to see Tubby out there sorting it all out. Almost to a fault, though, Waugh knew about staying put and soon it all turned around. Thereafter the West Indians were taken apart.

Indeed the home team's performance was so abject in the second innings that they were bowled out for 51. McGrath took ten wickets for next to nothing. Afterwards Lara was his usual self at the press conference, talking politely and apparently reasonably about the need for the West Indians to rally. Lara does not give much away. Humiliation was met with a charming defensive stroke. Meanwhile, debate raged about his leadership. Suddenly the home captain was the fellow in the spotlight.

Nothing seemed less likely than that these woebegone West Indians could square the series in Jamaica. Unfortunately the Australians were also unable to detect any danger. Careless batting on the opening day saw them dismissed for 256 with the captain alone standing firm. When their hosts subsided to 4/34 this collapse hardly seemed to matter. Then Lara went to work. Then the series really began.

Beneath the smile and the sweet talk, the Trinidadian is a cricketer with the game in his blood. Perhaps, finally, he had realised how much he had been distracted by frippery, how much he cared. No

AUSTRALIA V WEST INDIES, FIRST TEST
5–9 MARCH 1999, QUEEN'S PARK OVAL, PORT-OF-SPAIN, TRINIDAD

Toss:	**Australia**
Result:	**Australia won by 312 runs**
Man of the match:	**G.D. McGrath**

Australia (1st Innings)		R	BF	4	6
M.J. Slater	c Dillon b Collins	23	48	1	0
M.T.G. Elliott	lbw b Collins	44	208	1	0
J.L. Langer	c Jacobs b Walsh	5	36	1	0
M.E. Waugh	lbw b Walsh	2	10	0	0
S.R. Waugh (c)	c Jacobs b Dillon	14	43	1	0
G.S. Blewett	lbw b Ambrose	58	182	3	0
I.A. Healy (k)	lbw b Walsh	12	26	0	0
S.K. Warne	c Campbell b Ambrose	21	51	0	0
J.N. Gillespie	not out	28	76	3	0
S.C.G. MacGill	b Ambrose	0	1	0	0
G.D. McGrath	c Jacobs b Dillon	39	52	3	0
Extras	(lb 18, nb 5)	23			
Total	**All out**	**269**			
	121.3 overs at 2.21 rpo				

FoW				
	1–42	Slater	2–51	Langer
	3–53	M.E. Waugh	4–74	S.R. Waugh
	5–118	Elliott	6–153	Healy
	7–186	Warne	8–203	Blewett
	9–203	MacGill	10–269	McGrath

Bowling	O	M	R	W
C.A. Walsh	31	9	60	3
C.E.L. Ambrose	27	15	35	3
P.T. Collins	23	8	46	2
M. Dillon	26.3	4	69	2
J.C. Adams	14	2	41	0

West Indies (1st Innings)		R	BF	4	6
S.L. Campbell	lbw b McGrath	9	28	1	0
S. Ragoonath	run out	9	8	1	0
D.R.E. Joseph	lbw b McGrath	50	108	4	1
B.C. Lara (c)	run out	62	111	11	0
J.C. Adams	b MacGill	13	51	1	0
R.D. Jacobs (k)	lbw b MacGill	6	15	1	0
P.T. Collins	lbw b McGrath	1	16	0	0
R.I.C. Holder	lbw b MacGill	0	6	0	0
C.E.L. Ambrose	c Slater b McGrath	0	2	0	0
M. Dillon	b McGrath	0	8	0	0
C.A. Walsh	not out	0	0	0	0
Extras	(b 4, lb 2, nb 11)	17			
Total	**All out**	**167**			
	57.0 overs at 2.93 rpo				

FoW				
	1–16	Ragoonath	2–28	Campbell
	3–116	Joseph	4–149	Lara
	5–156	Jacobs	6–163	Adams
	7–163	Collins	8–163	Ambrose
	9–167	Holder	10–167	Dillon

Bowling	O	M	R	W
G.D. McGrath	14	3	50	5
J.N. Gillespie	12	3	34	0
S.C.G. MacGill	16	5	41	3
S.K. Warne	14	4	35	0
G.S. Blewett	1	0	1	0

Australia (2nd Innings)		R	BF	4	6
M.T.G. Elliott	c Joseph b Walsh	0	18	0	0
M.J. Slater	st Jacobs b Adams	106	205	12	0
J.L. Langer	c Jacobs b Dillon	24	40	3	0
M.E. Waugh	lbw b Ambrose	33	78	2	0
S.R. Waugh (c)	c Jacobs b Collins	0	5	0	0
G.S. Blewett	st Jacobs b Adams	28	76	1	0
I.A. Healy (k)	lbw b Walsh	0	5	0	0
S.K. Warne	b Walsh	25	55	1	0
J.N. Gillespie	c Lara b Ambrose	22	37	2	0
S.C.G. MacGill	b Walsh	0	2	0	0
G.D. McGrath	not out	4	4	1	0
Extras	(lb 7, w 1, nb 11)	19			
Total	**All out**	**261**			
	86.2 overs at 3.02 rpo				

FoW

1–7	Elliott	2–45	Langer
3–126	M.E. Waugh	4–127	S.R. Waugh
5–193	Slater	6–194	Healy
7–227	Blewett	8–257	Warne
9–257	Gillespie	10–261	MacGill

Bowling	O	M	R	W
C.A. Walsh	25.2	2	71	4
C.E.L. Ambrose	18	8	25	2
P.T. Collins	21	2	72	1
M. Dillon	14	1	57	1
J.C. Adams	8	1	29	2

West Indies (2nd Innings)		R	BF	4	6
S.L. Campbell	c M.E. Waugh b Gillespie	0	22	0	0
S. Ragoonath	lbw b Gillespie	2	27	0	0
D.R.E. Joseph	c Warne b McGrath	5	8	0	0
B.C. Lara (c)	c M.E. Waugh b Gillespie	3	2	0	0
J.C. Adams	lbw b McGrath	5	7	1	0
R.D. Jacobs (k)	lbw b McGrath	19	22	2	0
R.I.C. Holder	c M.E. Waugh b McGrath	4	11	1	0
C.E.L. Ambrose	lbw b McGrath	6	7	1	0
M. Dillon	run out	0	1	0	0
P.T. Collins	b Gillespie	0	6	0	0
C.A. Walsh	not out	2	3	0	0
Extras	(b 4, lb 1)	5			
Total	**All out**	**51**			
	19.1 overs at 2.66 rpo				

FoW

1–3	Campbell	2–8	Joseph
3–11	Lara	4–16	Adams
5–16	Ragoonath	6–31	Holder
7–47	Ambrose	8–47	Dillon
9–49	Jacobs	10–51	Collins

Bowling	O	M	R	W
G.D. McGrath	10	3	28	5
J.N. Gillespie	9.1	4	18	4

one was going to take his job away from him. He put his head down and he kept it down till he reached 99, whereupon he gambled on a reckless single. Even now the tension as the third umpire deliberated on the run-out appeal lingers. It was desperately close and an agonisingly long wait. At last a murmur spread around the ground which grew into a roar. The pictures were looking good. Lara was given the green light. He had reached his redemptive hundred.

Not for the first or last time, Lara found a staunch ally in Jimmy Adams. Adams occupied the crease for 407 minutes in scoring 94 and added 344 with his captain, a partnership that transformed the match and the series. Eventually Lara fell for 213 and though the Australians avoided the innings defeat they could not stop their opponents winning by ten wickets. One apiece.

Had it been a fluke? Could Lara keep carrying a weak side? Surely not. After recalling Ponting in place of Blewett, Australia dominated the opening days of the third and penultimate Test in Barbados. Waugh led the way, scoring a masterful 199 before he was grumpily leg before to an off-break. Ponting contributed a century and Australia secured an apparently decisive lead of 161. Then the fun started.

Courtney Walsh launched the fightback by taking five wickets as the visitors were wastefully bowled out for 146. Among the batsmen, only Warne passed 30. Chasing 308, the West Indians began badly and ended the fourth day on 3/85 after 47 overs batting, with Lara poised on 2 not out. The scene was set.

It is hard to remember a fifth day more exciting than 30 March 1999. Simply put, Lara played one of the game's truly great innings. Throughout a day that seemed to pass quickly yet also lasted an age, the Trinidadian did not waver. He set out to conquer his opponents and did so with a commanding display combining tight defence with sudden, flashing, exhilarating attack. He played late cuts with delicacy and pulls that thundered to the boundary. He produced sumptuous off-drives and even a one-handed sweep. Yet it was his impeccable footwork that most caught the eye.

Lara paced his innings beautifully and again found determined support from senior colleagues. At 5/105 the cause seemed lost. McGrath and Gillespie were taking wickets. McGrath sent down 44 overs in the innings. Rather than introducing a third fast bowler, Australia had again chosen both leg-spinners who between them took

1/117. Lara fed upon them ravenously. Lara was assisted by Adams (170 minutes), Ambrose (82 minutes) and, finally, Walsh, whose 0 not out counts among his finest innings, not least because he managed to keep out the best yorker Gillespie can ever have bowled.

Up until the nerve-racking last few minutes played in front of a boisterous crowd that flocked to the ground as the day wore on and news spread that Lara was set, the home captain was in control of himself and his opponents. Only with a few miserable little runs needed to complete the performance did he give so much as a ghost of a chance. When he did edge, the Australians missed the chance. Healy had been having a patchy tour. Certainly he had kept poorly in Jamaica. Over the years he had not been given his due, partly because he could be caustic and testy whereas Rod Marsh, no saint either, was ebullient. But he was an exceptional gloveman and deserved better than the empty outstretched glove that spared Lara at the critical hour. Since Warne was also performing well below his best, Waugh had to manage without strong contributions from two of his champions.

Lara finished the match with one more searing off-drive, where-upon he was chased and embraced by an even bigger congregation than had celebrated his century in Jamaica. Somehow Lara always knew when it was his moment, when history was ready to be made. Certainly he did not hesitate on the brink of records or shy away from posterity's garland.

Suddenly the West Indies led 2/1. It had all happened so quickly. Modern series do not allow either participants or observers to catch their breath. Antigua beckoned. Australia responded to its predica-ment by changing the balance of its attack, dropping the lesser of the spinners and including the versatile Colin Miller and Adam Dale, a skilful medium-pacer whose selection in the party suggested that the pace resources were under stress. Gillespie was injured.

Shane Warne was the man omitted. Great bowlers are sometimes left out early in their careers, before they have mastered their craft and made their names. Occasionally a great bowler may be omitted towards the end, as the rot sets in. Warne had been displaced mid-career and he was not pleased. He felt he deserved more loyalty from both his captain and the selectors but the truth was that he had not been bowling well. For the time being he was great only in his own mind. On the field he was an ordinary spinner struggling to find the deeds to match his incomparable wits.

Having made the first bold move of his captaincy, Waugh also managed to defy Ambrose long enough to reach 72 not out as his side stuttered to 303. Batting like Jimmy Barnes sings, Colin Miller contributed a robust 43. By now Lara was exhausted. Unable to construct a substantial innings he cut loose and promptly scored 100 from 84 balls. MacGill and Dale, especially, felt the full force of his fury. It was a thrilling but slightly redundant display.

No one else contributed much to the West Indian cause. Australia led by 81, scored another 306 as Langer produced a timely hundred at first wicket down and, as the local batting faltered once again, prevailed by 176 runs. The contest between Lara and the Australians had been drawn. Lara averaged 91. Sherwin Campbell was next with 28.

Steve Waugh was not much less impressive than his West Indian counterpart. He had taken responsibility for dropping Warne and had held his side together as Lara unleashed his assaults. Naturally he did not think much of the umpiring. He had always been convinced that umpires were poorly served by their five senses and therefore relied unduly on their sixth. As captain, his weak points were that he was not a lively enough presence on the field and he was reluctant to bowl spin and pace together. Nor was he much of a fellow for moving the field around. His attitude was, 'This is the field, bowl to it.' He would never abandon this position.

His strength was his judgement of character. And he had been Australia's best batsman. Nor did he miss a trick, drily pointing out that he had scored as quickly as Lara, a point that might otherwise have gone through to the keeper.

Waugh had survived his first trip as Australian captain. He was a strange leader, silently presiding over the most extraordinary affairs. He could seem dour, terse and unyielding, yet he did not try to stop his opponents playing attacking cricket, did not try to throttle them, preferring to back his players at all times, confident that they'd win more often than not. At times he resembled a kindergarten teacher, calm amid chaos. Sometimes he was so inactive that supporters wondered whether it was that he could not think of a way of changing the course of events or that he had been touched by some deeper wisdom wasted upon the rest of us. Certainly he could not be accused of blowing with the wind. He did not even bend with it.

Nor was the rest of Waugh's first year without its dramas. After the World Cup, the Australians returned home to welcome Pakistan and India. Both series would produce one memorable and illuminating match.

Pakistan had retained their singular rejection of form. At the tail-end of the century they were being especially unpredictable. Far from examining their talents and turning them into percentages, the Pakistanis seemed willing to let the wind blow where it might. Every player was distinctive. Each walked in his own way, thought his own thoughts. Every player knew that cricket was a game played against 11 opponents and 10 of your own side. Every player was blessed with a rare gift and a desire to take it to its limits. Restraint was their enemy, not failure. Even the understated characters were demonstrably subdued. In such a raw society, anonymity is death. Men need attention as plants need light. These Pakistanis had to develop faith in themselves or else disappear.

Nothing could be foretold about the series except that it would be eventful. The Pakistanis seemed to start every match in a spirit of 'wait and see'. They were spectators at their own contests, sometimes witnesses at their own executions. If there was a plan at all, it was not to have a plan. They could not win under lock and key. The philosopher who argued that man was born free but was everywhere in chains had not seen these fellows play cricket.

Hobart welcomed the Pakistanis with its customary hospitality and threatening winds. Already 1/0 down in the series, and forced to bat first on a mostly blameless surface, the visitors staggered to 222. Impatience was their undoing. Pinned down, their batsmen lashed out like cornered boxers. Scott Muller took 3/68. He had not found it easy to fit into the Australian side, lacking the social skills needed to slip smoothly into a group of established players and strong egos. He had expected to be treated as an equal and did not accept the junior role assigned to him.

Australia replied with 246 as Saqlain Mushtaq took six wickets. Waqar Younis also gave a superb performance, flinging down his break-backs as in his heyday. In the second innings the Pakistani batsmen surprised all and sundry by putting their heads down and working for runs. Inzamam contributed a typically unruffled century as the tourists reached 392, thereby setting a target of 369 to win.

The Pakistanis defended their total in the manner of men whose honour had been impugned. Rejected leg-before appeals held them back, and provoked friction between umpires and fieldsmen. Teams visiting Australia often feel they get a rough deal. Peter Willey, an imperturbable Englishman, and Peter Parker, a rotund Queenslander, were running the show.

Saqlain was expected to win the match for his side and the pressure took its toll. He seemed to bowl with one eye upon the scoreboard. Still, Azhar Mahmood took two wickets in two balls and by stumps on the fourth evening Australia had tottered to 5/188. Langer and Gilchrist had added 63 but the partnership couldn't last, could it?

It could and did. On a windswept afternoon and in front of 1704 people, some of them sober, the overnight pair set about the target in contrasting styles but with unfailing optimism. Langer was as gritty as an unfinished road. Like his captain he enjoyed the hardships of the game, the hurt, the physical confrontation, and the mental challenge. Gilchrist, the new kid on the block, was a fresher type, an outgoing, unassuming, amusing fellow liable to put his foot in it. Bumping into Bill Brown at breakfast that morning, Gilchrist had asked him how many he had scored in the great chase of 1948. Brown was twelfth man.

Off they went from the outset, sending the score rattling along. Langer worked for his runs with placements and scurried singles; his partner attacked the bowling with gusto. Feeling the pressure, Wasim Akram set pessimistic fields. His bowlers tried to win the match in a moment and not an hour, and sent down so many loose deliveries that before long the match was out of control.

Saqlain was swept to distraction and left the match a broken man. Pakistan's fielding became ragged as hope ebbed away. Pakistan had one chance to turn back the tide, an appeal for caught behind with Langer on 76. Peter Parker shook his head, although the edge had been heard in every part of the ground. It was a ridiculous decision that added fuel to the demands for the appointment of two independent umpires. Still, it was no worse than the infamous reprieves granted to Craig McDermott at the MCG in 1982, or those

AUSTRALIA V PAKISTAN, SECOND TEST
18–22 NOVEMBER 1999, BELLERIVE OVAL, HOBART, TASMANIA

Toss: Australia
Result: Australia won by 4 wickets
Man of the match: J.L. Langer

Pakistan (1st Innings)		R	BF	4	6
Saeed Anwar	c Warne b McGrath	0	7	0	0
Mohammad Wasim	c Gilchrist b Muller	91	122	12	0
Ijaz Ahmed	c Slater b McGrath	6	23	0	0
Inzamam-ul-Haq	b Muller	12	43	2	0
Mohammad Yousuf	c M.E. Waugh b Fleming	17	38	2	0
Azhar Mahmood	b Warne	27	72	2	0
Moin Khan (k)	c McGrath b Muller	1	3	0	0
Wasim Akram (c)	c Gilchrist b Warne	29	77	4	0
Saqlain Mushtaq	lbw b Warne	3	28	0	0
Waqar Younis	not out	12	18	1	0
Shoaib Akhtar	c Gilchrist b Fleming	5	6	1	0
Extras	(b 10, lb 6, w 3)	19			
Total	**All out**	**222**			
	72.5 overs at 3.05 rpo				

FoW				
1–4	Saeed Anwar		2–18	Ijaz Ahmed
3–71	Inzamam-ul-Haq		4–120	Mohammad Yousuf
5–148	Mohammad Wasim		6–153	Moin Khan
7–188	Azhar Mahmood		8–198	Saqlain Mushtaq
9–217	Wasim Akram		10–222	Shoaib Akhtar

Bowling	O	M	R	W
G.D. McGrath	18	8	34	2
D.W. Fleming	24.5	7	54	2
S.A. Muller	12	0	68	3
S.K. Warne	16	6	45	3
G.S. Blewett	2	1	5	0

Australia (1st Innings)		R	BF	4	6
M.J. Slater	c Ijaz Ahmed b Saqlain Mushtaq	97	195	10	0
G.S. Blewett	c Moin Khan b Azhar Mahmood	35	84	4	0
J.L. Langer	c Mohammad Wasim b Saqlain Mushtaq	59	106	4	0
M.E. Waugh	lbw b Waqar Younis	5	12	0	0
S.R. Waugh (c)	c Ijaz Ahmed b Wasim Akram	24	45	2	0
R.T. Ponting	b Waqar Younis	0	3	0	0
A.C. Gilchrist (k)	st Moin Khan b Saqlain Mushtaq	6	19	0	0
S.K. Warne	b Saqlain Mushtaq	0	1	0	0
D.W. Fleming	lbw b Saqlain Mushtaq	0	4	0	0
G.D. McGrath	st Moin Khan b Saqlain Mushtaq	7	15	1	0
S.A. Muller	not out	0	0	0	0
Extras	(b 2, lb 6, nb 5)	13			
Total	**All out**	**246**			
	80.0 overs at 3.08 rpo				

FoW		1–76	Blewett	2–191	Slater
		3–206	M.E. Waugh	4–206	Langer
		5–213	Ponting	6–236	Gilchrist
		7–236	Warne	8–236	Fleming
		9–246	S.R. Waugh	10–246	McGrath

Bowling	O	M	R	W
Wasim Akram	20	4	51	1
Shoaib Akhtar	17	2	69	0
Waqar Younis	12	1	42	2
Saqlain Mushtaq	24	8	46	6
Azhar Mahmood	7	1	30	1

Pakistan (2nd Innings)		R	BF	4	6
Saeed Anwar	b Warne	78	156	9	1
Mohammad Wasim	c McGrath b Muller	20	59	1	0
Saqlain Mushtaq	lbw b Warne	8	52	0	0
Ijaz Ahmed	c S.R. Waugh b McGrath	82	124	13	0
Inzamam-ul-Haq	c M.E. Waugh b Warne	118	191	12	0
Mohammad Yousuf	c Ponting b Fleming	2	10	0	0
Azhar Mahmood	lbw b Warne	28	60	4	0
Moin Khan (k)	c Gilchrist b Fleming	6	31	0	0
Wasim Akram (c)	c Blewett b Warne	31	74	3	0
Waqar Younis	run out	0	6	0	0
Shoaib Akhtar	not out	5	16	0	0
Extras	(lb 6, w 1, nb 7)	14			
Total	**All out**	**392**			
	128.5 overs at 3.04 rpo				

FoW

1–50	Mohammad Wasim	2–100	Saqlain Mushtaq
3–122	Saeed Anwar	4–258	Ijaz Ahmed
5–263	Mohammad Yousuf	6–320	Azhar Mahmood
7–345	Moin Khan	8–357	Inzamam-ul-Haq
9–358	Waqar Younis	10–392	Wasim Akram

Bowling	O	M	R	W
G.D. McGrath	27	8	87	1
D.W. Fleming	29	5	89	2
S.K. Warne	45.5	11	110	5
S.A. Muller	17	3	63	1
S.R. Waugh	4	1	19	0
M.E. Waugh	2	0	6	0
R.T. Ponting	2	1	7	0
G.S. Blewett	2	0	5	0

Australia (2nd Innings)		R	BF	4	6
G.S. Blewett	c Moin Khan b Azhar Mahmood	29	106	2	0
M.J. Slater	c Azhar Mahmood b Shoaib Akhtar	27	48	3	0
J.L. Langer	c Inzamam-ul-Haq b Saqlain Mushtaq	127	295	12	0
M.E. Waugh	lbw b Azhar Mahmood	0	1	0	0
S.R. Waugh (c)	c & b Saqlain Mushtaq	28	69	0	0
R.T. Ponting	lbw b Wasim Akram	0	5	0	0
A.C. Gilchrist (k)	not out	149	163	13	1
S.K. Warne	not out	0	0	0	0
Extras	(b 1, lb 4, nb 4)	9			
Total	**6 wickets**	**369**			
	113.5 overs at 3.24 rpo				

FoW

1–39	Slater	2–81	Blewett
3–81	M.E. Waugh	4–125	S.R. Waugh
5–126	Ponting	6–364	Langer

Bowling	O	M	R	W
Wasim Akram	18	1	68	1
Waqar Younis	11	2	38	0
Shoaib Akhtar	23	5	85	1
Saqlain Mushtaq	44.5	9	130	2
Azhar Mahmood	17	3	43	2

bestowed on Langer at The Gabba or Boon in Adelaide during the course of their excellent careers.

The Pakistanis allowed misfortune to prey on their mind and the match rushed away. At last, much too late, Langer was dismissed. The West Australians had taken the score from 5/126 to 6/364. Langer embraced his watching father and at the press conference explained that the noise heard as the ball passed by at the controversial moment had been the sound of his bat handle breaking. Some reporters managed not to laugh.

As the new year approached, Waugh could look back on his work with satisfaction. His players had survived numerous tight spots, had bounced back in the Caribbean and now in Hobart. Doubt had been stilled by the best possible method, a series of powerful performances produced by an adventurous side steadied by the hand of a canny captain. Waugh had managed to release his players. His team played enterprising cricket. And yet the confounded fellow did not seem to say or do anything. But, then, he never had been one for show.

One great match remained before 1999 could be consigned to the books. Pakistan had been crushed but the Indians had arrived, led by a great batsman but an inexperienced captain burdened with a coach, Kapil Dev, and some players not of his choosing. Sachin Tendulkar was still a youthful idealist who lacked the communication skills and authority needed to turn his outfit into a formidable force.

Waugh had much less to worry about as the Boxing Day Test approached. His team had won five successive Tests and although Gillespie's broken leg had not yet healed he had found the sort of fast bowler every captain likes to have in his armoury. Waugh had nursed enough bruises in his early encounters with the West Indies to know the power of pace. Ever since, he had been waiting to get his own back. It was nothing personal, just that the game owed him.

His prayers had been answered when Brett Lee hove into view. Suddenly Australia could hope to field a fierce pace attack of its own. Waugh was looking forward to standing at gully and watching the leather fly. Finally he had all the pieces in place.

Lee would live up to expectations. He seemed dashing and uncluttered and his face was more angelic than, say, Lillee's, but there was a discernible glint in his eye and a hint that he enjoyed the spotlight. Moreover, despite coming from Wollongong, on the coast of New South Wales, he had plenty of the bush in him, an honesty and steadfastness that told of a willingness to work and an ability to appreciate the simple things of life, a sunrise, a horse race, a beer in the evening and the chance to knock the blocks off as many batsmen as possible.

Lee's exceptional pace had often been brought to the attention of visitors and it was not all antipodean moonshine. He had been held back because, like most rookie fast bowlers, he took only two deliveries seriously, the yorker and the bumper. It was a position he was slow to abandon. Indeed it would take Lee until 2005/06 to understand the need to put overs, spells and days together, whereupon he became a proper pace bowler.

At this point, Lee could swing the new ball away from the bat but had not learnt to combine pace, control and movement. With the old ball, he tended to go wide of the crease and send down break-backs with an action that raised eyebrows. To his credit he stopped bowling this delivery when the consternation became widespread. Thereafter his beamer was the only delivery to provoke concern.

Lee's debut was everything his captain could have expected and the confrontation between Lee and Tendulkar was the highlight of the series. The pair came into conflict on the third day after the hosts had collected 405 between the showers. Lee's first spell had been impressive and effective. Throughout he resembled a colt running a few furlongs just for the fun of it. He took wickets with fast outswingers and searing inswingers that headed for the stumps like a guided missile and often struck wood without bothering to bounce. He charged through the Indian batting like a powerful beam penetrating the night.

Only one man defied the newcomer's pace. At the crease Tendulkar resembled St Paul's in the Blitz. Again and again, Lee raced to the crease, unleashed a thunderbolt and finished a yard away from his foe, snorting like a horse at the end of a race. Again and again, Tendulkar disarmed the missile, even responding with sallies of his own, drives and hooks that proclaimed that he was not afeared. As partners came and went, and aware that time was running out, Tendulkar moved from defence to attack, whereupon he produced a stream of thrilling strokes. Around him, India burned.

When Tendulkar reached three figures the crowd rose to him. Eventually he was caught on the boundary. Lee had taken 5/47 and, despite Tendulkar's defiance, Australia won the match.

An eventful year had ended on a high note for the Australians. Waugh had looked fate in the eye and had not blinked. Only two men had been able to withstand the force of the Australian onslaught— the two magicians of the age, Lara and Tendulkar. Both had been magnificent but the Australians would continue to cut a swathe through their opponents and, before long, even these great batsmen could not block their path. In many respects 1999 was the start of the Australian domination. It was a year that could have gone badly, a year that eventually went extremely well. Many challenges were met and overcome, and Waugh had almost forged his team. Langer, Ponting, Lee and Gilchrist had fought their way into the side, and all four were to be around for a long time.

13

MANY A SLIP

After surprising all and sundry by lifting the World Cup in 1987, the Australians were obliged to give way to stronger sides in not one, but two, subsequent tournaments. Far from continuing to dominate the 50-over game as a prelude to taking charge in the Test arena, they had stumbled along. Not until the end of the century would they recapture the World Cup, whereupon they retained it with aplomb by recording a third triumph, this time under African skies.

Pakistan had seized the trophy in 1992, overcoming England in the final. Imran Khan led the team in his imperious way, Javed Miandad provided the cement, a solidly built newcomer called Inzamam-ul-Haq drove the ball with innocent power and the bowling attack was built around Mushtaq Ahmed's cheerful deceptions and the incisive swing of a supremely gifted pace bowler, Wasim Akram. Not that the other players were exactly dull. Indeed it was one of the country's most mercurial teams. Pakistani dressing-rooms must be interesting places.

Relying on their usual familiar formula of a steady start, lots of singles and efficient fielding, the Australians floundered and did not reach the latter stages of a somewhat unsatisfactory tournament played on their own patch. To add insult to injury, their neighbours from across the Tasman beat them in the opening match and throughout played a more enterprising game. Border and Simpson could not match the brilliance of Martin Crowe's chop and change tactics. Nor did any of the Australians perform remotely as well as New Zealand's inspired and inspirational leader. Alas New Zealand lost their captain towards the end of their semi-final and their dreams went with him. Pakistan prevailed and promptly gave thanks, Imran lifted the trophy and spoke of worlds beyond cricket.

Mark Taylor took the team to the 1996 World Cup, the second played in the subcontinent. Threats and explosions had by now become part of the cricketing experience. Proud, neglected tribes were ever more stridently demanding a homeland or protesting against imposed borders. Moreover the conflict between the modern and medieval had become even more desperate as old and scared religious leaders railed against changes in the ways of the world that were rendering irrelevant all that they valued. Unwilling to adjust, these supposed sages let loose upon the world a wave of angry, agitated young men and women, suicide bombers and so forth, by way of redemptive cleansing. History has shown that whenever anyone tries to make the world a cleaner place, racially or religiously, an awful lot of people die.

Violence might have become part of the international cricketing experience, but that was not to say that the sport had found it easy to adjust to the dangers. In the 1980s New Zealand had abandoned a tour of Sri Lanka after a bomb had exploded outside their hotel in the capital city, killing innocent people. The bombs were not aimed at the cricketers but what consolation was that? Accordingly the Australians were alarmed when the draw for the 1996 World Cup sent them to meet the co-hosts in Colombo. To make matters worse, numerous nasty letters were received, and read by wives and vulnerable types within the touring party.

After debating the matter long and hard, Taylor and his men refused to go to Sri Lanka. As far as they were concerned it was neither a personal nor a political decision, merely a precautionary one. Naturally their hosts felt aggrieved. Matches of this sort are few and far between. Tournaments of this significance are long in the making. The Africans would be similarly upset when their first World

Cup was spoiled by the refusal of some western teams to fulfil their obligation to play in Zimbabwe.

At least the Australians were not suffering from towering self-congratulation as they conceded their match in Colombo. The West Indies also withdrew from their commitment, at which point, displaying rare unity, the subcontinental countries organised a match among themselves. It went well and peaceably.

Before the start of the 1996 tournament, Mike Coward of *The Australian* had an idea that was, even by his demanding standards, inspired. In this land of oracles and gurus he visited the country's most eminent astrologer who, by a stroke of luck, lived in Vishakhapatnam, where Australia was to make its first appearance. Armed only with an open mind, Coward asked for a prediction and was advised to come back in a few days, as time was needed to consult charts. Upon his return, Coward was informed that the winner of the World Cup could not be foretold with any certainty. His disappointment was eased, though, when the astrologer added that he could divulge the finalists. Sri Lanka would play Australia.

Mr Coward's numerous readers were hooked. Since the Sri Lankans were rank outsiders and Australia had given away two points, an encounter in the final seemed a long shot. On the other hand, Sri Lanka had been presented with two wins without bowling a ball and the Australians were strong.

Both teams reached the semi-finals. Sanath Jayasuriya dominated the early rounds, attacking from the first ball, piratically cutting and carving his team into powerful positions, thereby giving the middle order plenty of time to consolidate. Sri Lanka's batting was strong and seasoned and the bowling and fielding were tight enough to put pressure on every opponent. And the momentum was with them.

Not that Jayasuriya or Kaluwitharana, his swashbuckling opening partner, contributed much to the semi-final, played against India in Calcutta. Both were caught at third man in the first over of the match. Nevertheless the Sri Lankans reached 251 on a breaking pitch.

Even at the time Azharuddin's decision to bowl first that sweltering day at Eden Gardens seemed odd. But then, captains are inclined towards perversity. Not so long ago, while I was still captaining the minor county, *The Daily Telegraph* asked me to cover one of Devon's matches whereupon I found myself criticising my own puzzling decision to bat first on a greentop!

Azharuddin would later claim that he had been misled by a curator convinced that his pitch was going to last the distance, in which regard the gentleman concerned was not alone among fellows of his ilk. By and large groundsmen are a gloomy lot, persuaded that players and weather gods have joined in a conspiracy to defeat them. At the time darker motivations were not suspected by those seeking to explain Azharuddin's decision. Perhaps it was, after all, just a mistake. That was the problem in the aftermath of the bookmaking scandal. No one could any longer tell what was real.

In any event, India started well and then fell apart. Towards the end, thirsty, hungry, their hopes shattered and a sense of betrayal in the air—at the best of times conspiracists are as thick on the ground in the subcontinent as petals after a wedding—the crowd started to burn wood and paper and to throw water bottles onto the field.

As it happened *The Age* had decided to hold the day's last edition to include the result of this match and my attendant column. Relieved to find the contest petering out, I had already begun dictating my article to the young man responsible for setting it into the paper and pressing the button on the last few thousand copies. Accordingly, the sight of trouble brewing, and Clive Lloyd's consequent stopping of the match, in his capacity as match referee, was not received with any particular warmth either by your correspondent or the helpful fellow in Melbourne.

Obliged to start again, and working off the top of my head and against an advancing deadline, I managed to dictate another 750 words, whereupon the ground settled down and Lloyd, blast him, decreed that the contest could resume. Fresh top required. Informed of this development, my contact remained surprisingly calm. No sooner had this version been completed than the riots resumed and the match was abandoned once and for all. Alas it was necessary to start again and to throw together a fourth and final attempt at the summit. My heroic accomplice played his part and a few hours later the last edition was dropping on the doorsteps of inner Melbourne.

Eventually I was able to leave the press box and to fade into a crowd beaten into submission by lathi-wielding policemen, and also hushed by embarrassment at their own excesses. One forlorn-looking boy summed it up. 'India bad today,' he said. It was unclear whether he was commenting upon the match or the misbehaviour but it did not matter because he was right either way. Calcutta was proud of its sporting reputation and next day the newspapers and streets were full of apologising locals. Not that Calcutta is exclusively a cricketing city. Indeed it is India's footballing stronghold. Might soccer have become the national game had the city retained its influence over the country?

Of course the first three versions of the saga never saw the light of day. Nor did the final product reach Bengal, sales of Australian papers being somewhat sluggish in the region. In both cases it is probably just as well. For once, though, I felt like a proper reporter! As it happened I was the only Australian journalist at the match. Everyone else had flown to Chandigarh to cover their team's encounter with the West Indies the next day.

On this occasion my rudimentary approach to reporting was an advantage because it permitted an immediate response to developments. Generally it was a handicap because it was exhausting, besides which my writing was almost illegible. My reluctance to change was caused by a suspicion that my work might suffer from the formalising of the process and an old dog's stubborn resistance to new tricks.

The penny didn't drop until years later, when I spent a few days wandering around in the strawberry-growing hills outside Pune. As usual children kept requesting autographs—Indians have a strong attachment to paper. Asked for their names, the first three supplicants replied 'Emil'. It seemed odd that so many youngsters in Panchgani had the same first name but eventually I realised that they wanted my email address. If a bunch of ragged country boys could master email then surely it was not beyond the powers of a Cambridge graduate. So it proved. Not for the first or last time, I had been an ass.

Australia's semi-final was compelling. After losing its first four wickets for 15, Mark Taylor's team recovered to 8/207 thanks to an unbeaten 72 from Stuart Law and a characteristically creative 69 from Michael Bevan. An abrasive man, Law was not to be given many days in the sun, a solitary Test and a few one-day matches alone recognising an outstanding talent. He was not inclined to toe the party line and had the suspicion often found in country cousins (he had been raised among the resentments of rural Queensland) of the golden boys of the metropolis. His relationship with the Waughs was prickly, not least because of the way the newcomer spoke his mind on the field.

When the West Indians were at 2/165 in the 41st over, with Chanderpaul and Richardson in full cry, it seemed that the Australians must fall. Not a bit of it. As *Wisden* drily reported, 'West Indies pulled off an extraordinary defeat'. Juggling the batting order by demoting the proper players and promoting Roger Harper and Ottis Gibson or, rather, the panic that prompted such a move, was responsible for the disaster. Richardson watched from the bowler's end as successive batsmen lurched between desperate defence and reckless attack.

That is not to say that Australia did everything right. Warne was given only nine overs and still managed to take four wickets, a performance that secured him recognition as Man of the Match. Law was asked to bowl leg-spin rather than his usual medium pace. Not until the last few overs of a 100-over match did the Australians seem to have even the remotest chance of winning. *Wisden* was right. Their opponents beat themselves.

Mike Coward's astrologer had been correct. Australia and Sri Lanka were indeed to meet in the final to be played in Lahore. No one sensible disregards astrology, palmistry and the rest of it. Although charlatans abound, there have been too many puzzling events witnessed by intelligent sceptics such as my friend Fabian Muir, who once amused himself in Paris by attending a séance, in company with some other shrewd lawyers. Stunned by the experience, he returned with an even more sceptical Norwegian girl and was startled as messages were received in Norwegian (her hand was on the bottom of the pile). So violent was the response that the stone flew off the table whereupon Fabian left the room at a fair clip.

In truth the final was disappointing. The stadium was only half-full as the match began on a foggy morning, and the atmosphere was hardly electrifying as the outsiders collected the winning runs on a dew-ridden evening. Perhaps it was simply that the semi-finals had been so eventful that critics, crowd and players were exhausted.

After Australia had stuttered along against varied slow bowling enjoying the dryness of the ball and the support of enthusiastic fieldsmen, the vibrant underdogs lost their openers but were steadied by Asanka Gurusinha—'the Great Guru'. Eventually the stage was set for the old-timers to guide their team to the greatest victory in its history.

Aravinda de Silva reached a superbly controlled hundred and, with four overs to spare, Arjuna Ranatunga drilled the remaining runs whereupon the celebrations began. Australia had been beaten by a daring, thoughtful and superior opponent.

Naturally and justifiably Sri Lanka's victory provoked wild celebrations on the island and the players went home not just as champions but as heroes. Ranatunga's Napoleonic leadership was praised, and his craftiness in inspecting conditions the previous evening was widely thought to have been crucial, for he realised that after nightfall the ball would become too slippery to hold. Ranatunga's fearlessness and willingness to confront the Australians had been crucial to the confidence of his mostly youthful and impressionable team. Not long before, the Sri Lankans had toured Australia where their captain had been provocative, bold and not at all cowed by reputations or local customs. Like Gavaskar, Ganguly and Ian Chappell in their different ways, Ranatunga established the identity of his side, asserted its ability, emphasised its nationality, celebrated its uniqueness. It was a release, not just for a team but for an entire nation. No one, before, had dared to cock such a snook.

Disappointment at the final must not be regarded as an attempt to rain on a wonderful achievement that temporarily unified a wartorn country. Sri Lanka played thrilling cricket, deserved to win and was hardly to blame for the subdued atmosphere to be found in the stadium. Indeed the winners' only fault was to celebrate victory not too well but too long. Not until their dismal performance at the next World Cup would the Sri Lankans accept that the past was indeed another country.

Mark Taylor did not get another chance to lift a World Cup. Before the next competition was staged in England, the selectors broke new ground by appointing separate captains for the different disciplines of Test and 50-over cricket.

For many critics, splitting the Australian captaincy was an act of sacrilege. Often, and only half in jest, they described it as the second most important office in the country. Of course, no one and nothing could challenge the status of the President of Collingwood Football Club. When the news broke that Mark Taylor would remain captain of the Test side but Steve Waugh was to replace him as leader of the 50-over outfit, the loyalists protested long and loud.

Never having thought about sport in quasi-religious terms, my reaction was more restrained. Cricket's greatest lesson is to take every ball on its merits. However, those objecting to the splitting of the captaincy were not merely worried about the compromising of a position. More pertinently, they were concerned about the weakening of the captain's authority. Suddenly Taylor could speak only to the Test players. He could advise and encourage, shape and direct the five-day side but as soon as the time came for the coloured clothes to be distributed he would be replaced by a team-mate with different opinions and strategies. Months might pass before he met the one-day specialists. Beyond doubt it was an imperfect situation.

Such objections might have merit, but the decision could also be defended as the lesser of two evils. Taylor was not worth his place in the 50-over side. His continued selection was handicapping the team and imperilling his own standing. His scratchy form at the start of the innings, lumbering work in the field and sluggish running between wickets weakened the side. If they retained him as 50-over captain, the selectors would be following the supposed English custom of choosing the captain and then the side.

Should Taylor, though, be sacked as captain of the Test side merely because he could no longer command a place in the one-day side? Wouldn't that attach undue importance to the shorter version of the game? Notwithstanding the manifest disadvantages of the solution arrived at by the selectors, the fact remained that they had fulfilled their duty to pick the strongest sides for the two competitions. By and large the same players stand out in every form of the game. At the margins, changes may be required. Fifty-over matches often end in a flurry with not much between the teams. A run needlessly lost, or a run stolen as a child pinches an apple, can determine the outcome. Moreover winning and losing are infectious. Taylor had become a liability. He had to go.

Nor was Taylor the only senior player dropped. A younger gloveman was also summoned to replace Ian Healy, a jug-eared fellow called Adam Gilchrist, a lively all-rounder who had been forced to cross the Nullarbor in search of opportunity because New South Wales' selection panel had allowed Phil Emery to play too long.

Such was Australia's commitment and loyalty towards distinguished sporting servants that the newcomer was booed when he walked onto the field. Nor was he striding out in front of Healy's staunchest supporters at The Gabba but on his own patch in Sydney. Obviously it was nothing personal. The fact that Healy was an abrasive, ruthless, clinical performer did not matter. He was a champion, and he had made it obvious he wanted to play.

To make matters worse, Waugh made a faltering start to the captaincy. Uncertain of his support, unable to locate his distinctive voice, he began by imitating his predecessor. As might be expected, it did not work. Not until Waugh found the confidence to follow his own instincts did his work improve. Leadership's loneliness can be disconcerting. It is not a part-time job. A room falls silent when a captain speaks. Woe betide the newly appointed cricket captain who does not accept that his life has changed. Waugh also missed his first few matches in charge, whereupon Warne seized his chance.

Warne led the team with a characteristic mixture of flair and opportunism. Daring, team-spirited and considerate, Warne impressed former leaders and inspired a loyal following among younger players. From the outset he was a more innovative captain than Waugh, who tended to rely on systems. Warne was in touch with the game's ebb and flow, and had the nerve to act upon his hunches. He had the fearlessness of the gambler. Warne had hoped that his chance to lead the side might eventually come but suspected that reservations about his lifestyle might preclude promotion. He was right about that. He would be overlooked next time as well, and the captaincy given to a younger man who had accepted the need to confront his failings.

Not long after his appointment, and still under scrutiny, Waugh found himself taking his side to England in an attempt to win the 1999 World Cup. His team made a dreadful start, losing to New Zealand on a slow and low-bouncing pitch in Cardiff, and to Pakistan in a high-scoring match in Leeds. Waugh seemed to need crises to lure him from his shelter. Some leaders are made for war, others for peace. Somehow the warriors find a scrap.

Waugh had various problems. His coach, Geoff Marsh, was a likeable but limited man whose team meetings were somewhat uninformative. Moreover, the team management had imposed a 'no grog' rule in an attempt to curtail the high jinks detected in the West Indies. The players quickly became tetchy and Waugh was seen as an isolated figure trying to prop up an apparently doomed outfit.

After a fortnight of mostly dismal performances, the Australians looked like a beaten side. Something drastic was needed to stop the favourites going home early, with their tails between their legs. Waugh was partly to blame for his team's predicament. Theoretically sound, his policy of giving the new ball to his swing bowlers and saving McGrath for the middle of the innings had backfired. He had wanted to bring together his tightest and best bowlers, McGrath and Warne, at the very moment his opponents were trying to raise their tempo. Instead of surprising opposing teams, the strategy upset his own side's equilibrium.

With hindsight, Waugh would admit that it did not make much sense to deny the finest pace bowler in the world the opportunity to use the new ball. His strategy confused his players. Captains must carry their players along with them. Although they tried hard to make it work, the Australians did not believe in the tactic. A team unconvinced by its own strategy has gloomy prospects.

In the nick of time, Waugh had the good sense to consult his most independent-minded team-mates, including Tom Moody and Damien Fleming. He needed to be told truths he knew but had forgotten. They reminded him that aggression was Australia's game and recommended a return to basics. No one familiar with the country's history could doubt the wisdom of their advice. A long team meeting followed and thereafter the Australians were a different side.

At his next press conference, Waugh said that his team needed to win its next seven matches and added that he considered the task to be within its capabilities. Finally the fighter had been released. Not for the first or last time, events would prove him right. Of course the vindication was partly due to luck and partly to his own efforts. Waugh's predictions often came true because he made them come true. Despite his subdued exterior, he had a bit of Muhammad Ali in him, not least in his defiance of dangers he had created.

From this moment onwards, Waugh's team was on the attack, a strategy he applied relentlessly and sometimes without the required subtlety. History may judge him to have been an unusual captain, a man of years as opposed to minutes, at once naive and seasoned, cynical and idealistic. His approach made him an outstanding captain for the first four days of a Test but vulnerable to an opponent still in with a chance at the start of the last day. His refusal to prey upon nerves by slowing the game down meant that the late-charging opponent might succeed. Under his captaincy, Australia would lose astonishing matches in Barbados, Headingley, Antigua and Kolkata, all of them on the final afternoon. Waugh gave inspired opponents room to manoeuvre. Thanks to him, Test cricket became a faster game. And throughout he stood silently at gully, chewing the cud, thinking up ways of taking a wicket.

Waugh's style of captaincy was shaped by the 1999 World Cup tournament. At this time of crisis, at this turning point, he decided to concentrate on his strengths. He applied the things he knew and the things he had discovered. At last he knew the sort of captain he wanted to be, needed to be. He could not pull rabbits from hats but he had his own truth to convey. And it was this. He knew how to win. It was the making and breaking of his captaincy.

Ruthlessness bordering on gamesmanship could be detected in Australia's next match against senior opposition. Thanks to the curiosities of an odd points system, Australia needed to beat the West Indies but wanted them to progress. As soon as victory was certain, and to widespread bemusement, Waugh (19 from 73 balls) and Bevan (20 from 69) patted back easy deliveries. It was a calculated attempt to stop New Zealand reaching the next stage and bringing with them their earlier victory over Australia. Typically, Waugh accepted responsibility for the strategy, both at the crease and afterwards in the press conference. Sportsmanship be damned. He had not written the rules. Why should he allow his side to be handicapped by their absurdities?

Happily for the game, the ruse did not work. The Kiwis advanced anyhow and brought with them the indignation of the slighted neighbour. Confirmation that revenge is indeed a dish best served cold would come in Perth several years later when Stephen Fleming and his men did their utmost to stop Australia reaching the final of the World Series.

Notwithstanding these shenanigans, Australia progressed to the next stage and now needed to win only five successive matches. It was a normal state of affairs. Any team trying to win a knockout tournament must put together a string of victories. By the end of the following week, India had been trounced and the Zimbabweans put in their place. McGrath bowled economically with the new ball in both matches. Suddenly a spring could be detected in the step of a previously hangdog side. Australia was moving into the final stages as a team on the rise. Three more matches remained. Now every country was in the same boat. Opponents had been given a chance to subdue the Australians and had fluffed it.

Moreover the next two matches were to be against the same opponent, a team just as desperate, hungry and capable as the Australians, Hansie Cronje's South Africans. On 13 June 1999, at Leeds, Steve Waugh played his most famous one-day innings. At first a South African victory seemed to be inevitable but no match was over while Steve Waugh was at the crease. Gradually the Australian score mounted. Before long every ball was an agony and most seemed to bring a single or a boundary. Once his eye was in and his spirit aroused, none of the great players of the era chased as well or hit the ball as fiercely as this lean and hungry predator. Not that he attacked hot-bloodedly. Far from it. It was the combination of chilly manner, clarity of thought and ferocity of intent that made him dangerous. Herschelle Gibbs ought not to have taken any chances with that infamous catch at mid-wicket. It is not wise to give such a man a second chance.

At first in bursts, and then with an arrow's certainty, the Australian captain took his team towards its target. As the gap closed a bystander said, with more admiration than surprise, 'The so and so's going to do it, you know!' And so he did. Australia overtook South Africa's 271 in the final over, with Waugh on 120. Even from the stands you could tell he had that look in his eye. It was the inexorable way the score kept mounting. Waugh was not living on hope. He expected to win.

Four days later the same teams met again, this time in Birmingham, with the winner to proceed to the final at Lord's where the Pakistanis were waiting. Both sides thought they had the measure of Wasim Akram's rag, tag and bobtail side and accordingly regarded their own encounter as akin to a final.

For the second time in a week, the gap between the teams was wafer thin. For a second time it depended more upon human fallibility than cricketing skill. Whereas the first match was won by an epic innings, the semi-final was not won at all. After 100 overs of confrontational cricket not a single run separated the sides. Almost throughout, South Africa played the better cricket and once again it took a telling intervention from a great Australian cricketer to thwart them.

Pinned down by top-class bowling from Shaun Pollock and Allan Donald, Australia stumbled to 213, a modest score on a fair pitch surrounded by tempting boundaries. Steve Waugh and Michael Bevan had held the innings together after their side had slipped to 4/68. South Africa moved comfortably to 0/48 and seemed bound to reach the final. Against any other side, Cronje's men would surely have finished the job. The Australians were another matter. Since their return to the fray, the South Africans had been unable to conquer them. Something always seemed to go wrong. Often rough justice was blamed. Some detected a deficiency in the South Africans' thinking, an inability to overcome an opponent they held in high regard, a tendency to step back after inflicting a wound. Did the South Africans truly believe the deed could be done?

Shane Warne was their other problem, and he struck three times as the chase faltered, removing Gibbs with one of his most incendiary leg-breaks, then Gary Kirsten and then, crucially, and helped by a slice of luck, Cronje himself as the ball flew to slip off his boot. From 4/61, the Africans fought back. Jacques Kallis and Jonty Rhodes rallied their side and Pollock contributed 20 in 14 balls. The Australians made mistakes. Paul Reiffel dropped a catch and then, with the ground in a ferment and the South African press corps urging on their side, he let another slip through his grasp at long-off. To add insult to injury, the ball crossed the ropes without bouncing.

Suddenly South Africa needed to score nine runs in the last over with their last pair in occupation. Yet it was no ordinary last pair. The man on strike counts among the fiercest hitters the game has known, a determinedly understated character by the name of Lance Klusener, a fellow whose outlook brings to mind Keith Miller's observation that no one who has had 'a Messerschmitt on his arse' could worry about anything in sport. Klusener has seen Zulu women bearing babies scanning the skies for rain. He read books before he walked the crease. Sporting heroes are not cartoon characters but human beings trying to hang on to their souls.

As Sanath Jayasuriya changed the course of the 1996 campaign with his destructive batting against the new ball, so Klusener had become the most feared batsman of the 1999 competition. Armed with half a tree trunk and skilled at striking attempted yorkers over boundaries, Klusener had spread panic among his opponents. Great hitters have that effect. Everything happens so quickly. Sometimes it happens on the way to the crease. Captains cannot hide their anxiety. Bowlers feel under extra pressure. Bad deliveries are sent down, catches dropped, foolish risks taken and suddenly an erratic over has been bowled and 20 runs conceded.

By the start of that last over, Klusener had already reached 23, from 12 balls. A blunder by Waugh had left the final over in the hands of Damien Fleming. Moreover the Victorian was defending a short straight boundary. He started around the wicket, searching for yorkers. Klusener met the first two balls with controlled clouts that sent the ball speeding through the air to the boundary. As a rule he preferred not to lift the ball too high, relying on flat shots that denied fieldsmen time to intercept.

Scores were level. South Africa was one run shy of reaching the final of the World Cup. One of cricket's hardest hitters was on strike. That his partner was a relative bunny hardly mattered. At least Allan Donald was unlikely to lose his head. Waugh went across to talk to his crestfallen bowler. Later he was to say that, after the second boundary, he had thought that his team 'might be in a bit of trouble'. A bit of trouble?!

After a long consultation, captain and leather-flinger decided that moving over the wicket was the best bet, a tactic calculated to deny Klusener the freedom he needed to swing his arms with impunity. In short, and belatedly, Australia decided to bowl stump to stump. You miss, I hit.

Of course Waugh also brought his field in to save the single. No point trying to protect the boundary. A tap into an untenanted area and it was over. He had to close the gaps and force Klusener to take another risk, to go for another big shot. It was Australia's only chance. Four balls left.

In many respects Klusener was now the man under pressure. Things change quickly in one-day cricket. Suddenly the South Africans were expected to win, ought to win, had the odds heavily on their side. Not that the swashbuckling batsman looked worried. He was exactly the man his country needed on strike.

Fleming's third delivery was full and straight. Anxious not to hit across the line, Klusener drove it back down the pitch. He shouted at his partner to stay in his crease. It had been a good delivery but three further chances remained. Amid the bedlam in the ground, and the turmoil in his own mind, Donald did not hear the call and started rushing down the pitch in search of the glorious, elusive run. The ball was intercepted and at last the fast bowler responded to the screams of his partner to turn back. Donald is a remarkable athlete but even he could not change direction swiftly enough to recover his ground before the shy arrived at the stumps. Fortunately the throw missed by inches and South Africa breathed again.

Now Klusener blundered. An eternity passed between deliveries, time for him to go down the pitch to settle his partner. Donald had been shaken by the close shave. Desperate not to let down his side, and realising the dangers of risky running, he decided to hold his crease till it was safe to leave. On another day Klusener might have anticipated Donald's reaction. But, then, he had plenty on his own plate.

Fleming's fourth delivery was as precisely pitched as its predecessor. Klusener's response was just as measured as he drove the ball back past the bowler, slightly to the on-side of the stumps, towards Mark Waugh, not that the fielder's identity seemed to matter. Realising that the ball was heading a few yards away from the fieldsman, and calculating that a run could be taken, Klusener started to rush forwards, yelling at his partner to follow course. Donald, though, had been watching the shot and regarded the circumstances as disconcertingly familiar. Accordingly, and unaware of his partner's intentions, he turned back towards his crease determined to lie low and fight another day.

It all seemed to happen in slow motion. Klusener kept advancing, Donald kept retreating. Waugh stopped the ball, returned it to the bowler who relayed it to the wicket-keeper who removed the bails with no opposing batsmen in sight. Donald had been run out. Reprieved Australians rushed from all corners of the ground to join the celebrations. The press box fell eerily silent as the South African contingent mourned and the Australians tried to gather their thoughts. Only those in the rooms can describe the reaction of Hansie Cronje and his players. From a distance they looked stunned.

Finals of any sport rarely live up to expectations. Too much is at stake. Moreover the players are often worn out. By and large cricket has been lucky with its World Cup finals. The less-inspiring ones have produced surprise winners whose triumphs have been celebrated with glee. Alas the 1999 final was the dullest of them all. Pakistan was to blame. Wasim Akram's side went down with scarcely a whimper.

Afterwards rumours spread that Pakistani players had been out partying the night before the match. Suggestions that senior players had been paid a million dollars to lose the match refused to go away. The Pakistanis could not complain that the stories were given credence. They only had themselves to blame. Apparently four players had been given $US25 000 each to throw the match against Bangladesh.

Still, it required a leap of the imagination to believe that even a side capable of throwing a qualifying match during a World Cup could cast aside the wealth and fame that accompany World Cup winners to their grave. Cynics suggested that the Pakistanis did not think they could win and therefore decided to pocket the loot. Optimists hope they merely had a bad day. At any rate, Pakistan was dismissed cheaply and the match was over by mid-afternoon.

Waugh had looked defeat in the eye and prevailed. Australia was top of the Test and one-day rankings. A few more mountains remained to be climbed, not least in India. Nevertheless Australian cricket had come a long way, and could legitimately hope to maintain its dominance for the next few years.

AUSTRALIA V SOUTH AFRICA, WORLD CUP SEMI-FINAL
17 JUNE 1999, EDGBASTON, BIRMINGHAM, UK

Toss: South Africa
Result: Match tied
Man of the match: S.K. Warne

Australia		R	BF	4	6
A.C. Gilchrist (k)	c Donald b Kallis	20	39	1	1
M.E. Waugh	c Boucher b Pollock	0	4	0	0
R.T. Ponting	c Kirsten b Donald	37	48	3	1
D.S. Lehmann	c Boucher b Donald	1	4	0	0
S.R. Waugh (c)	c Boucher b Pollock	56	76	6	1
M.G. Bevan	c Boucher b Pollock	65	101	6	0
T.M. Moody	lbw b Pollock	0	3	0	0
S.K. Warne	c Cronje b Pollock	18	24	1	0
P.R. Reiffel	b Donald	0	1	0	0
D.W. Fleming	b Donald	0	2	0	0
G.D. McGrath	not out	0	1	0	0
Extras	(b 1, lb 6, w 3, nb 6)	16			
Total	**All out**	**213**			
	49.2 overs at 4.32 rpo				

FoW				
1–3	M.E. Waugh	2–54	Ponting
3–58	Lehmann	4–68	Gilchrist
5–158	S.R. Waugh	6–158	Moody
7–207	Warne	8–207	Reiffel
9–207	Fleming	10–213	Bevan

Bowling	O	M	R	W
S.M. Pollock	9.2	1	36	5
S. Elworthy	10	0	59	0
J.H. Kallis	10	2	27	1
A.A. Donald	10	1	32	4
L. Klusener	9	1	50	0
W.J. Cronje	1	0	2	0

South Africa		R	BF	4	6
G. Kirsten	b Warne	18	42	1	0
H.H. Gibbs	b Warne	30	36	6	0
D.J. Cullinan	run out	6	30	0	0
W.J. Cronje (c)	c M.E. Waugh b Warne	0	2	0	0
J.H. Kallis	c S.R. Waugh b Warne	53	92	3	0
J.N. Rhodes	c Bevan b Reiffel	43	55	2	1
S.M. Pollock	b Fleming	20	14	1	1
L. Klusener	not out	31	16	4	1
M.V. Boucher (k)	b McGrath	5	10	0	0
S. Elworthy	run out	1	1	0	0
A.A. Donald	run out	0	0	0	0
Extras	(lb 1, w 5)	6			
Total	**All out**	**213**			
	49.4 overs at 4.29 rpo				

FoW

1–48	Gibbs	2–53	Kirsten
3–53	Cronje	4–61	Cullinan
5–145	Rhodes	6–175	Kallis
7–183	Pollock	8–196	Boucher
9–198	Elworthy	10–213	Donald

Bowling	O	M	R	W
G.D. McGrath	10	0	51	1
D.W. Fleming	8.4	1	40	1
P.R. Reiffel	8	0	28	1
S.K. Warne	10	4	29	4
M.E. Waugh	8	0	37	0
T.M. Moody	5	0	27	0

14

END OF THE WAUGH

By the end of that astonishing year of 1999, Steve Waugh had established himself as an outstanding batsman and as a successful captain. A World Cup had been won, the West Indies had been thwarted and England had been forced into a period of self-examination. Fearing that his side might rest on its laurels, and appreciating the need for constant challenges, Waugh sought ways of reinvigorating his players. It was not just their games that had to be stimulated; their minds, too, required attention. He had seen the West Indians fall into decline as they had started to celebrate themselves as opposed to Caribbean cricket. Laziness is the death of any sporting team.

Waugh recognised the need to excite his men. As a thinker he has something in common with Sherlock Holmes, who set out to eliminate everything false on the grounds that whatever remained, however improbable, was the truth. Approaching the problem from an unusual angle, Waugh decided to surprise his team by inviting them to think and create. As a rule, dressing-room conversations remain on a safe and superficial level. Not wanting to appear vulnerable before their peers, players make jokes, tease each other and try to fit in. Later it is the banter that they miss most, the mutual teasing that indicates acceptance. Many men yearn for the security provided by groups.

Having won a World Cup, and eager to till his own ground, Waugh found the confidence to pursue his ideas. On overseas tours, players found themselves obliged to give talks to their team-mates about their own enthusiasms and also aspects of Australian life and cricketing history. At such times men reveal themselves, intentionally or otherwise. By opening up, they became better understood by their comrades and perhaps even themselves. History provides context and meaning. Interests convey and explain character. Understanding builds tolerance.

By asking players to make such presentations, Waugh took a considerable risk. He could have been laughed out of court. Doubtless his record helped. Cricketers admired him and wanted to copy him, yet the inscrutable figure had not given much away. As captain he opened the door to his mind. Clearly he was also confronting himself, and the persona that he knew was a limitation even as it proved a success. Not that he regarded his way as definitive. After a Test match in Delhi, he talked in depth to Greg Baum, whose subsequent article was fascinating. After describing his preparation and mental state throughout his innings, he said that he'd like to read similar pieces about other batsmen, whose approaches might be different but no worse for that.

Waugh's reward for showing his hand was a team in which relationships moved beyond the superficial. It was not all behind closed doors. Australian achievers from many fields were invited into the rooms to address the players. It was not so much a matter of raising players' spirits as seeking inspiration. Waugh knew that success entailed sacrifice and believed the point could best be conveyed by outsiders. Convinced that the struggle was an end in itself because it pushed a man to his limits, daring him to care and to commit, he especially enjoyed reading *Life is So Good*, Richard Glaubman's book about George Dawson, an African-American who learned to read at 98, and admired Ernest Shackleton, the great explorer who left his ice-bound ship and his men and went in search of rescue. They knew he'd come back to save them. Waugh wanted to be Shackleton. He could not see why cricketers should seek examples only from within their own ranks.

Obviously cynics would not accept Waugh's ideas and so, as opportunity arose, he brought into the side men capable of responding to his style of leadership. He put them alongside proven champions, thereby forging a formidable outfit. Naturally he wanted under his stewardship the players who had most to offer, those with a mental toughness and ambition to match his own. Unable to rely on his inheritance, he had to build his own side. The World Cup had been a close shave. He did not want to walk down that path any more. There were new worlds to conquer.

Waugh's support for Justin Langer and Matthew Hayden counts among the most significant achievements of his captaincy. It also gave him a core of colleagues answerable only to him. Neither might have been given another chance had another candidate been appointed. Mark Taylor had not thought much of Hayden, and some of the selectors shared his reservations. The Queenslander was regarded as too slow, both of foot and wit, to succeed in the Test arena. Although he could plunder State attacks on predictable Australian pitches, he lacked the wherewithal needed to meet the multifarious challenges of international cricket. Or so it was long contended. Hayden himself tended to prove the point when chances were offered. His early career was a self-fulfilling prophecy.

Langer was dismissed as an earnest but limited batsman. Courage and determination could only take a man so far, or so the argument ran. Sooner or later the player was bound to be found wanting. It was a viewpoint that was not lightly cast aside. Indeed, long after his second coming had proved effective it could be heard still in distinguished circles. Nor did the sight of the West Australian repeatedly carting the bowling around from the first ball of the first over affect his casting as a 'blocker'. Every innings was described as 'nuggety'. As it turned out, though, the nuggets were pure gold. Langer would be dismissed as one of Waugh's 'boys'—one England captain dismissing him as a 'teacher's pet'—yet his record speaks for itself.

Perhaps Waugh saw a little of himself in both men. It would not be such a bad criterion. Manifestly he thought they deserved another chance. Accordingly he supported Hayden's selection, first for a home series against the West Indies and afterwards for a tour of India. Considering the banana-bender's reputed incompetence against spin, it was an audacious move. Moreover modern teams travel without strength in reserve. Hayden would have to play.

Over the next five years, the Queenslander turned himself into one of the most destructive batsmen the game has known. Clearly his swagger was skin deep. Supported, he flourishes. Doubted, he retreats. Waugh's unstinting support released the powerful opener like a dog from a cage. His feet started to move and the runs started to flow. Not until Ricky Ponting fought to retain him for the Oval Test in 2005 would he play remotely as well under the new captain. Once Ponting showed his faith, though, Hayden surged again.

Once Hayden felt comfortable, he was formidable. He intimidated bowlers, threatening them with booming drives, forcing them to withdraw their length and with it much of their threat. That is not to say that shorter deliveries troubled him. As much as the straight drive, the pull was the key to his game. Indeed it is the most distinctive feature of Australian batting. Over the past 25 years, there have not been many visiting batsmen who have pulled as well as their Australian counterparts—Michael Vaughan, David Gower, Martin Crowe, Viv Richards and Richie Richardson are the only ones that come to mind. Doug Walters, Ian Chappell, Ricky Ponting and Matthew Elliott are particularly expert exponents of a shot that, more than any other, allows batsmen to dictate terms. Steve Waugh always refused to attempt the stroke, reasoning that it was risky and that runs could be collected quickly enough without it. It was a refusal that denied him the mastery expected from strong Australian batsmen and the acclaim of those who value domination over efficiency.

Some players fell away under Waugh, most notably Michael Slater, an attacking player whose brain had become feverish. Slater's problem's came to a head on the 2001 tour of England. Throughout the series he was hopping around at the crease. Nor were his manoeuvres the preparations of a batsman eager to move into line and also to delay his commitment to going forwards or back. Instead he darted around in an agitated and unpredictable manner that indicated his state of mind better than any words.

Many batsmen feel they cannot stand still as the ball is released yet realise that no final decision can be made until the length and direction of the ball have been determined. Accordingly they make a precisely timed and repeated movement of their own choosing. Some batsmen step slightly forward, others step back and marginally across. In both cases the weight is not finally committed so that the batsman can move again. In truth it is more of a rock than a step, a means of starting the response. Provided the batsman does not lose his bearings the movement is not damaging. Mark Waugh's last slide was put down to slowing reactions and a loss of motivation, yet his preparatory movements also deteriorated as his feet began pointing towards mid-off as opposed to cover point, thereby opening his chest and leaving him vulnerable. Especially when it is unconscious, turning the back foot to the wrong angle renders almost impossible the correct execution of strokes of any sort. By and large Australian batsmen have preferred to stand still till the ball is well on its way.

Slater lost his place in the team for the last match of a forgettable and predictable 2001 Ashes tour. He had been dropped before, not least after an especially rash stroke in the first over of the 2nd innings of the Delhi Test match of 1996. Now Langer replaced Slater at The Oval and scored a hundred. For several years thereafter the new pair would bat productively together, forming one of the most effective partnerships the game has known. Much to Kerry O'Keeffe's amusement, they charged down the wicket to hug each other as another milestone was reached.

In retrospect, that Oval Test of 2001 had far-reaching consequences for the careers of several players, and not only those at the top of the batting order. Australia had comfortably retained the Ashes so it ought to have been a match of little significance. By its end, though, not only the new Australian opening partnership had been settled. Steve Waugh's position had been irrevocably weakened by a stubborn, widely admired decision that took a heavy toll upon his body and would have a profound effect upon his career.

Waugh was not fit to play at The Oval. He ought not to have taken part. Raised by Border, who played with broken bones, realising that he could not ask for a runner but determined to evoke the attitude needed to win dead rubbers, Waugh decided to play on one leg. Hobbling up and down the pitch, cracking boundaries, protecting himself in the field and avoiding quick singles, he nursed himself through the five days. Oh yes, and he scored 157.

At the time Waugh's performance was regarded as a statement of Australian durability. In retrospect it was a foolish mistake. Inevitably Waugh's injury worsened during his long innings and the hours spent in the field. By the end of the Test he could hardly walk, let alone sprint. His preparations for the ensuing home series against New Zealand were, not surprisingly, affected.

Although his century provoked admiration, Waugh was never quite the same again. Intended as an expression of defiance, his innings marked the beginning of the end of his captaincy. In some respects he was unlucky. Had New Zealand arrived down under a few weeks later with a weak captain and not much of a plan, his poor condition might not have been noticed. Instead the Kiwis arrived as a hardened team with their wits about them. The Australians were tired, with a wounded and distracted leader. Despite the limitations of his attack, sensing vulnerability, and exploiting it with debonair skill, Stephen Fleming was able to alarm his counterpart.

Both Waughs had poor series against New Zealand. Fleming's field placements were a talking point. Capitalising on weakness, and applying his strategy without any hint of compromise, the visiting captain was able to disconcert the Australian middle order, and especially his counterpart. He seemed to relish the chance to be the aggressor, attacking the twins' back-foot games, defying them to respond. Crucially, Fleming carried his side along with him in his unrelenting attempt to prick the Australian balloon. Some of them had been waiting years for such an opportunity.

Guided by intelligence, driven by the numerous frustrations accumulated in a life spent in the shadows of a noisome neighbour and with the confidence of a settled and underestimated side, the New Zealanders were a handful. Had a clear catch behind the wicket been given out on the final afternoon in Perth, they might have taken the spoils. Instead Steve Waugh was spared and they had to settle for three draws in a rain-ruined series. Australian umpiring had long been a bone of contention, and the situation was not improved by Daryl Harper's failure to dispatch Justin Langer when he was plumb leg before in the first over of the campaign.

As it turned out the Kiwis' main weak point was not so much the umpiring, in which area their own fellows were not beyond criticism, as their inability to break their opponents' opening partnership.

Everything else had been worked out. In an attempt to upset his usual line of attack, Fleming and his men had developed a strategy of leaving alone as many of Glenn McGrath's deliveries as possible. Although the paceman garnered a couple of wickets as the batsmen shouldered arms, the ploy was seen to work. Although it seemed negative, the plan was the result of constructive analysis. Fleming was playing the Australians on his own terms, an approach the English would follow with even more success in 2005.

Doubtless the Kiwis enjoyed this sight of a feared middle order reduced to a state of anxiety. It wasn't just the twins. Damien Martyn was confronted with a teasing field including several men placed at point and gully. In his own, understated way Fleming was taunting his hosts, and they did not like it. Moreover the visiting bowlers carried out the plan better than anyone could have anticipated. In many respects it was the funniest Test series staged on Australian soil since the Whitlam era.

Neither Waugh met the challenge. Suddenly both were starting to show their age. They looked heavy-footed. Mark's subsequent failures against an otherwise pathetic Pakistani side sealed his fate. Fortune deserted him in his final campaign as Shoaib Akhtar roused himself sufficiently to hurl him out in Colombo, where the first match was played for security reasons (previously Australia had avoided the place on the same grounds). Shoaib has extraordinarily flexible joints, and is allowed to fling the ball under revised legislation. His ferocious reverse-swinging yorkers also caused the umpires to scrutinise the ball. Not that they admitted as much at the time.

Despite his sluggish form against New Zealand, Steve Waugh survived a little longer. Before long, he would lose his place in the one-day side. A few months later his place in the Test side would be in jeopardy, and it would take that famous innings against England in Sydney to save him. Twelve months later he would be saying his goodbyes with another resilient contribution at the SCG, this time against India. Between times he was forced to rest his body as much as he could.

Hitherto Waugh had paced himself extremely well. He was a crafty fellow. In his last few seasons, the Australians stopped practising as hard, curtailing fielding drills and spending less time warming up on the morning of a match. Typically Waugh turned the situation to advantage by pointing out that his players needed to rest and that strong teams could ignore fashion. Previous generations had not stretched or played soccer on the field.

Waugh played against Pakistan in Colombo and Sharjah and struggled against Shoaib, but he managed a hundred in the final match of a hot and miserable series, a landmark reached with some sudden sixes. Once again 'old Stone-face' had summoned from somewhere exactly the right innings at exactly the right time. Not that the Pakistanis offered much opposition. Indeed their performances count among the most lamentable seen on any cricket field. One match ended in two days.

Waugh led Australia in the Ashes campaign of 2002/03 and acquitted himself pretty well. He knew that the selectors were ready to replace him. By now dropped from the one-day side, it became a matter of record that Waugh had been promised nothing beyond the Ashes series. Sydney rallied to his cause, his devotees furiously arguing his case on talkback radio and on the front pages of local newspapers. Outsiders could be forgiven for regarding it as a closing of the ranks. In fact Waugh was a national figure who had been supported through numerous struggles and whose triumphs over adversity had attracted the hearts and minds of many supporters.

Nasser Hussain's ill-advised decision to bowl first in the opening Test played at The Gabba helped Waugh to lead his side to another comfortable victory over their traditional enemy. By the time the teams reached Melbourne for the Boxing Day Test, the result of the series had been decided. Even so, it was a crucial match for a captain uncertain about his future.

Waugh batted well in the first innings at the MCG and even his more strident critics began to admit there were still signs of life in the old dog. The odds had begun to swing in favour of his retaining his post should he decide to continue playing. Waugh's second effort was another matter. Australia needed to score only a few dozen runs to win the match. For the first time in the tour, Steve Harmison found his full measure of pace and bounce. He made Waugh look foolish as he parried, edged and ducked before losing his wicket cheaply to

Caddick. Convinced that slowing reflexes and loss of nerve had cost Waugh his wicket, reporters started writing their obituaries. Waugh explained that he had been suffering from a migraine and had almost turned back on his way to the wicket. After years of uncomplaining service, he deserved the benefit of the doubt.

Nevertheless Waugh arrived for the last match of the series, in his Sydney stronghold, with plenty on his mind. England batted competently on a firm pitch and Waugh's turn at the crease did not come till the middle of the second afternoon whereupon he marched out in his Charlie Chaplin way to find his team in trouble at 3/56. It was a throwback to his early experiences in the Australian side. Over the last few years Waugh's defiance had become almost a liability.

As far as reporters were concerned he could not have come to the wicket at a worse time. Friday afternoons are tricky because the next day's papers are so thick that the printers start rolling hours earlier than usual. Provided Waugh fell cheaply or scored a quick 30 or else was unbeaten on 60 or so it might not matter. Unfortunately his intentions were otherwise. As usual his red handkerchief was in his pocket, a lucky charm that had become an emblem. Cricketers' superstitions are extraordinary. Every toilet seat in the dressing-rooms must be down before Neil McKenzie can hope to score runs. Adam Gilchrist always puts his right foot on the field first as he makes his way to the wicket.

Waugh started smoothly on a dry pitch and for the rest of the day found a command that had hitherto proved elusive. Characteristically effective clips off the pads—the Waughs seldom missed chances to score through the leg-side—mingled with drives through the covers played off either foot. Wickets had been falling and as day headed towards evening he was joined by Gilchrist, an unselfish colleague and his vice-captain to boot. He could not have hoped for a more encouraging partner.

Waugh moved past 50 and the 6 p.m. deadline was fast approaching. At least the story was clear. 'Defiant Waugh', and so on, and so forth. Everyone set about constructing a piece that could cover most bases. No one thought the blighter might reach three figures. Then some Jonah pointed out that play was bound to continue till 6.45. From the crowd's perspective, this was wonderful news. Television and radio were also pleased. Cricket writers and sports editors were appalled. Waugh had always been inclined to catch the moment. And this was some moment.

History relates that Waugh completed his hundred off the last ball of the day, an attempted yorker sent down by Richard Dawson, a young off-spinner who had studied at Exeter University. Kerry O'Keeffe and Jonathan Agnew caught the moment perfectly on ABC Radio. None of the journalists had seen much of that overwhelming last hour. Right at the end we saw the back-foot drive, heard the tumult and watched as Waugh was paraded around the ground. Many spectators were in tears and even politicians were moved. Somehow Waugh had once again risen above himself. Had he been swept along by a tide of emotion, as the romantics claimed? Or had he been solely intent on proving his point to sceptical selectors? Had it been a bit of both?

Two hours later, cricket writers packed their bags and went home, hoping that their descriptions of an event they had barely seen would satisfy readers of the morning papers. Waugh left at about the same time. The dressing-room had been in turmoil. Everyone knew that they had seen an extraordinary performance from an extraordinary man. The next day Waugh was dismissed in the second over and England won the match. None of it seemed to matter. People had found in their champion a quality they wanted to uncover in themselves.

After keeping the selectors waiting for a considerable time, Waugh decided to keep playing. A quiet spell followed as Waugh prepared for a home series with an Indian side determined to retain the Border/Gavaskar Trophy. Before the series began, Waugh announced his intention to step aside at its completion. Everyone had assumed he'd try to keep playing till the tour of India in 2004, where he had unfinished business.

As usual, opinion was divided about Waugh's motivation for announcing his retirement months before the event. Cynics dismissed it as an attempt to turn a tough series into a farewell tour. Sympathisers said it reflected Waugh's desire to stop the speculation so that everyone could concentrate on the cricket. In the event, Waugh's announcement would prove a distraction and the home captain and his team would lack their usual composure throughout the series. It did not help that newspapers encouraged fans to wave red handkerchiefs whenever their hero appeared on the ground.

Waugh's attempt to leave gracefully was not helped by his running out of Damien Martyn in the first Test in Brisbane. Waugh simply ran past his partner after a mix-up had left both exposed. Inconvenient figures were published showing that while the Australian captain had been involved in numerous run-outs, he had seldom been the victim. Soon afterwards, rain stopped play for the day, which meant that there was precious little else to write about. Waugh was taken to task and he responded angrily. Much to the bemusement and, later, amusement of seasoned reporters, he was still raising the matter several days later. Some thought he protested too much. Meanwhile Sourav Ganguly saved his side with an outstanding innings.

Thankfully the rest of the series was memorable for different reasons, as Virender Sehwag and Rahul Dravid served their team superbly, a cavalier and a roundhead working in impressive harmony. After the draw in Brisbane, India secured an unexpected and inspired victory in Adelaide as Ajit Agarkar's outswingers undid batsmen committed to attack. Swing has always troubled batsmen intent upon immediate destruction of the ball.

Despite Sehwag's brilliant contribution on Boxing Day and more staunch resistance from Dravid, India was well beaten at the MCG and the sides arrived in Sydney for Waugh's last stand with the series all square. Since India held the trophy, the Australians had to win.

In truth, it was not much of a match. The pitch was slow and hardly changed during the course of five somewhat grumpy days. Exhaustion, emotional as much as physical, was widespread. Brett Lee lost his run-up and was forced to bowl several feet behind the popping crease. Tendulkar eschewed risk, cut out his off-side strokes and scored a double century. Ganguly's side batted interminably and then did not enforce the follow-on. India set an apparently impossible target of 705 and the last few hours were spent in the company of Stephen Rodger Waugh as he successfully parried his opponents' every thrust. Ganguly held back in the manner of a man daunted by his opposite number and fearful that he might any moment launch the sort of withering counterattack that had been his signature. Frozen into inactivity, Ganguly neither crowded the bat nor changed his bowlers around. Perhaps he, too, was weary. Momentous cricket series used to be spread over several months. Now they are completed in a few weeks.

Waugh may, indeed, have contemplated a last dash for victory. Or he may have been bluffing, fooling his counterpart into defending. It was always hard to tell his intentions. In the event he settled for a sudden, unsatisfactory rush for three figures, a charge regarded by some as self-indulgent and praised by others as an attempt to entertain a disappointed crowd. This time the sceptics had a case. Or perhaps, for the first time in his career, Waugh really did not care what anyone thought or wrote.

Eventually Waugh was held on the boundary, whereupon he stalked from the field, half little boy embarrassed by all the fuss, half retiring champion acknowledging his faithful supporters. The Waugh era was over.

What had it meant, the depth of the feeling in the SCG as Waugh scored his hundred against England and 12 months later bade farewell? Why had so many people become so attached to this enigmatic, unyielding figure? Was it his triumphs over adversity? Or the sense that he was an outsider asking no quarter, giving no quarter? Was he not the eternal, silent, uncomplaining warrior? Was it simply that he had been a fine servant? Was it nationalism? Australia likes to win and wants to be admired, and through Waugh, Australian cricket had achieved both. Has any other cricketer been on the winning side so often? Waugh had reached over the heads of players and critics alike and into the hearts and minds of followers of the game. And his appeal had been international. Other sportsmen might bring magic into the lives of their supporters. Waugh brought more human qualities, strengths that seemed to be within our own grasp.

AUSTRALIA V ENGLAND, FIFTH ASHES TEST
2–6 JANUARY 2003, SYDNEY CRICKET GROUND, NEW SOUTH WALES

Toss: England
Result: England won by 225 runs
Man of the match: M.P. Vaughan

England (1st Innings)		R	BF	4	6
M.E. Trescothick	c Gilchrist b Bichel	19	40	2	0
M.P. Vaughan	c Gilchrist b Lee	0	7	0	0
M.A. Butcher	b Lee	124	276	19	0
N. Hussain (c)	c Gilchrist b Gillespie	75	149	8	0
R.W.T. Key	lbw b Waugh	3	27	0	0
J.P. Crawley	not out	35	142	3	0
A.J. Stewart (k)	b Bichel	71	86	15	0
R.K.J. Dawson	c Gilchrist b Bichel	2	9	0	0
A.R. Caddick	b MacGill	7	29	0	0
M.J. Hoggard	st Gilchrist b MacGill	0	5	0	0
S.J. Harmison	run out (Langer/MacGill)	4	4	1	0
Extras	(b 6, lb 3, nb 13)	22			
Total	**All out**	**362**			
	127.0 overs at 2.85 rpo				

FoW

1–4	Vaughan	2–32	Trescothick
3–198	Hussain	4–210	Key
5–240	Butcher	6–332	Stewart
7–337	Dawson	8–348	Caddick
9–350	Hoggard	10–357	Harmison

Bowling	O	M	R	W
J.N. Gillespie	27	10	62	1
B. Lee	31	9	97	2
A.J. Bichel	21	5	86	3
S.C.G. MacGill	44	8	106	2
S.R. Waugh	4	3	2	1

Australia (1st Innings)		R	BF	4	6
J.L. Langer	c Hoggard b Caddick	25	44	3	0
M.L. Hayden	lbw b Caddick	15	11	2	0
R.T. Ponting	c Stewart b Caddick	7	6	1	0
D.R. Martyn	c Caddick b Harmison	26	71	4	0
S.R. Waugh (c)	c Butcher b Hoggard	102	135	18	0
M.L. Love	c Trescothick b Harmison	0	6	0	0
A.C. Gilchrist (k)	c Stewart b Harmison	133	121	18	0
A.J. Bichel	c Crawley b Hoggard	4	9	0	0
B. Lee	c Stewart b Hoggard	0	1	0	0
J.N. Gillespie	not out	31	83	2	1
S.C.G. MacGill	c Hussain b Hoggard	1	5	0	0
Extras	(b 2, lb 6, w 2, nb 9)	19			
Total	**All out**	**363**			
	80.3 overs at 4.51 rpo				

FoW				
	1–36	Hayden	2–45	Ponting
	3–56	Langer	4–146	Martyn
	5–150	Love	6–241	Waugh
	7–267	Bichel	8–267	Lee
	9–349	Gilchrist	10–363	MacGill

Bowling	O	M	R	W
M.J. Hoggard	21.3	4	92	4
A.R. Caddick	23	3	121	3
S.J. Harmison	20	4	70	3
R.K.J. Dawson	16	0	72	0

England (2nd Innings)		R	BF	4	6
M.E. Trescothick	b Lee	22	21	4	0
M.P. Vaughan	lbw b Bichel	183	278	27	1
M.A. Butcher	c Hayden b MacGill	34	66	4	0
N. Hussain (c)	c Gilchrist b Lee	72	181	9	0
R.W.T. Key	c Hayden b Lee	14	26	1	0
J.P. Crawley	lbw b Gillespie	8	15	1	0
A.J. Stewart (k)	not out	38	82	3	0
R.K.J. Dawson	c & b Bichel	12	35	1	0
A.R. Caddick	c Langer b MacGill	8	26	1	0
M.J. Hoggard	b MacGill	0	10	0	0
S.J. Harmison	not out	20	23	4	0
Extras	(b 9, lb 20, w 2, nb 10)	41			
Total	**9 wickets declared**	**452**			
	125.3 overs at 3.60 rpo				

FoW					
1–37	Trescothick	2–124	Butcher		
3–313	Hussain	4–344	Key		
5–345	Vaughan	6–356	Crawley		
7–378	Dawson	8–407	Caddick		
9–409	Hoggard				

Bowling	O	M	R	W
J.N. Gillespie	18.3	4	70	1
B. Lee	31.3	5	132	3
S.C.G. MacGill	41	8	120	3
A.J. Bichel	25.3	3	82	2
D.R. Martyn	3	1	14	0
S.R. Waugh	6	2	5	0

Australia (2nd Innings)		R	BF	4	6
J.L. Langer	lbw b Caddick	3	8	0	0
M.L. Hayden	lbw b Hoggard	2	6	0	0
A.J. Bichel	lbw b Caddick	49	58	8	0
R.T. Ponting	lbw b Caddick	11	16	2	0
D.R. Martyn	c Stewart b Dawson	21	79	2	0
S.R. Waugh (c)	b Caddick	6	11	1	0
M.L. Love	b Harmison	27	50	3	0
A.C. Gilchrist (k)	c Butcher b Caddick	37	29	7	0
B. Lee	c Stewart b Caddick	46	32	9	1
J.N. Gillespie	not out	3	36	0	0
S.C.G. MacGill	b Caddick	1	2	0	0
Extras	(b 6, lb 8, w 3, nb 3)	20			
Total	**All out**	**226**			
	54.0 overs at 4.19 rpo				

FoW					
1–5	Langer	2–5	Hayden		
3–25	Ponting	4–93	Bichel		
5–99	Waugh	6–109	Martyn		
7–139	Love	8–181	Gilchrist		
9–224	Lee	10–226	MacGill		

Bowling	O	M	R	W
M.J. Hoggard	13	3	35	1
A.R. Caddick	22	5	94	7
S.J. Harmison	9	1	42	1
R.K.J. Dawson	10	2	41	1

15

PUNTER TAKES CHARGE

Ricky Ponting took the Australian side to the 8th World Cup, played in Africa as autumn descended upon the continent in March 2003. Since it was Africa's first opportunity to stage a large cricketing tournament and thereby confirm its democratic capabilities, the preparations were completed months in advance and down to the last detail. A huge contingent of volunteers was collected, especially in South Africa, mostly black men and women determined to show their newly liberated country in the best possible light.

Ali Bacher was responsible for organisational matters. A controversial figure with hands in many pies, he was a former captain of his country and an intimate of Joe Pamensky, one of whose companies had provoked the interest of corporate investigators even as it caused distress among its investors. Bacher had many enemies and just as many admirers. Hansie Cronje had been one of his most severe critics, an attitude founded upon a suspicion of his former boss's alleged opportunism. Seldom has a kettle been called black by such a pot!

Regardless of their views of his curious mixture of Machiavelli and morality, everyone agreed that Bacher was a superb administrator.

And so it proved. The matches played in South Africa could not have flowed more smoothly along. It was hardly Bacher's fault that the competition was spoilt by the refusal of two western nations to play matches in Zimbabwe and Kenya.

New Zealand's reluctance to visit Nairobi was founded upon painful memories of the carnage witnessed outside team hotels in other parts of the world. Stephen Fleming's side, and its predecessors, had been dogged by bad luck. Terrorist bombs had exploded outside their hotels in Sri Lanka and Pakistan, and tours had been abandoned. That none of the violence had been directed at them was of little consequence.

When the players received official warnings about security in the Kenyan capital they took them seriously. Nightmares were awoken. Some of the players wanted to play the match, others were anxious to withdraw. Fleming knew that, for the first time, he had a team capable of lifting the trophy. Withdrawing would imperil their position, especially in the unlikely event of their hosts reaching the second round. The team considered flying in and out of the country on the day of the match, but eventually a vote was taken. Going to Kenya was not unanimously supported so the Kiwis conceded the match.

Amid such celebrations as a soccer-mad country could muster, Kenya promptly beat Sri Lanka and reached the semi-finals. It was a farcical situation. Notwithstanding the trauma of past events, New Zealand should have played the match. It is hard to believe that the security men were not being unduly cautious.

England wanted to boycott their fixture in Harare, but without losing the points. The wriggling and wrangling they undertook in their attempt to justify their position removed any remaining vestige of credibility. England had played an important part in negotiating the Lancaster Gate Agreement that established the newly independent country's constitution and the Foreign Office, represented by Peter Carrington and Lord Soames, had helped Mugabe to secure a majority in the first free election by turning a blind eye to his tactics. Nor had the English made a fuss when Mugabe sent his North Korean trained troops to subdue supposedly hostile elements in Matabeleland, a task they accomplished by the simple method of mass murder.

Having accepted the invitation to participate in the World Cup, England had manoeuvred itself into an untenable position. Worse, the players were being advised by posturing dimwits. Officials tried to find a solution that would allow them to keep their points and not cost them any money by way of penalty, conduct that sat ill with their protestations of principle. At first they insisted that they were withdrawing for security reasons. Anticipating conflicts of interest and opinion between nations, the ICC had taken the precaution of listing the exceptional circumstances under which a team may legitimately withdraw from an official commitment, and security was among them.

England could not prove that its conduct fulfilled one of the established criteria. Obviously the security issue was a furphy. As far as visitors were concerned, Zimbabwe was safe. Apart from anything else, the terrorists were running the country. Eventually the English realised another excuse was needed. Officials argued that the Zimbabwean regime was so despicable that a boycott was not merely legitimate, but morally mandatory. Unfortunately they could not persuade their own government to agree to this.

In reply, the ICC and other countries pointed out that nothing much had changed since the competing nations had agreed to take part in the tournament. They could have added that hypocrisy is rife in the matter of sporting boycotts. No such remedy had been proposed after the Ndebele and Tamil massacres of the 1980s. Nor were any of the newly indignant opposed to sporting contact with the repressive regimes ruling China, Burma and several African countries. Zimbabwe had a horrible government, but not the worst on the continent. Meanwhile the British prime minister was shaking hands with Colonel Gaddafi.

Unable to convince other countries about the legitimacy of their grievance, the English turned their guns on the ICC, painting it in such a poor light that the game's ruling body promptly decided to decamp to Dubai. The ICC is not a vast and malevolent bureaucracy but a small administration serving the game and answerable to a Board consisting of the leading cricketing nations. Moreover the magnitude of its task needs to be understood. Cricket is the most unruly of games. Ten nations play Test match cricket. Two of them have been at loggerheads for 50 years. Two have suffered massacres ignored by the rest of the world, the victims being Ndebele and Tamil. One has been bankrupted by a wicked Stalinist, another is ruled by a military dictator. One is emerging from centuries of racist rule, another lives on the breadline. Two have been fighting in Iraq. Another thinks mostly about rugby. The West Indies does not even exist.

Nor are the complexities restricted to nations. Within cricket's small family can be found Hindus, Muslims, Buddhists, Christians and statisticians. Like Joseph's coat, players come in many colours. Yet for decades cricket was predominantly a white man's game. Until 1960, a black man could not captain the West Indies. Until 1991, a black man could not play for South Africa. Until recently, both Lord's and the BBC were infected with men who had made money under apartheid. While English paternalists were running the game, these differences did not matter but now, thankfully, the old power had been ditched. The ICC reflects its component parts.

Isolated, England boycotted its meeting with Zimbabwe and sacrificed the points at stake. Supporters bleated impotently but Zimbabwe and Kenya progressed to the latter stages of a compromised competition.

Meanwhile Ponting and company had problems of their own to confront. Australia's first match was against Pakistan at The New Wanderers Stadium in Johannesburg. No sooner had journalists reported for duty than news arrived that Australian officials had called an emergency press conference at the team hotel. Rumours started spreading and Shane Warne's name was mentioned. At that moment, the rest of the team arrived at the ground.

At the appointed breakfast hour, Warne appeared alongside a grim-faced James Sutherland, Australian cricket's young CEO. By now reporters had gleaned that a routine drugs test had found a banned substance in the leg-spinner's sample. The news was explosive. Sutherland explained that Warne intended to read a statement and no questions were to be allowed. Warne admitted that he had taken an illegal substance, expressed his regrets about letting the side down, and informed a stunned audience that he was flying home and would take no further part in the tournament.

Warne's downfall had its origins in a shoulder injury incurred as he dived to intercept a straight drive while bowling in a one-day match. Desperate to play in the World Cup, he had been dismayed to hear that his chances of recovering in time were slim. The rest must be the merest conjecture. Somehow Warne's conduct is always open to varying interpretations, generous and harsh. The detected substance can assist sportsmen in two ways. It is a diuretic, helping them to reduce weight. Warne is insecure and vain. Prone to burliness owing to a professed fondness for pizzas and other calorie-laden repasts, he wanted to improve his shape, not least to help his bowling. In recent weeks he had been looking trim and fit. Warne never eats healthy food. He eats burgers and so forth, or starves.

Unfortunately the substance can also be used to screen the presence of steroids calculated to build strength and hasten recovery. During the inevitable and hysterical inquest into his behaviour, Warne protested that his mother had given him a pill to help him to control his weight while he wasn't playing. Later it emerged that two different pills had been taken, a revelation that did little to improve the Victorian's reputation as a reliable witness. Cynics remained convinced that he had been taking steroids in an attempt to recover in time for the World Cup. A doctor who was staying at my house, Dr Nothling, grandson of Otto, Bradman's replacement in 1928/29, contended that Warne's recovery had not been unusually swift.

Eventually, Warne was suspended for a year, a sentence regarded as mild in many quarters. Australian cricketers are regularly informed about the contents of the banned list, and are well aware of the consequences of being caught with a prohibited substance in their bloodstream. The suggestion that a vastly experienced international sportsman might take an unknown pill, not once but twice, seemed far-fetched. Critics could be forgiven for thinking that Warne had gambled and lost.

Back at The Wanderers, the Australians had fought back strongly from a poor start. Pakistan was an overrated side full of famous players whose best days were behind them. A sporting field is an examination room on which a player is constantly reminded that he is only as good as his last performance. Waqar Younis and Wasim Akram should have been replaced but a young country craves heroes, besides which the allegiances that affect Pakistani cricket do not always tolerate progressive thought. Only the Australian Labor Party is worse affected by factions.

Andrew Symonds chose a fine moment to produce the innings of his life. A curious player whose game can be raw, impassioned, versatile, powerful, inspired and alarmingly rough, Symonds had reputedly been enraged by Warne's untimely departure and took it out on the Pakistani bowling. Clubbing the ball with controlled fury, he scored a stirring century that took his team to a total beyond the range of a compromised opponent. Symonds had been the man chosen to replace Steve Waugh. Not for the first or last time, the selectors' judgement had been vindicated.

Australia continued to play forceful cricket until they met England in the coastal town of Port Elizabeth. Hitherto Brett Lee had been the bowler of the tournament. His ability to swing the new ball at high pace and then return to disrupt the middle of the innings with a second burst had been invaluable. Throughout his career his problem had been his lack of trajectory. A bowler with a high arm can make the ball bounce even from a fullish length. In contrast, Lee tended to skim the surface unless he was pounding down a bumper. This allowed batsmen to drive balls landing short of the half-volley.

Steve Waugh had encouraged Lee to attack. Ponting was less willing to risk losing control of the match and told Lee that economy was part of his remit. Once he became accustomed to his new instructions, Lee responded superbly. When the ball was swinging, he went for wickets confident that the odds were favourable. If a tight spell was required or the ball was refusing to move, he adapted his game. Years later it would take another conversation with Mark Taylor, over a beer in a pub, to turn Lee into a truly formidable force. Finally the penny dropped. It was possible to be aggressive and patient, fast and mean, fiery and disciplined. Throughout the 2005/06 home season, Lee was not merely the best fast bowler in his country. He was the best and fastest bowler anywhere.

Lee only bowled one bad spell in the entire competition, but it came against England in this important match. Trying to win the match in a few overs, he banged the ball down and was repeatedly hooked and cut by the belligerent English openers, Marcus Trescothick and Nick Knight. England galloped along but was checked mid-innings as Andy Bichel and colleagues took the game back to basics.

Chasing a modest target on an awkward surface, the Australians began to go into a decline. Bichel, though, had been waiting a long time for his opportunity and had no intention of going down without a fight. Always a willing bowler, he had developed into a hard-hitting lower-order batsman. He joined Michael Bevan at the crease, with his team down and almost out. Nasser Hussain was the English captain, a tough, stubborn man hard enough to knock a team into shape but lacking the lighter touch needed to take it to glory.

England was not yet used to the idea of beating Australia. In these matters, thought is father to the deed. Hussain sat back, playing the percentages, keeping his patterns. Australia advanced, Bevan pushing the ball into gaps, Bichel thinking and belting. Hussain did not dare to take the gamble that might have brought a wicket. He did not want to risk his advantage on a plunge. His team seemed to be paralysed with a mixture of fear and excitement. Thrown the ball with a few runs needed, James Anderson tried a slower ball and stood transfixed as Bichel clouted it into the stands. The next ball, Andrew Caddick's half-hearted chase after a boundary indicated his state of mind. The critics had been right. England needed a new captain and a more aggressive mentality. Within a year, both would have been put in place.

Australia stormed past Sri Lanka in a semi-final memorable mainly for Adam Gilchrist's decision to walk after his sweep had ended up in his opposite number's gloves. Gilchrist's unexpected gesture provoked widespread debate among commentators and colleagues because it challenged entrenched perceptions. Supporters said he was an honest, uncomplicated country boy trying to meet Bradman's famous challenge to leave the game in a better state than he found it. Sceptics argued that he had a political and corporate agenda. What was certain was that the gloveman had set a standard for himself, a point that was not immediately grasped. His reluctance to appeal when he did not think the batsman was out would become a bone of contention in a side known for its ability to work the umpires as a prime minister works a room.

Despite the early loss of their liveliest batsman, the Australians romped into the final at Johannesburg. There they were to meet an Indian side that had started badly before rallying. An early defeat had led to players' cars and homes being stoned. Rahul Dravid and Sachin

Tendulkar had appealed for calm, saying that the players were trying their hardest. Presented with an easier than expected passage, and at their best against Pakistan as Tendulkar produced one of his most sumptuous innings, India charged into the final.

Alas, the final was an anti-climax. None of the senior Australian batsmen had been batting fluently, a situation that might not last. Given the opportunity to bat on a friendly pitch by an Indian captain misled by the untimely appearance of a few discouraging clouds, the Australians slaughtered a woebegone attack. Ganguly's decision to bowl was timid. Australia can only be beaten by confrontational opponents.

From the moment Matthew Hayden demolished Zaheer Khan's nervous opening over, the outcome was inevitable. Hayden was at his bullying best and the bowlers wilted. Ricky Ponting emerged at the fall of the first wicket to play a scintillating innings and Damien Martyn was even more creative. Chasing a mammoth total, India's hopes did not survive the opening over as Tendulkar first struck a boundary and then lost his wicket seeking another. It was a poor shot and derision was poured on his head, but he had been given an impossible task. It was Ganguly and his bowlers who deserved to be in the dock. India was a beaten side long before the chase began.

Ponting's brilliant innings and his team's triumph gave the young leader the authority he needed to become the fully fledged Test captain of his country. His next major assignment followed hot upon the heels of his predecessor's emotional retirement. Sri Lanka was the destination. Previously about as comfortable on turning subcontinental pitches as a cellist on the drums, Ponting scored heavily and led his side to a hard-earned but solid victory. His players worked hard in muggy heat and retained the sense of purpose detected under Steve Waugh. If anything the side looked fresher. Dressing-rooms containing older players, let alone ageing captains, are seldom the most invigorating places.

Ponting's side beat the Sri Lankans 3/0 and was clearly well placed to win the forthcoming series in India, where the Australians had not won for 35 years. Among his predecessors, Taylor had failed on the subcontinent, and Waugh had fallen short in a thrilling series. Border had come closest, drawing two of the three matches played and tying the first Test of the series, an epic played at Chepauk in Madras that

tends to be forgotten, though not through any fault of my distinguished colleague Coward.

Unfortunately injury prevented Ponting taking the side to India
in the spring of 2004. He was not fit to play till the fourth and last
Test of the campaign. Luck plays its part in sport. Had Ponting been
in charge from the outset he would have emerged with his reputation
enhanced. Instead he was forced to remain in Australia while his
replacement, Gilchrist, and his coach, John Buchanan, went to work.

Between them, the Australian thinktank had developed a plan to
contain the Indian batsmen. Previously V.V.S. Laxman, Virender
Sehwag and Rahul Dravid had been prolific against the Australians.
They had scored quickly and on both sides of the wicket. On his first
tour to India, Warne had been reduced to aiming at off-stump to
a heavily manned off-side field, a strategy that slightly slowed the
scoring and wholly reduced the leg-spinner's menace. The batsmen
had forced him to play the game on their terms. He recognised his
mistake and has never repeated it.

Another tactic was needed. Buchanan argued that the bowlers
ought to keep the ball full and straight, seeking leg befores and clean
bowleds as opposed to outside edges. They'd deny the batsmen
confidence and rhythm by setting strangling fields so they could not
collect boundaries except by taking risks. There would be no opportunity for the Indian batsmen to dominate.

Gillespie and company applied the strategy superbly. High-class
batsmen were held in check. Rather than a bull fight, each Test
became a game of cat and mouse. Of course it helped that the Indians
had their own problems, with Ganguly struggling for form and
Dravid proving that he was human. Not that victory came easily for
the Australians. Australia won the first match but the second hung by
a thread when a deluge interrupted play on the fifth and final day.
India had needed about 200 more runs on a reliable pitch. The uninhibited drives played by Sehwag in the last over of the fourth day had
left the locals confident of squaring the ledger.

Nagpur settled the issue. To the Australians' delight, an especially
independent curator prepared a well-grassed wicket in the City of
Oranges and no amount of urging could make him shave it. Ganguly
was furious and at the last minute withdrew from the match, either
in disgust or after suffering a setback. You pay your money and you

take your choice. Amid much trumpet blowing, Tendulkar had returned from injury to play. It was not much of a pitch for an under-prepared batsman and he had a miserable time. The Australians bowled with controlled hostility and romped to victory as the ball moved about. Not that it was unplayable, but India looked like a beaten side. The Australians celebrated a fine team effort.

Ponting might have been better advised missing the entire series. He had joined the team in time to watch the decisive victory, had seen even the mighty Tendulkar struggle as he hurried back into the fray. He must have felt like an outsider. It does not take long for a team to develop its own ethic, particularly on tour. An exciting young batsman called Michael Clarke had taken the chance to play some breathtaking innings, Lee and Watson were training almost fanatically hard and a rare team spirit had been built. It is not easy for anyone, let alone a young captain, to come in cold.

Also, despite Waugh's best efforts, the Australians still had a way of losing dead rubbers. Waugh had tried to change this habit by the simple device of publicly challenging his players, before a series began, to win every match. But this time, the Australians had thought only about winning the series, a deed that had been done. Ponting had little to gain from taking part. On the other hand, Australian captains don't like missing matches. Border had held the record for most consecutive Tests played, and Taylor and Waugh had followed his example. By their reckoning, a captain belongs on the bridge. Ponting must have been desperate to get back, and to play his part in the achievement.

A gentlemanly former Indian Test cricketer had prepared a dustbowl in Mumbai, and the hosts chose three spinners. Australia had to manage without Warne, whose last-minute injury exposed the folly of leaving behind the country's only other top-class spinner. Two novices, Nathan Hauritz and Cameron White, had been brought along—for the experience, the selectors insisted. Critics could be forgiven for thinking that the coach, in particular, did not appreciate MacGill's overall contribution.

In the event Hauritz, the only finger-spinner in the party, was preferred to the emerging leggie. Ironically Hauritz had spent the winter trying to slow down his delivery by way of improving his powers of deception. An accurate one-day bowler, he had accepted

213

that he needed to widen his skills in the longer version of the game. On this surface, though, spinners simply needed to send the ball down hard, land it on a length and let the pitch take care of the rest.

To add to his problems, Ponting lost the toss. Nevertheless, as the fourth innings began, Australia was in a winning position. By then Michael Clarke had taken six wickets for a few rupees as India collapsed in the face of his pacy but unsubtle left-armers. Hauritz had bowled too slowly for the conditions and had been punished by a reviving middle order led by Laxman, relishing the opportunity presented to him by his captain to bat at first wicket down.

Australia needed to score 107 to win. Wickets started to fall at first in a trickle and then in a flood as batsman upon batsman was unable to cope with a surface that had lasted as long as peace at a children's party. Dravid's tactics were inspired and nerveless as he defied expectations by relying on his young finger-spinners in preference to Anil Kumble, his vastly experienced specialist. Amid a cacophony of sound that spread around the ground like rolling thunder, not sparing a packed, almost overwhelmed press box, the Indians won by 13 runs.

Ponting invited Gilchrist to join him as he accepted the Border/Gavaskar Trophy. His team had secured the series and brought home a great prize, but he had missed most of it. Worse, he had presided over the solitary defeat. Slow to replace or protect Hauritz, his captaincy seemed to have lost its edge. Englishmen watching events unfold in Mumbai must have felt that recovering the Ashes was no longer quite such a distant prospect.

And the Englishmen had been watching. Michael Atherton had covered the first two Test matches for his newspaper and had informed his countrymen that the Australian pace attack was in decline. Had he been able to stay for the entire series he might also have reported that the Australian captain had been weakened by an unnecessary loss.

AUSTRALIA V INDIA, WORLD CUP FINAL
23 MARCH 2003, THE NEW WANDERERS STADIUM, JOHANNESBURG, SOUTH AFRICA

Toss: India
Result: Australia won by 125 runs
Man of the match: R.T. Ponting

Australia		R	BF	4	6
A.C. Gilchrist (k)	c Sehwag b Harbhajan Singh	57	48	8	1
M.L. Hayden	c Dravid b Harbhajan Singh	37	54	5	0
R.T. Ponting (c)	not out	140	121	4	8
D.R. Martyn	not out	88	84	7	1
D.S. Lehmann					
M.G. Bevan					
A. Symonds					
G.B. Hogg					
A.J. Bichel					
B. Lee					
G.D. McGrath					
Extras	(b 2, lb 12, w 16, nb 7)	37			
Total	**2 wickets**	**359**			
	50.0 overs at 7.18 rpo				

FoW   1–105 Gilchrist   2–125 Hayden

Bowling	O	M	R	W
Zaheer Khan	7	0	67	0
J. Srinath	10	0	87	0
A. Nehra	10	0	57	0
Harbhajan Singh	8	0	49	2
V. Sehwag	3	0	14	0
S.R. Tendulkar	3	0	20	0
D. Mongia	7	0	39	0
Yuvraj Singh	2	0	12	0

India		R	BF	4	6
S.R. Tendulkar	c & b McGrath	4	5	1	0
V. Sehwag	run out	82	81	10	3
S.C. Ganguly (c)	c Lehmann b Lee	24	25	3	1
Mohammad Kaif	c Gilchrist b McGrath	0	3	0	0
R. Dravid (k)	b Bichel	47	57	2	0
Yuvraj Singh	c Lee b Hogg	24	34	1	0
D. Mongia	c Martyn b Symonds	12	11	2	0
Harbhajan Singh	c McGrath b Symonds	7	8	0	0
Zaheer Khan	c Lehmann b McGrath	4	8	0	0
J. Srinath	b Lee	1	4	0	0
A. Nehra	not out	8	4	2	0
Extras	(b 4, lb 4, w 9, nb 4)	21			
Total	**All out**	**234**			
	39.2 overs at 5.95 rpo				

FoW				
	1–4	Tendulkar	2–58	Ganguly
	3–59	Mohammad Kaif	4–147	Sehwag
	5–187	Dravid	6–208	Yuvraj Singh
	7–209	Mongia	8–223	Harbhajan Singh
	9–226	Srinath	10–234	Zaheer Khan

Bowling	O	M	R	W
G.D. McGrath	8.2	0	52	3
B. Lee	7	1	31	2
G.B. Hogg	10	0	61	1
D.S. Lehmann	2	0	18	0
A.J. Bichel	10	0	57	1
A. Symonds	2	0	7	2

16

ENGLAND
EXPECTS . . .

The Australians who arrived in England for the 2005 Ashes
series were, outwardly, their old cocky, intimidating selves. It
was a front that hid concerns and confusions within the
touring party, as well as complacency among the selectors. Before a
ball had been bowled, an email arrived from a senior player observ-
ing that tough days lay ahead. But it was not merely a tale about
Australian selectors' errors, or a coach who was treading water, or
senior players who had spent too much time together.

England had changed. The old country had a winning team, and
winning is a habit. Moreover these Englishmen were well-balanced,
well-coached, well-led and hungry. England had been in a cricketing
ferment for months before the Australians even arrived. After eight
successive defeats the nation sensed that its time had come. Steve
Waugh had gone, England was second in the rankings and a new
Galahad had been found. Several of the Australians had been playing
county cricket with mixed results. Suddenly they were seen to be
human, perhaps even vulnerable. Before Christmas every seat had
been sold. Cricket was back on the back pages. It was on the front
pages, too. England scented blood.

The hunger was tangible. Jonathan Agnew, the BBC's generally genial correspondent, suggested that winning the Ashes would be as big an event as lifting the soccer World Cup in 1966. Every Englishman of a certain age can remember that victory, can name the England side, half the Germans and even that nice moustachioed Russian who persuaded himself that Geoff Hurst's shot had crossed the line. Hurst scored a hat-trick, Martin Peters added a fourth. Nobby Stiles snapped at numerous ankles, Bobby Charlton was majestic, brother Jack presided over the penalty area, Bobby Moore was serenity itself, Gordon Banks was flawless, Alan Ball was everywhere. It was a dreadful, dirty World Cup but England won.

And these Ashes were bigger than that? Agnew's comment also begged a question. What went wrong in between? English soccer held its own until the 1970s; English cricket flourished until 1981 but then began its long slide into the doldrums. England's national deterioration started in the same decade. The idea that sport exists apart from other forces is preposterous, and certainly given short shrift by C.L.R. James and John Arlott. Sport's location as the last item on news broadcasts and on the back pages of newspapers is merely a convenience.

The way a country plays cricket reflects broader forces in its society. West Indian cricket displays a lack of managerial experience, while a generation of players is following the same path as black popular music, from sorrow to cheerfulness and on to self-indulgent anger (and, hopefully, beyond). The current Indian team captures the new confidence of a country no longer torn between western affluence and ancient customs but prepared to look both in the eye and to take the best each has to offer.

By the same token, the inexorable collapse of English sport in the 1980s was caused by factors beyond the incompetence of those directly involved. A nation had lost its identity, no longer knew itself. England became an inward-looking land. Thatcherism had run its course and the country was drifting midway between her discipline and promise of renewal held out by Blair's New Labour. Into the vacuum marched greed, selfishness and egoism. The cult of the 'celebrity', yobbos, puritanism and prurience combined to bring the country to its knees. Comedy and creativity suffered. Reality television and endless confessional chat shows took their place.

In the years between Thatcher's neo-rationalism and Blair's

modernism, England suffered from a lack of conviction. Forced to choose between a return to Anglo-Saxon straightforwardness or the higher sophistication of Northern Europe, it floundered. Both are coherent positions. There is no halfway house. Education collapsed and newspapers went from bad to worse as Rupert Murdoch exacted vengeance for past snubs.

English cricket could hardly hope to remain immune from such nationwide debilitation. Sporting success depends on a supreme gathering of the will. Without belief, nothing can be accomplished. Those who arranged the singing of 'Jerusalem' before each Test match in the 2005 Ashes series had grasped the point.

For 15 years, English sport was sustained by strong individuals such as Sebastian Coe, Steve Ovett and Nick Faldo, but now soccer fell foul of the yob culture. Cricket also lost its head, with rebel tours, contrived matches, lob bowling, and worse, and these at the highest levels. Ian Botham and Paul Gascoigne were the champions of the age. Unsurprisingly neither cricket nor soccer could find an English manager or coach capable of confronting the prevailing culture.

England had to choose between its stoical past and the intelligence of Europe. Eventually soccer, or rather the chairmen of ambitious clubs, took the European route. Desperate to break the cycle, the more advanced officials asked Frenchmen, Swiss, Swedes and Germans to take charge of their teams. Scotsmen and Irishmen were also summoned. Accordingly the culture of the game started to improve, though the news took an unconscionable time to reach Leeds and Newcastle. Nor was it only a question of management. Others steps were taken to brighten the game. Lighter balls, drier pitches and less tolerant referees helped. Television brought money and glamour.

Soccer also had the sense to embrace the local African communities. Not that it had much choice, for their talent and commitment could not be missed. Every year more and more black Africans appear in the colours of famous English clubs. Athletics, too, has been strengthened by their contributions. Inclined to be slower starters, Asians will follow in their wake.

Before long other clubs responded to the challenge by raising their own standards. Anyone doubting the extent of England's football revival need only consider the performances of Bolton, Wigan and Charlton, smaller clubs guided towards the top by managers cut from the local stone.

The irony is that there was nothing wrong with England or Englishmen in the first place. It is a great country with a proud history that has produced Shakespeare, *Dad's Army* and Reggie Perrin. Bad habits had crept in, that is all.

Cricket had some particular problems. At Somerset, once, a prolific visiting batsman was supposed to be pressing for runs on the last morning against some moderate bowling supported by an inviting field. Instead he blocked. It became clear that he wanted and expected Somerset to introduce even worse bowlers who would toss the ball up without making the slightest effort to get him out. Chris Tavare obliged and the opponent scored an easy unbeaten hundred before the declaration.

The cynicism was appalling. A fortnight earlier, Neil Fairbrother, the batsman concerned, had scored a hundred against the West Indies. Not that he ought to be singled out. Just that this particular match lingers in the mind. If the evidence of Don Topley and Jack Bannister is taken seriously (as it ought to be), matches were occasionally fixed over weekends towards the end of the summer when sides met in different competitions.

Nor was the collapse of the cricketing culture the only problem facing the game. Previously, private schools and mining towns had been reliable sources of cricketing talent. Professional cricket had its origins in Nottingham, the city of Chartism, the city where craftsmen dared to appreciate the value of their work. Harold Larwood and Bill Voce emerged from a proud and independent tradition. But the mines had been closed.

The decline of the Empire and the collapse of the economy after the Second World War took a toll on the schools, and the families that kept them in business. Inevitably the idea of education for its own sake proved unsustainable. Stoic and classical traditions were replaced by consumerism. Money had to be put on the table.

It took England a long time to realise that both cricketing supply lines had dried up. Eventually the need for an effective domestic structure was grasped. Eventually a plan was put in place. Four-day cricket, central contracts, two divisions and an Academy followed. Attention was also paid to the 'recreational game'. Minor counties started playing three-day matches. Urban clubs were pushed towards longer matches. In 1995 clubs routinely played 46-over games with two—usually ageing—trundlers allowed to bowl 23 overs apiece. Now it was 55 overs a side with limitations on the bowlers. Believe me, it is a young man's game.

English cricket also had the sense to tap into stronger sporting cultures. Unable to find men of distinction in its own ranks—Mike Brearley was otherwise engaged and Ken Barrington had died too young—officials asked Australians to run its Academy and several county teams. An African educated in the strong ethics of Prince Edward's School in Harare became the national coach. Beyond doubt these men have helped to instil strong values in their charges.

Nor was England content merely to catch up. Despite the protests of the senior counties, Lord's decided to give 20-over cricket a go. Now the rest of the cricketing world is copying England.

England's sporting culture had improved in leaps and bounds. Australia was not meeting the familiar downtrodden, inept opponent. Ponting and his players were taking on an entire sporting nation, one that after many years of drift and decay had put its mind to the pursuit of excellence.

Andrew Flintoff was the proverbial icing on the cake. His emergence was no more inevitable than that of Shane Warne or Glenn McGrath. Indeed it took five years for the boy to become a man. Not until the culture of the game was strong did his talent start to emerge. Flintoff would become the pivotal figure of the 2005 Ashes series, as Botham had been in 1981. In some respects, his performances eclipse those of his mighty predecessor because he had to confront a heavier burden of expectation. Botham ambushed a poorly led opposition. Flintoff engaged a formidable opponent in hand-to-hand combat.

In many ways, the two great allrounders reflect their ages. Moreover the Englishmen have common ground. Both appreciate the simple pleasures to be found in country life, seem to expand in white clothes and relish the roars of the crowd.

Not even Botham's harshest critic can disregard the generosity of spirit felt by his pals, his selflessness on the field, the brilliance of his play. Flintoff is no saint either, a bluff all-rounder, a player intent on cracking skulls as well as cricket balls, a man highly regarded in many quarters but not immune to the allure of the tabloids. Yet their differences are more telling. Flintoff is a gentler, quieter, simpler man, able to live with the silences. Whereas Botham possessed a violence of temper and ferocity of will that allowed him to reach into himself for powers beyond the ordinary, Flintoff prefers to rely on his skill and think his way to success. Botham could let go, Flintoff stays in control. Botham gambled, was prepared to buy wickets. Flintoff hardly ever bowls a bad ball. Botham relied on swing and surprise, Flintoff depends on pace and disguise. At heart, and Trafalgar Square notwithstanding, he is a reserved and orthodox cricketer.

Botham was captivated by the moment, Flintoff observes and intervenes. Botham defied the odds, Flintoff plays them. Botham relied on inspiration, Flintoff on power. Botham dived into fame as a duck dives into a pond. He knew it was for him. Even as a teenager, he was not scared of exposure or the heat of battle. He pretended not to care that ancients dismissed him as a wild youth enjoying a run of luck, but it hurt. It is odd that man can at once defy failure and fear rejection. Botham's ferocity towards his enemies is founded on this fear. He must destroy those he cannot carry along with him. And he is good at it.

Botham was lucky in his early days. He spent his formative years under the stewardship of Brian Close and Tom Cartwright, the heart and the brain, the Churchill and Attlee of cricket. Cartwright instructed his pupil in the crafts of swing and cut bowling, Close brought out the fighter in him. Mike Brearley and Ken Barrington, another coupling of head and heart, came next, relishing the spirit of their young charge as he displayed an audacity they had never known.

Flintoff was a late developer. For years he was dismissed as lazy and overrated. He was overweight and for an unconscionable period failed to fulfil his ability. Perhaps humility lay behind his uncertainty, a suspicion that fame and glory might not suit him or that he was not ready for them. Far from plunging devil-may-care into the pond, Flintoff trod warily around its edges. Perhaps, too, he was haunted by the spectre of coming responsibility.

Flintoff arrived in the world of turbulent triumph as an adult, not as an intrepid and impressionable youth, and managed it better than his predecessor. By 2005 he had become a source of strength, not merely to his team but to the entire game, even to the country.

A sympathetic coach and a supportive captain played their parts in his rise. Duncan Fletcher provided the stability, Michael Vaughan offered the encouragement and Kevin Pietersen became his release valve.

From the moment their plane touched down at Heathrow airport, the Australians knew they had their hands full. Usually it is the other way around. Usually the bombardment begins in Perth. To make matters worse, the tourists immediately suffered a telling defeat.

Four years earlier, Steve Waugh had arrived in England with a plan. Determined to give his hosts the sort of thrashing they had not experienced since the days of William the Conqueror, he devised a strategy calculated to establish his team's superiority before the Test series began. To that end he studied the fixture list, observed that several one-day matches were to be played before the start of the series and decided to put them to use. He began talking about the new tactics he intended to introduce in the 50-over series. Of course he did not reveal his intended innovations, responding to enquiries by growling, 'You'll see 'em when you see 'em.'

As usual, 'old Stoneface' was ahead of the game. His strategy was immediately clear. From the first ball he let loose his pace attack. He placed aggressive fields and told them to go for wickets. In short he set out to destroy the English batting before it had time to settle. It was a withering statement of intent. One-day cricket was supposed to be a batsman's game. Matches were supposed follow a pattern.

Waugh's bowlers executed the plan to perfection. They were helped by pitches that remained as damp as a romantic's handkerchief and a sun that made the sort of fleeting appearances more often associated with peanuts in a pub. Not the sort of conditions in which to encounter Glenn McGrath and his band of brothers. The ball moved around obligingly and the batsmen were left groping as if playing Blind Man's Bluff. Every doubt was redoubled.

England had learned from the experience. In 2005 the boot was on the other foot and the first 20-over engagement in Southampton would be significant. By the end of a one-sided match the Australians knew they were in for a long hard fight.

By all accounts the atmosphere in the ground bordered on the ecstatic. England had been waiting a long time to have a proper tilt at the Aussies. Paul Collingwood and the African pairing of Kevin Pietersen and Andrew Strauss attacked with bravado and continued to do so despite a mid-innings clatter. None of these players bore the scars of past defeats at the hands of the Australians. They played with an optimism that was positively antipodean. England enjoyed the sight of the much-vaunted visiting pacemen being carted around the south coast. The Australians were, unmistakeably, rattled.

The feeling that the Australians were vulnerable was growing. Andrew Symonds appeared at a match in Cardiff still bearing the effects of a night on the tiles. Ponting dropped him and a suspension was imposed but the Queenslander ought to have been sent home. Bangladesh won the match by five wickets after Ponting foolishly decided to bat on a damp pitch, whereupon Damien Martyn pottered along at his own pace.

The Australians also lost to England but managed to reach the final and the match was tied. Subsequently the Australians prevailed in a three-match series played against their oldest foes, but the seeds of doubt had been sown. The Australians were not functioning as a disciplined and united fighting force and the start of the Ashes campaign was only a few days away.

Perhaps, too, England was motivated by another event, an outrage that unified even as it devastated. During the 50-over series, with the Australians and their hosts in Leeds and due to play their next match in the capital city, news arrived that bombs had exploded on the London Underground and on buses in the centre of town. Broken bodies, blood, jagged metal and haunted faces lined the streets. Many casualties were suffered, many lives ruined. Terrorism's ugly face and hateful outlook had come to town.

For a few days, the cricket seemed surreal. Then the smoke drifted away and everyone understood that the show had to go on, for to do otherwise was to admit defeat. Part of the reason the cricket was such fun was that it provided a sunny counterpoint to the black nastiness. Perhaps, though, the intense patriotism of the crowds can be understood only with the bombs in mind.

17

AUSTRALIA MEETS ITS MAKER

Everyone was agog for the Ashes. As the hour of battle approached, not even Eden Gardens at its most frenetic could have produced a higher level of anticipation than that sensed in every English cricketing community. After many years of almost inevitable defeat, now the prospect loomed of two proud and powerful cricketing forces meeting in a conflict of uncertain outcome. Hopes were high that this would be the greatest of all cricketing duels between these longstanding foes. Astonishingly the deeds would prove as mighty as the promise.

After the one-day matches had been played, with England dominating the single 20-over match and the visitors rallying to take the spoils in the 50-over competition, the teams came to Lord's ready for the fray. And a vast throng came with them.

Suffice it to say that the first day of the first Test surpassed all expectations, in which respect it would typify the series. By lunch the crowd was bubbling. Probably no hats were thrown into the skies as wickets fell but they might as well have been.

England began well. From the first ball the bowlers ran in hard and went for wickets. In a trice memories of inhibited past perform-ances were banished. This was a different England, an aggressive team ready for a fight. The Australians were not given time to settle. Not that they were being all that circumspect. Instead they went for their strokes, hooking, driving on the rise and running between wickets in the manner of men fleeing Lee van Cleef. On many previous occasions the Australians' attempt to seize the initiative had been rewarded. This time they were dismissed in 40 overs.

That England had the bowlers to exploit a firm pitch was reward for the selectors' foresight in promoting a tall paceman blessed with an extra yard of pace. Steve Harmison was outstanding. Whirling away from the Pavilion End, and bowling without any hint of the hesitancy seen in South Africa, where he had been about as accurate as a secret service report, he troubled every batsman. Justin Langer took a blow to the arm, Ricky Ponting and Matthew Hayden were late with their hooks and struck on the head.

Between innings England's bowlers must have been pleased with themselves. Then it was McGrath's turn. Even by his own elevated standards, the veteran's performance was spellbinding. Bowling with hypnotic precision, he dismembered his opponents. Not a ball, not a thought strayed from the correct path. Everything was part of the infernal plan.

Presented with a surprise lead, the Australians struggled for a second time. It had been years since they were made to work as hard for runs as they were between lunch and tea on the second day. Another wicket and England was back in the contest. Another 30 runs and the Australians were in charge. Twice the visitors edged away only to be pegged back. Hardly a stroke was played in front of the wicket. Successive batsmen were forced to protect their bodies and wickets.

Finally the decisive moment came as Michael Clarke was dropped. Suddenly the Australians broke out. Suddenly the batting did not look difficult or the bowling menacing. Suddenly strokes were finding gaps. Suddenly the travails of the afternoon were forgotten. Yet they were not a figment of our imagination.

Michael Vaughan's side had let their chance slip. Heavy defeat came on a damp fourth day before a Sunday crowd that had hoped for much more. The English were not disgraced, merely outplayed. Greatness undid them. They managed to remove Adam Gilchrist cheaply twice but could not stop the bowlers. On the third and almost final day Shane Warne had produced one of his most compelling performances, using every word in the leg-spinning vocabulary and adding several of his own creation. It was a mesmerising, entertaining and destructive contribution. Only Kevin Pietersen called his bluff. Indeed the African forced his chum to bowl into the rough from around the wicket.

In hindsight, the English might have been bolder. The Australians can be accused of precisely the opposite offence. Perhaps that was the problem. Neither side had found the right tempo. Adjusting from the rush of 50-over cricket into the more considered approach generally favoured in the longer game is not easy.

Already it was hard to see Australia losing when both McGrath and Warne were playing. And they didn't.

Everything changed on the first day of the second Test at Birmingham. The Australians had a rotten morning. Losing McGrath in a training accident was bad enough. Ricky Ponting made matters worse by choosing to bowl, a decision taken days before the match. Sensible captains do not make up their minds about a pitch until an hour before play begins. Doubtless he did not want to risk undermining his players by changing course after McGrath's injury. Even so it was a mistake, and he would pay for it.

From the outset it was clear that Ponting had committed a howler. Hoping to see the ball swinging around, the Australian captain must have been aghast to find it ambling down the wicket like an old-timer down a country lane. England's openers were able to drive on the bounce. Had the Australians bowled well or luck sided with them the toss might not have mattered. The reverse was the case. Cricket exacts its revenge upon those taking liberties.

Much had changed in the home camp. Defeat had not broken the Englishmen. Instead, they had absorbed its lessons, accepted they had been too timid and decided to attack. They scored 400 in a day. The openers set the pace and Flintoff kept up the onslaught. At Lord's he had resembled Hercules at a sewing machine. Pietersen played the shot of the afternoon, a back-foot flip past mid-on. They are the most dangerous pair since Bonnie and Clyde. Of course it helped that the boundaries had been shortened; ten sixes were struck and some of them cleared the rope but not the fence.

The next morning, Matthew Hayden departed first ball. Forgetting the old adage that a man is prisoner of his words and master of his silences, he had observed before the match that England had little chance of causing an upset. He stroked his first ball to short cover. Michael Vaughan would set clever fields for the Queenslander throughout the series, pushing mid-off deep and straight and placing a man for the miscued drive.

Something stirring was needed from the Australian captain and Ponting responded with a succession of superbly timed strokes. Bouncers were tapped behind square leg with the ease of a man removing the top from an egg. Full deliveries were dispatched with a full blade. In a trice the Australian captain had reached 50 as his side rattled along at five runs an over.

Vaughan tossed the ball to Ashley Giles. Determined to attack his hosts at their weakest point, Ponting tried to soft-sweep a ball not full enough for his purposes. A lobbed catch to short fine leg was the result. Ponting did not have a happy match.

Eventually the Australians needed to score 282 to win. Warne had taken 6/46 in England's second innings. With McGrath injured, he stood between Australia and slaughter. Perhaps it helped that he felt at home among the English, had built a house in Hampshire and was thinking about settling in the country. He has always needed to be wanted. Living among Englishmen must have steeled his resolve. A man can only take so much teasing.

Brett Lee had bowled his heart out in an attempt to make amends for his wild display on the opening day. England's second effort had been sustained by Flintoff who hit the ball with such force that the stadium, let alone the boundaries, did not seem big enough to contain him.

When Australia slumped to 7/137 and then to 8/175 as Clarke was confounded by a beautifully conceived and executed slower ball from Harmison, the match seemed to be over. My first suspicion that the hosts still doubted themselves came at breakfast next morning as supporters repeatedly asked for a prediction. With two lame wickets to fall and the Australians needing to score another 106 runs they wanted a prediction?! Such was their respect for the fighting spirit of the Australians.

Ashes cricket has seldom produced any match as tense, as utterly compelling as this second Test on this second Sabbath of the series. The cricket was spellbinding as the Australian tailenders tried to bring off one of the game's greatest escapes in the face of fierce bowling. A wicket was lost as Shane Warne trod on his stumps. Even then the visitors refused to lie down. Lee and Kasprowicz nibbled away at the target till it came agonisingly close. It was hard to believe what was happening, yet there it was before our very eyes, and those of a huge and excited audience. England fretted. Afterwards the players admitted that they, too, had been petrified.

Lee almost won the match with a sumptuous off-drive that unfortunately found its way straight to a boundary fieldsman. By now even puzzled Australian reporters thought their team might prevail but then came that last, desperate moment as a low catch was held. Had Lee's drive found a gap or Kasprowicz's parry fallen safely it might have been another story.

England owed much to Flintoff's gigantic contribution. The Lancastrian had set about the Australians with pace, power and bravado. It was the sort of performance more often read about in cartoons after the hero has munched upon spinach or donned a cape the better to summon the valour that captures the imagination. Flintoff looked the Australians in the eye and did not blink. He grew in stature with every meaty blow, every roaring delivery.

Although Flintoff plays his cricket aggressively, no meanness can be detected in his game. Great sportsmen are above all that. As his comrades celebrated victory Flintoff walked across to console Lee. Afterwards everyone agreed that the sight of him putting an arm around his erstwhile opponent was the finest of the summer. It confirmed the size of his heart and indicated that England could, perhaps, be expected to take the spoils. An English arm around an Australian, a jubilant crowd, 'Jerusalem' echoing around a ground. How could they lose? To add to the Australians' woes, there had been talk in the papers about a row between Ponting and Warne over the captain's decision to bowl.

The Australians repaired to Old Trafford with the series all square. The mood of the series had changed dramatically. England had become the aggressor. The Australians had been pushed back. Ponting had been out-thought and outmanoeuvred. Aggressive English bowling and tight, precisely placed fields had restricted Australia's batsmen. Ponting was becoming increasingly frustrated about England's use of substitutes and the way the ball was reverse

AUSTRALIA V ENGLAND, SECOND ASHES TEST

4–8 AUGUST 2005, EDGBASTON, BIRMINGHAM, UK

Toss:	**Australia**
Result:	**England won by 2 runs**
Man of the match:	**A. Flintoff**

England (1st Innings)		R	BF	4	6
M.E. Trescothick	c Gilchrist b Kasprowicz	90	102	15	2
A.J. Strauss	b Warne	48	76	10	0
M.P. Vaughan (c)	c Lee b Gillespie	24	41	3	0
I.R. Bell	c Gilchrist b Kasprowicz	6	3	1	0
K.P. Pietersen	c Katich b Lee	71	76	10	1
A. Flintoff	c Gilchrist b Gillespie	68	62	6	5
G.O. Jones (k)	c Gilchrist b Kasprowicz	1	15	0	0
A.F. Giles	lbw b Warne	23	30	4	0
M.J. Hoggard	lbw b Warne	16	49	2	0
S.J. Harmison	b Warne	17	11	2	1
S.P. Jones	not out	19	24	1	1
Extras	(lb 9, w 1, nb 14)	24			
Total	**All out**	**407**			
	79.2 overs at 5.13 rpo				

FoW				
	1–112	Strauss	2–164	Trescothick
	3–170	Bell	4–187	Vaughan
	5–290	Flintoff	6–293	Jones
	7–342	Giles	8–348	Pietersen
	9–375	Harmison	10–407	Hoggard

Bowling	O	M	R	W
B. Lee	17	1	111	1
J.N. Gillespie	22	3	91	2
M.S. Kasprowicz	15	3	80	3
S.K. Warne	25.2	4	116	4

Australia (1st Innings)

		R	BF	4	6
J.L. Langer	lbw b S.P. Jones	82	154	7	0
M.L. Hayden	c Strauss b Hoggard	0	1	0	0
R.T. Ponting (c)	c Vaughan b Giles	61	76	12	0
D.R. Martyn	run out	20	18	4	0
M.J. Clarke	c G.O. Jones b Giles	40	68	7	0
S.M. Katich	c G.O. Jones b Flintoff	4	18	1	0
A.C. Gilchrist (k)	not out	49	69	4	0
S.K. Warne	b Giles	8	14	2	0
B. Lee	c Flintoff b S.P. Jones	6	10	1	0
J.N. Gillespie	lbw b Flintoff	7	37	1	0
M.S. Kasprowicz	lbw b Flintoff	0	1	0	0
Extras	(b 13, lb 7, w 1, nb 10)	31			
Total	**All out**	**308**			
	76.0 overs at 4.05 rpo				

FoW

1–0	Hayden		2–88	Ponting
3–118	Martyn		4–194	Clarke
5–208	Katich		6–262	Langer
7–273	Warne		8–282	Lee
9–308	Gillespie		10–308	Kasprowicz

Bowling

	O	M	R	W
S.J. Harmison	11	1	48	0
M.J. Hoggard	8	0	41	1
S.P. Jones	16	2	69	2
A. Flintoff	15	1	52	3
A.F. Giles	26	2	78	3

England (2nd Innings)

		R	BF	4	6
M.E. Trescothick	c Gilchrist b Lee	21	38	4	0
A.J. Strauss	b Warne	6	12	1	0
M.J. Hoggard	c Hayden b Lee	1	27	0	0
M.P. Vaughan (c)	b Lee	1	2	0	0
I.R. Bell	c Gilchrist b Warne	21	43	2	0
K.P. Pietersen	c Gilchrist b Warne	20	35	0	2
A. Flintoff	b Warne	73	86	6	4
G.O. Jones (k)	c Ponting b Lee	9	19	1	0
A.F. Giles	c Hayden b Warne	8	36	0	0
S.J. Harmison	c Ponting b Warne	0	1	0	0
S.P. Jones	not out	12	23	3	0
Extras	(lb 1, nb 9)	10			
Total	**All out**	**182**			
	52.1 overs at 3.49 rpo				

FoW

1–25	Strauss	2–27	Trescothick
3–29	Vaughan	4–31	Hoggard
5–72	Pietersen	6–75	Bell
7–101	Jones	8–131	Giles
9–131	S J Harmison	10–182	Flintoff

Bowling	O	M	R	W
B. Lee	18	1	82	4
J.N. Gillespie	8	0	24	0
M.S. Kasprowicz	3	0	29	0
S.K. Warne	23.1	7	46	6

Australia (2nd Innings)		R	BF	4	6
J.L. Langer	b Flintoff	28	47	4	0
M.L. Hayden	c Trescothick b S.P. Jones	31	64	4	0
R.T. Ponting (c)	c G.O. Jones b Flintoff	0	5	0	0
D.R. Martyn	c Bell b Hoggard	28	36	5	0
M.J. Clarke	b Harmison	30	57	5	0
S.M. Katich	c Trescothick b Giles	16	21	3	0
A.C. Gilchrist (k)	c Flintoff b Giles	1	4	0	0
J.N. Gillespie	lbw b Flintoff	0	2	0	0
S.K. Warne	hit wicket b Flintoff	42	59	4	2
B. Lee	not out	43	75	5	0
M.S. Kasprowicz	c G.O. Jones b Harmison	20	31	3	0
Extras	(b 13, lb 8, w 1, nb 18)	40			
Total	**All out**	**279**			
	64.3 overs at 4.33 rpo				

FoW

1–47	Langer	2–48	Ponting
3–82	Hayden	4–107	Martyn
5–134	Katich	6–136	Gilchrist
7–137	Gillespie	8–175	Clarke
9–220	Warne	10–279	Kasprowicz

Bowling	O	M	R	W
S.J. Harmison	17.3	3	62	2
M.J. Hoggard	5	0	26	1
A.F. Giles	15	3	68	2
A. Flintoff	22	3	79	4
S.P. Jones	5	1	23	1

swinging. He ought to have raised these matters before the series began. Now it would sound like sour grapes. Yet the dressing-room was full of chitter-chatter about these distractions.

There was worse to come in Manchester. For four days the Australians bowled badly and batted without conviction. By the fifth morning the game seemed to be up. England had been the better-organised and more coherent team. A cricketing machine had been brought to a halt by a resolute, ruthless and hungry opponent. Nothing in sport is better than the sight of a tightly run, aggressive team playing a daring and disciplined game.

Although playing badly, Ponting and his men were not prepared to admit defeat. To save the match they had to bat an entire day on a worn surface. Around the country the excitement was palpable. No tickets had been sold for the fifth day. Why would they have been? Australia had taken 11 days to take a 3/0 lead in the previous Ashes series. So it was first come first served. And come they did. As officials arrived at dawn, long queues wound, snakelike, around Old Trafford. Supporters had been waiting since 3 a.m. for the gates to open, behaviour which is expected at the Last Night of The Proms, but for cricket? In England?

It seemed as if the whole country wanted to watch the match. School holidays allowed thousands of children to join the merry throng. Cricket in England has become a notably younger game. One player even sports blue hair! Old Trafford could have been filled three times over. They closed the gates an hour before play and thousands of disappointed followers were shooed away. Attempts to erect a screen in the city centre were thwarted by policemen concerned about public order.

No sooner had play started than the crowd had reason to celebrate. Matthew Hoggard tried his off-cutter first ball and rejoiced as the leather kissed Justin Langer's outside edge. England's least effective bowler had removed the visitors' most stubborn batsman. With a single delivery. But the crowd knew that the Australians would not go quietly and settled in for a long and gripping struggle.

At lunch Australia still had eight wickets in hand and a chance of saving the match. Damien Martyn's was the third wicket to fall as Steve Bucknor failed to detect an inside edge so blatant that the Australian captain made his thoughts known to the errant Jamaican.

Worse followed. Unable to read Flintoff's swing, Simon Katich flailed and flashed until an edge was held at third slip. Nor could Adam Gilchrist survive his tormentor's pace and movement.

Ponting stood his ground with the determination of a captain prepared to sweat blood to save his side. Seldom has a captain defied the run of play as magnificently as he did in his country's hour of greatest need. As Australia slept, its captain produced one of the finest defensive innings of recent times and much the best of his career. It might have been Steve Waugh out there, or Ken Barrington.

As usual he started shakily. Like those gramophones of yesteryear, Ponting takes a while to warm up. Occasionally he played across the ball, the middle of his bat alone curtailing the bowler's yelp for leg before. Once the Tasmanian had taken his bearings he set about building the sort of colossal score required by his side. By doing so, he confirmed that he is a batsman of many parts and a responsible leader of the team. Captaincy is a piece of cake when everything is falling into place.

Of course Ponting could not save the match on his own. Shane Warne kept him company until the last hour began. Brett Lee hung on desperately. Then calamity befell the captain. After 411 defiant minutes, he pulled and the ball brushed his glove. He left with head bowed, a fine batsman who had played the innings of his life. As one spectator put it, 'You wouldn't be dead for quids!'

Seldom has any match produced the agony and ecstasy felt by players and spectators alike as this epic contest approached its climax. Seldom have louder roars been heard at any sporting arena, but Ponting's tailenders did not let him down. Seldom have two such Test matches been played within a fortnight.

Thanks to Ponting and the rain that denied the hosts almost an entire day, the series still stood all square. Could Australia regroup? It didn't seem so as the fourth Test started.

Luck had deserted Ponting. McGrath had played in Manchester and though not fully fit had managed to take a few wickets as England pressed for runs in its second innings. Now he was forced to withdraw for a second time on the morning of the match. Cricket has a nasty habit of kicking a team that's down. England knew the feeling. It had been happening to them for years.

Ponting had needed to call correctly. Nottingham had provided a flat pitch and his pace attack had been reduced to the bare essentials. Instead Michael Vaughan and his men had been given a priceless opportunity to rub salt into their opponent's gaping wound.

It is hard to convey the feebleness of the Australian performance on the first day of the fourth Test. Put it this way: England's openers added 105 runs without much difficulty and no one was surprised. On a firm, first-day pitch, the cream of Australian bowling failed to make any impression. Ponting placed a field of two slips and a gully, after only ten overs. Confidence was low in the Australian camp. Before long Australia supporters were saying, 'Maybe we can get a draw.' A draw? Against the Poms! It had, indeed, come to that.

Some of the wounds were self-inflicted. Fourteen no-balls in 20 overs is not good enough from a schoolboy side, let alone an international outfit enjoying excellent facilities and with a highly paid coach. Bad luck had only a small part to play. A few edges eluded the stumps, but the batsmen were on top. Hardly an appeal was heard, barely a ball was missed. All too soon the spinner was introduced. Not much fun bowling slow to established openers on a flat pitch on the first morning of a Test.

Almost inevitably, Warne took the first wicket, with his team's first stroke of fortune. Before long he was bowling in that hypnotic, compelling way. But he needed a little help from his friends. Warne has a huge heart and plenty of artistry and artfulness. Even he, though, could not beat the second-best side around on his own.

Despite the awfulness of the first day, the Australians came within a whisker of bringing off one of the great victories in Test match history. Forced to follow-on after another abject display with bat and ball, they found themselves defending 128 on an amiable fifth-day pitch. Ponting and his players were magnificent as they tried to defend the indefensible. The visitors strained every muscle and imperilled every bone as they sought victory amid the ashes of defeat. Every run brought a roar from a passionate Nottingham crowd. The news that Robin Hood had slain the Sheriff could hardly have been better received. Every wicket was followed by a gasp. Hardly a soul could watch. As the target came closer even the most decorous English reporters could scarcely contain themselves. It had been a long time.

Warne was, again, magnificent and Lee was superb. Between them they took 7/82 but still it wasn't enough. To their immense relief, the Englishmen prevailed by three wickets. Afterwards everyone knew they had taken part in one of the finest matches played since, well, since Birmingham and Old Trafford. The Australians had nothing to regret except the result. Their representatives did them proud. Try as they might, Ricky Ponting and Shane Warne could not conjure a victory out of thin air, but both men were mighty in defeat. Ponting was his old energetic self in the field. Already he had batted beautifully and without any luck and as captain he chivvied his players along and tried to make the most of slender resources.

About the only black mark against him was his outburst as he returned to the pavilion after being run out by one of England's numerous athletic substitutes. In truth Martyn had called him for a tight run, an error that proved costly. Still, the sight of Ponting snarling at a complacent home coach boded well. He had become a tad civilised. Now he needed to take the fury into his captaincy.

The fourth Test at Trent Bridge was a reminder never to discount the chances of a proud Australian team. Had Aleem Dar had even a moderate match they might have pulled it off. Instead he made numerous, obvious mistakes, and each time at the visitors' expense. The Australians have often enjoyed the blessing of the umpiring gods and now were feeling their wrath. Umpires are affected by the mood of a match. Moreover the Englishmen had learned to appeal with the same conviction as their opponents.

Supporters expected the Australians to make changes for the fifth and final Test at The Oval, specifically to include Stuart MacGill in an attempt to add menace and variety to an ailing attack. Instead they stayed put. By choosing only four bowlers they played into England's hands. Australia had to take 20 wickets.

Cruelly, Ponting once again lost the toss. Again, the new-ball bowlers were ineffective. Again, Shane Warne papered over the cracks. His first spell lasted 18 overs and he was never quite the same again. Although he has a short run, he puts a lot of energy into each ball and also concentrates hard. At full strength his deliveries leap off the pitch like electrocuted salmon. By tea he was as red as the Mayor of London's robes. By stumps the only parts of his anatomy still working were his head and his heart.

On the second day, Warne had to watch from the pavilion as his batsmen replied to England's 373—Warne had led the charge with 6/122. He must have been astonished to see them leave the field mid-afternoon when the light deteriorated. The innings was well underway. Justin Langer and Matthew Hayden had just patted each other's backs by way of acknowledging their first century-opening partnership of the series. Neither appeared in any particular difficulty. England had played an extra batsman and was running out of ideas. In truth it did not seem to be much of a time to leave the field.

The English side must have been delighted by this unexpected withdrawal. The last thing they expected was that the Australians might be prepared to shorten the game. Moreover a precedent had been set. Visiting supporters had not expected to see an Australian pair with 100 runs to their name and victory needed to save the Ashes leave the field without the assistance of a crane, an undertaker or else in response to the raising of an umpire's finger.

Next day Matthew Hayden revived his career with a wilful innings. Something had changed in him during the days before this match. Repeated failures at the crease forced him to reconstruct his game. He examined his mistakes and realised that he needed to start working harder. Every man loses his path. Survivors recognise the fact and get back on track.

A lower-order collapse secured England a lead of six runs. Then came a frustrating and disturbing fourth afternoon, another Sabbath, as England tried to protect its position. The match was being played in mid-September, a fortnight later than usual. Bad light was bound to be a factor.

England lost a wicket and Michael Vaughan appeared, intent on convincing the umpires that it was pitch black out there. McGrath helped the English cause by sending down a ridiculous bouncer. The umpires indicated that it was too dark for pace so Ponting called Michael Clarke into the fray. Vaughan continued to complain and, feebly, the umpires fell for it. Not another ball was bowled. Three hours' play was lost. A vast crowd and a huge television audience around the world were cheated. Not that the spectators seemed to mind.

What followed was remarkable. No sooner had the umpires taken the players from the field than some bright spark decided that what the crowd needed was a chance to join some shrill chanteuse in a rendition of 'Land of Hope and Glory' and the splendidly rabble-rousing 'Jerusalem'. The words were even provided on the big screen in case some poor soul had forgotten them.

Before long the crowd, at any rate that part of it not cringing with embarrassment, was in full voice. A visiting team had been invited to play a series of matches only to be subjected to this jingoistic self-glorification. They had come from a country that has fought side by side with its host in four wars. Numerous foreigners had also arrived to support their team. Thousands of children were watching.

But the worst of it is the bright spark was probably right. An opportunity to sing patriotic songs was exactly what the public seemed to crave. Despite having paid a premium for their tickets, large sections of the crowd cheered when highly paid umpires decided, not once but twice, that the light was too gloomy for highly skilled and highly paid batsmen to face slow bowlers.

The spectators were, manifestly, more interested in England winning than in watching cricket. They were happy because the interruption meant that their team had a better chance of securing the draw. To that end they were content to spend hours twiddling their thumbs.

Even when cricket was played the mood of the crowd bordered on the demented. To watch the faces of English supporters in the public stands when an Australian wicket fell was to see a mixture of hatred and hysteria. Not the least shock experienced while sitting among spectators was the discovery that the people singing about Andrew Flintoff were not inebriated students but well-heeled 40 year olds.

A few humorous souls in the stands did their best to lighten the mood. One self-parodic bunch raised their umbrellas in an attempt to convince the umpires it was raining. Nearby Australians promptly removed their shirts and started to sunbathe. By and large the crowds had been sporting, and they had surpassed themselves in Birmingham and on the fifth day at Old Trafford. Plainly, though, an unhealthy spirit was lurking beneath the surface. Perhaps it was the bombs.

Having chosen four bowlers and left the field for bad light on the second day, the Australians had contributed to their own downfall. Now they faced the task of taking nine wickets *and* scoring the required runs in a single day. Astonishingly they almost made it. Had Warne taken a comfortable and crucial slip catch a fighting touring team might have squared the series. Instead Pietersen was spared and Lee was frustrated. That Warne was the culprit counts among cricket's most savage ironies.

After surviving Lee's torrid spell before lunch, and changing from defence to attack, Pietersen changed the course of the match in a few minutes. His assault on Lee brought 37 runs in three mostly short-pitched overs as Ponting's gamble in unleashing his fastest bowler backfired. Hooking and straight driving with courage and panache, the African blasted his adopted country to safety. He had already clouted Shane Warne for six over mid-wicket, twice. With every missed chance, every passing minute and every fierce blow, the Australians felt their grip on the trophy slipping away.

Eventually it was all over. Pietersen reached his hundred, bad light fell across the land, the players shook hands and England went to celebrate in Trafalgar Square. The Australians went home. What had it all meant? Why had it all meant so much? A bloke armed with a handful of leather tries to remove an opponent bearing a hunk of wood. As has been said a thousand times, it's only a game. But is it? Or is it an opportunity to express individuality, to explore talent, to play in a team, to represent a pub, club, county or country, to show that you exist?

England had recaptured the Ashes. Unsurprisingly the series took a toll on both sides. England went to Pakistan and hardly won a match. Australia recovered as a team, but most of the players suffered setbacks. Martyn, Kasprowicz, Clarke, Katich and Gillespie were dropped. Gilchrist was exhausted. Warne and Hayden suffered from viruses. Langer was injured. Only Ponting and Lee survived unscathed—both surpassed themselves in 2005/06—and they were periodically fractious.

The Australians will soon recover the Ashes. Cricket is the national game, the Poms are the natural rivals and the Australians have come a long way since the dark days of the mid-1980s. A strong culture has been built around the game. England deserved its victory but their opponents will be back.

Indeed the process began almost as soon as the players reached home. A committee led by Border and Taylor was formed to consider the lessons of the tour and to propose improvements. Meanwhile the selectors dropped underperforming players and set about finding effective replacements.

The Australians have no intention of accepting defeat as part and parcel of the game of cricket. For all sorts of reasons they want the Ashes back. An emerging nation needs its benchmarks, a sporting nation needs its trophies. Border had set Australian cricket on the victory path in 1987. Twenty years later the ambition remains, the hunger endures.

INDEX